ENDURING WESTERN CIVILIZATION

The Construction of the
Concept of Western Civilization
and Its "Others"

Edited by
SILVIA FEDERICI

Westport, Connecticut
London

Copyright Acknowledgments

Chapter 3, "True West: The Changing Idea of the West from the 1880s to the 1920s," by Chris GoGwilt, revised from the "Epilogue" to *The Invention of the West: Joseph Conrad and the Double-Mapping of Europe and Empire* by Chris GoGwilt (Stanford, CA: Stanford University Press, 1995) is used with the permission of the publishers, Stanford University Press. © 1995 by the Board of Trustees of the Leland Stanford Junior University.

Material from Arnold Toynbee, *A Study of History,* vol. V (London: Oxford University Press, 1939) is reprinted with permission of Oxford University Press.

Library of Congress Cataloging-in-Publication Data

Enduring Western civilization : the construction of the concept of
   Western civilization and its "others" / edited by Silvia Federici.
     p. cm.
   Includes bibliographical references and index.
   ISBN 0–275–95154–5 (alk. paper). — ISBN 0–275–95400–5 (pbk.)
   1. Civilization, Western. 2. Civilization, Western—
Historiography. I. Federici, Silvia.
CB245.E54   1995
909′.09812—dc20   95–7985

British Library Cataloguing in Publication Data is available.

Copyright © 1995 by Silvia Federici

All rights reserved. No portion of this book may be
reproduced, by any process or technique, without the
express written consent of the publisher.

Library of Congress Catalog Card Number: 95-7985
ISBN: 0–275–95154–5
     0–275–95400–5 (pbk.)

First published in 1995

Praeger Publishers, 88 Post Road West, Westport, CT 06881
An imprint of Greenwood Publishing Group, Inc.

Printed in the United States of America

The paper used in this book complies with the
Permanent Paper Standard issued by the National
Information Standards Organization (Z39.48–1984).

P

In order to keep this title in print and available to the academic community, this edition was produced using digital reprint technology in a relatively short print run. This would not have been attainable using traditional methods. Although the cover has been changed from its original appearance, the text remains the same and all materials and methods used still conform to the highest book-making standards.

Contents

Acknowledgments   vii

Introduction   ix

Part I. A Genealogy of "Western Civilization"   1

   1. Greece: Aryan or Mediterranean?
   Two Contending Historiographical Models   3
   Martin Bernal

   2. On the Scottish Origin of "Civilization"   13
   George C. Caffentzis

   3. True West: The Changing Idea of the West
   from the 1880s to the 1920s   37
   Chris GoGwilt

   4. The God That Never Failed: The Origins
   and Crises of Western Civilization   63
   Silvia Federici

       Satirical Appendix: Oedipus and the Coup   91
   Sol Yurick

Part II. One or Many Civilizations? — 117

5. Mathematics and Eurocentrism — 119
   George Gheverghese Joseph

6. Orientalism, Political Economy, and the Canonization of Indian Civilization — 137
   John Roosa

7. African Languages and European Linguistic Imperialism — 161
   Alamin Mazrui

8. They Came Before the Egyptians: Linguistic Evidence for the African Roots of Semitic Languages — 175
   Nicholas Faraclas

Index — 197

About the Contributors — 209

Acknowledgments

Many people have contributed to make this book possible. Among them I want to thank in particular George C. Caffentzis, Les Levidow, Gabriella Federici, Dina Valli, Peter Linebaugh, Linda Longmire, Dan Coughlin, Sohnia Sayres, Russ Harrison, Ariel Salleh, Rip Bulkeley, Mario Fenyo, Sam E. Anderson, Arthur Powell, Marylin Frankestein, Monty Neil, John Willshire, Peter Fraser, Kay Williamson, Robin Horton, Mariarosa Dalla Costa, Iain Boal, and Nancy Kelley. Special thanks go to Nancy Lucas, who has helped me prepare the manuscript for publication; Sharon Ross, Coordinator of the Hofstra Academic Computer Lab; and to Dr. James Sabin and Elisabetta Linton of Greenwood Publishers.

Introduction

Scarcely a day goes by without our reading or hearing of "our inherited cultural tradition," the "typical values of western civilization," "the idea of European coherence" —or, more simply, "our western traditon," "our western values," "our western culture." No set of ideas has become more commonplace, none been more assiduously drummed into our ears. . . . It is noteworthy that [the unity of "western European culture"] has emerged as a dogmatic assertion precisely at the moment when . . . the interpretation of history upon which it is based has been shattered by historical criticism and discarded by historical scholarship; and it is perhaps still more noteworthy that the weakening and undermining by professional historians of the historical premises underlying this theory has failed to detract from its effectiveness as a political dogma. (Barraclough, 1955: 31–32)

We are thus before a moral and political dilemma of no mean proportions when we talk about the relevance of the concept of civilization to our current problems in the late twentieth century. It will not do to try to hide the dilemma by abandoning the concept and avoiding the difficult analysis. Rather, let us embrace it as the central issue of our time. (Wallerstein, 1991a: 224)

What do we mean by "Western Civilization"? Today, this question is more important than ever, considering the prominent role that in recent times the notion of Western Civilization has played in academic and political debates. Throughout the 1980s, "Western Civilization" was at the center of the controversies that accompanied the demand for multicultural education and pedagogical reform in American colleges (*Partisan Review*, 1991; Pratt, 1992). More recently, in the broader political arena, we have witnessed the revival of ideologies that portray world politics as dominated by a "clash of civilizations," as in the scenario proposed by Samuel Huntington in a number of widely publicized articles (Huntington, 1993a, 1993b; Melloan, 1993). There is also a widespread perception that "Western Civilization" is undergoing a historic crisis, and indeed all the trendiest philosophical schools—postmodernism, feminist theory, afrocentrism, deconstruction—have defined themselves as alternatives to, or critiques of, "Western Civilization."

Yet, it is evident that no more clarity presently exists concerning the meaning of this concept than at the time Barraclough was commenting on the sudden popularity of the term (Barraclough, 1955). For despite the prestige currently enjoyed by postmodern theories, which stress the constructed character of all meaning, little effort has been made, by defenders and critics alike, to investigate the content of this concept. Much work has been devoted to demonstrating that the teaching of the "Classics of the Western tradition" does not meet the pedagogical needs of a multiethnic population of students, whose cultural backgrounds and concerns are unrepresented in a Eurocentric curriculum. It has also been objected that Western Civilization cannot provide the perspective from which world history is conceptualized, for such a move perpetrates the belief in the cultural superiority of Europe. Few, however, have asked how the concept of Western Civilization has been constructed, what historical status it can claim, or have suggested that Western Civilization is a fiction. More than that, in taking an oppositional stand against "Western values," the new cultural vanguards have contributed to naturalize "Western Civilization," so that the concept is now increasingly used as a self-explanatory term, a term of absolute reference, and above all a neutral term.

There are good reasons, however, to challenge this trend. The most immediate reason is that the language of "Western Civilization" creates a shadow play whereby real processes are mystified in a way that precludes transformative action, as has often happened during the recent debates. Certainly, the fact that the "Western Civilization" canon was made the central question in the discussion of pedagogical reform has increased our awareness of the pedagogical needs of our ethnically diversified student population (Butler and Walter, 1991; Gates, 1992; Gless and Herrnstein Smith, 1992; Olguin, 1991). But it has also fostered the illusion that pedagogical reform can be conceived as a shift in cultural paradigms. Moreover, it has detracted attention from more substantive issues such as the ever diminishing support given by government to education, and the perils posed to academic freedom by the military's penetration of academic life and by the subordination of education to narrowly defined economic goals.

The "Western Civilization debate" has also perpetrated the myth of a Western/non-Western cultural divide, thus giving some intellectual credibility to a politics of cultural blocs that is particularly dangerous in the present conjuncture. For hardly had the Berlin Wall fallen and the debate on the "end of history" gotten under way than the flag of "Western Civilization" was raised again in conservative political circles, to evoke the specter of a coming world dominated by cultural conflicts, where "the West" will be naturally pitted against "the Rest," and cultural differentiation will inevitably be a source of lethal division among humankind (Huntington, 1993a, 1993b).

Last but not least, an unquestioning, naturalizing approach to "Western Civilization" precludes both an understanding of the reasons for its enduring currency and a proper evaluation of the prophecies concerning its imminent crisis. For it is not the first time that "Western Civilization" has sustained radical challenges. Already in the post–World War I and World War II period, the specter of the "decline of the West" haunted the political imagination of the European and American elites. Moreover, for almost four decades every liberation movement in the "Third World" has defined its goals in opposition or as an alternative to "Western Civilization." Yet, in each case "Western Civilization" has endured. While undergoing changes in rhetoric and objectives, it still managed to present itself as a model, under the guise of "modernization," to the new nations of the "Third World" (Black, 1966).

What guarantees, then, that the present challenges are the harbingers of a qualitatively new situation and are not instead ushering in a rationalization process, which may leave the substance of "Western Civilization" unaltered, while giving it more congenial attires for the imperatives of the day? To phrase this question from a different angle: How can we be sure that in moving from a world order dominated by the ideology of Western Civilization to one committed to cultural diversity, we do not mistake for genuine change the very modifications that will allow the old ideology to survive?

This question is crucial both at the level of curriculum reform and world-historical change. As it has often been noted, far from contradicting each other, cultural universalism and cultural particularism have played a complementary function in recent history. In the postcolonial period, for instance, the promotion of cultural particularism was put at the service of "Westernization," as revitalizing select aspects of indigenous cultures conferred an aura of autonomy to societies that were otherwise being reshaped according to the universalizing requirements of the world market (Federici, 1989: 79; Roosa, in this volume: 151–52). At the curriculum level as well, multiculturalism may be nothing more than a token reform or a means to equip students with the skills needed to operate in a global economy. Indeed, for all the defenses of "Western Civilization" by powerful conservative intellectuals and institutions, the corporate world recognizes the need for a globally wise workforce and is now creating a new genre of books and a subspecialty of business consulting that instrumentalizes multiculturalism to the demands of profitability. Among the main forces driving multiculturalism are the U.S. military and intelligence services, which, no less than corporate entrepreneurs, are demanding a personnel capable of operating in a global context and therefore equipped with a multicultural training. In this context, we should not be surprised if a new, more sophisticated version of "Western Civilization," with a more multicultural and gender-conscious facade, should emerge from the present debates, serving to make corporate capital and the U.S. military appear as "civilizing" agents in their new global missions.

It can also be argued that after 500 years of "Western" intervention in the "Third World," no world culture has remained intact (Olguin, 1991) and, vice versa, that many of the celebrated achievements of "the West" have been obtained through the incorporation of the accumulated knowledge of "non-Westerners" (Reed, 1988). Where, then, should we draw the line between what is internal and what is external to "Western Civilization"? And to what extent can we turn to its "Others" as an alternative to the present cultural configuration?

These questions cannot obviously be answered by any one book. They do point, however, to the need for a better understanding of the historical reality that lies behind the concept of "Western Civilization" and the relation between the West and its Others. This is where this volume makes its contribution.

Written from a multidisciplinary viewpoint, the essays contained in this volume trace the development of the concept of Western Civilization and examine the reasons for its endurance, unsettling many standing beliefs. Prime among these beliefs is that which concerns the very existence of a "Western tradition," as the book shows that Western Civilization is a recent ideological invention, dissimulating under a cultural mantle the worldwide expansion of capitalist relations. From this point of view, the book can be seen as an attempt to reconstruct the discourse of "the West" in its diverse applications; but the purpose of this volume is not simply to bring to light the structures of the Western Civilization discourse and the devices by which it has succeeded to maintain a semblance of coherence. Rather, its objective is to understand the political potential of this concept and to highlight the practices it has mystified and justified. In so doing, not only do the contributors unearth a conceptual history whose knowledge is indispensable for any critical usage of the term, but they also make it possible for us to connect the past to the present and treat Western Civilization not as a relic demanding our assent or dissent, but as a code, continuously redefined, for processes still unfolding today. For if it is the case that the ideology of Western Civilization has served to legitimize the advance of capitalism, then we can see that this process is not confined to "the age of expansion," but is being realized today on a planetary scale. We can also see that Western Civilization cannot be challenged by a shift in cultural models, nor can we pursue the study of "other cultures" without reckoning with the forces that are presently shaping their course and threatening their survival. Short of that, we risk bringing to the classroom images that, like the light of expended stars, come from worlds that no longer exist, or are recreated, for new imperial purposes, in our own cultural institutions.

Thus, one of the main lessons to be drawn from this book is the need to transcend any debate purely framed as a contrast between cultural unity and cultural diversity, for "the central issue of our time" is rather how a world can be constructed where culture is no longer a means of mystification and discrimination. It is to this project that this volume is dedicated.

Part I provides a genealogy of the concept of "Western Civilization." In an indirect polemic with Jacques Derrida's deconstruction of "Western Logocentrism," this section argues that "Western Civilization" may very well be the "creation myth of the white man," but it is a myth whose origins are not undecidable, nor are they to be found (or rejected) by perusing the ancient struggle between logos and mythos in Plato's texts, as Derrida would have us believe (Derrida, 1982; Young, 1990). For the lesson to be drawn from the essays contained in this section is that "Western Civilization" was produced in surprisingly recent times and for preeminently political reasons, which tells us more about the intentions of the elites that have promoted it than about Hellas and Ptah.

An important contribution in this direction is Martin Bernal's essay, which recaptures the main themes of his famous *Black Athena*. Bernal has argued that the dominant account of the origin of Ancient Greek civilization—which he defines as the Aryan Model—stands in contrast to how the Ancient Greeks conceptualized their history. Bernal shows how the political and racist assumptions generated by the European colonial expansion served as the prime factor behind the intellectual shift from the Ancient to the Aryan Model. He challenges the idea of Western Civilization as a self-propelled cultural project, recognizing its vital dependence on many borrowings and appropriations.

George C. Caffentzis traces the origins of the concept of "Civilization." The literature on this topic is enormous (for example, Elias, 1978, 1982; Stocking, 1987). Caffentzis, however, covers uncharted ground, demonstrating that "civilization" cannot be understood only as a conceptual scheme, devised by Enlightenment philosophers to rethink the stages of social formation nor as a moral ideal, nor (in the fashion popularized by Norbert Elias) as the development of new mediated codes of courtly and bourgeois behavior. As his analysis of eighteenth-century Britain demonstrates, "civilization" was the historical process that paved the way for the expansion of capitalist relations which, in Europe, no less than in the colonies, required the destruction of the aboriginal cultures, in this case the destruction of the mode of life of the Scottish Highlanders. Thus, in Europe as well, "civilization" was not a vehicle for the transmission of tradition, but the end of tradition; not the guarantor of the cultural "heritage," but its destroyer; not the expansion of liberties, but their restriction; above all, it was not the expression of a European/Western ethos, but the project of a limited elite, which thousands resisted, arms in hand.

Chris GoGwilt also challenges the hypothesis of a continuous Western tradition. He shows that the concept of Western Civilization, in its contemporary meaning—as the signifier of a unique cultural development within world history—originated in the Russian debates of the second part of the nineteenth century, to be appropriated later by the European elites in the context of major political dislocations that changed the map of Europe and its role in the colonial world. In GoGwilt's reading, "Western Civilization" can be taken as the expression neither of a continuous Western tradition nor of Eurocentrism, insofar as the concept originated in response both to new divisions within Europe and to a rejection of Europe as a unitary cultural entity.

Silvia Federici examines the development of the concept of Western Civilization in the context of the political realities which it mystifies. She shows that "Western Civilization" has endured because it was never a cultural creature, designed to prevail or fall on the basis of its cognitive or ethical merits. Nor were the elites who produced it ever committed to one unique set of values, as suggested by the common but misguided identification of "Western Civilization" with the precepts of eighteenth-century rationalism. More than faithfulness to any particular cultural claim, what has allowed "Western Civilization" to endure has been the exceptional backing it has received both from governmental institutions and from a body of conceptual *bricoleurs* who, from time to time, have retooled it to meet the challenge of its opponents. Federici concludes, however, that the adjustments by which "Western Civilization" has been rescued have made its intellectual status not unlike that of the Ptolemaic hypothesis during the Copernican revolution.

Part I ends with a satirical rendition by Sol Yurick of *Oedipus the King*, one of the most classic texts in the Western Civilization curriculum. Yurick tests the adage that the present recreates the past. He takes us back to the student revolts of the late 1960s, which on American campuses inaugurated the contemporary mobilization against the canon, and he asks provocative questions. What if these revolts—he inquires—undermined not only the Establishment's control over the present but also its control over the past? What if Oedipus, Jocasta, Creon, and even Sophocles, inspired by the '68ers, became suspicious of their situation and expanded their roles to investigate the political maneuvers implicit in their textual fate? Building from the available variants to the Oedipus myth, the play humorously answers these questions. In this process, it reveals the monetary and imperialistic machinations of the Oedipus tale, which link the past with the present, and destabilize our view of how and in whose interests "Western Civilization" was created.

Part II discusses the politics of "multiculturalism," showing how a crucial aspect of the European and U.S. world dominance has been their ability to define other cultures. Thus, the essays contained in this second section sound a cautionary note against the tendency to conceptualize cultural choices as a contrast between universalism and particularism.

George Gheverghese Joseph criticizes the teaching of mathematics, perhaps the most canonic discipline in the arsenal of "Western knowledge," which has been used time and time again to uphold the superiority of the European races and therefore is especially in need of multiculturalization. He argues that a Eurocentric math approach undermines the students from non-Western cultures and distorts the very nature and history of mathematics. He also points out, however, by appealing to the example of nineteenth-century British imperial policy, that an expanded cultural awareness is not necessarily a sign of social improvement, as long as our interest in other cultures is not accompanied by a move toward more egalitarian relations.

John Roosa traces the canonization of "Indian civilization," or "Indology," back to the early phase of British colonialism, showing how British imperial officers encouraged the "discovery" of Indian tradition. Most important, he points out how Indology was genetically connected to the rise of political economy, insofar as both shared the sponsorhip of the East India Company and were complementary in their goals. Roosa expands on some of the themes elaborated by Edward Said's *Orientalism* (Said, 1978); but while Said reconstructs only the strategies internal to the Orientalist "discourse," Roosa traces in detail the connection between Indology and the imperial context.

Alamin Mazrui challenges the tenet embraced by some African cultural nationalists which states that the shift from the use of European to the use of African languages in contemporary African life (at the institutional and educational levels) is an essential aspect of mental decolonization and anti-imperialist struggle. He shows how both European and African languages served the objectives of colonial rule and continue to be functional to the expansion of market relations in contemporary Africa. Mazrui argues that control over the means of communication is by far more important than any specific linguistic practice in the maintenance of the status quo.

Nicholas Faraclas presents an interesting hypothesis concerning the African origin of the Semitic languages which have been considered among the mother tongues of "Western Civilization," tracing their dispersion back to the diaspora that followed the drying of the once green Sahara. He argues that unbiased scholarship will have to recognize the importance of Africa to the history of "Western Civilization" and that the study of African history also challenges the criteria scholars have used to decide what constitutes a civilization.

REFERENCES

Barraclough, G. (1955). *History in a Changing World*. Oxford: Basil Blackwell.
Black, C. B. (1966). *The Dynamics of Modernization: A Study in Comparative History*. New York: Harper and Row.
Butler, J. E., and J. C. Walter. (1991). *Transforming the Curriculum. Ethnic Studies and Women's Studies*. Albany: State University of New York Press.
Derrida, Jacques. (1982). *Margins of Philosophy*. Trans. Alan Bass. Chicago: Chicago University Press.
Diamond, Stanley. (1974). *In Search of the Primitive: A Critique of Civilization*. New Brunswick, N.J.: Transaction Books.
Federici, Silvia. (1990, Fall). "The One and the Many in Linguistics." *Journal of Humanism and Ethical Religion* 3(1): 68–85.

Gates, Henry Louis, Jr., (1992). "The Master Pieces: On Canon Formation and the African-American Tradition." In Darryl J. Gless and Barbara Herrnstein Smith, eds., *The Politics of Liberal Education*. Durham, N.C.: Duke University Press

Gless, Darryl J., and Barbara Herrnstein Smith. eds. (1992). *The Politics of Liberal Education*. Durham, N.C.: Duke University Press.

Huntington, Samuel P. (1993a). "The Coming Clash of Civilization Or, the West Against the Rest." *New York Times*, June 6.

———. (1993b, Summer). "The Clash of Civilizations?" *Foreign Affairs* 72(3): 21–49.

Loden, Marilyn, and Judy B. Rosener. (1991). *Workforce America! Managing Employee Diversity as a Vital Resource*. Homewood, Ill.: Business One Irwin.

Melloan, George. (1993). "Cultures in Conflict on the Global Battlefield." *Wall Street Journal*, August 16, p. A16.

Olguin, R. A. (1991). "Towards an Epistemology of Ethnic Studies: African American Studies and Chicano Studies Contributions." In J. E. Butler and J, C. Walter, eds., *Transforming the Curriculum. Ethnic Studies and Women's Studies*. Albany: State University of New York Press, pp. 149–68.

Partisan Review. (1991). "The Changing Culture of the University" Issue. LVIII(2).

Pratt, Marie L. (1992). "Humanities for the Future: Reflections on the Western Culture Debate at Stanford." In Darryl J. Gless and Barbara Herrnstein Smith, eds., *The Politics of Liberal Education*. Durham, N.C.: Duke University Press, pp. 13–31.

Reed, Ishmael. (1988). "America: The Multinational Society." In Rick Simonson and Scott Walker, eds., *Multicultural Literacy*. St. Paul, Minn.: Greywolf Press, pp. 155–60.

Simonson, Rick, and Scott Walker, eds. (1988). *Multicultural Literacy*. St. Paul: Greywolf Press.

Thompson, Laura. (1973). *Culture in Crisis, A Study of the Hopi Indians*. New York: Russell and Russell.

Wallerstein, I. (1991a). *Geopolitics and Geoculture: Essays on the Changing World-System*. Cambridge: Cambridge University Press.

———. (1991b). "The Modern World-System as a Civilization." In I. Wallerstein, ed., *Geopolitics and Geoculture: Essays on the Changing World-System*. Cambridge: Cambridge University Press.

———. (1991c). "The Renewed Concern with Civilization(s?)." In I. Wallerstein, ed., *Geopolitics and Geoculture: Essays on the Changing World-System*. Cambridge: Cambridge University Press.

Part I

A Genealogy of "Western Civilization"

1

Greece: Aryan or Mediterranean? Two Contending Historiographical Models

Martin Bernal

In 1978, when Edward Said published *Orientalism*, he argued that, far from being shaped by disinterested scholarship, Orientalism as "a mode of discourse" corroborated by "supporting institutions, vocabulary, scholarship, imagery, doctrines" was largely a self-referential system, developed in conjunction with Western imperialism for which it served important functions (Said, 1978: 2). Orientalism, in other words, was more valuable "as a sign of European-Atlantic power over the Orient" than "as a veridic discourse about the Orient" (Said: 6).

The publication caused a furor among orthodox Orientalists, and in June 1982 there came the official response. Writing in *The New York Review of Books*, the eminent historian of the Middle East, Bernard Lewis, counterattacked. Lewis used the tactic of *reductio ad absurdum*. He imagined a hypothetical situation in which modern Greeks supposedly objected to what they saw as the biases of classical scholarship and consequently tried to overthrow it. Lewis presented this situation as analogous to that of modern Arab malcontents questioning the scholarly objectivity of Orientalism. Thus framed, the charge inevitably appeared ridiculous.

In response to Lewis, in *The New York Review of Books* of August 12, Said argued that there could be no comparison between the pure scholarship of the classicists and the use of Orientalism as a handmaid of imperialism. He contrasted the great liberal German Hellenist Ulrich Willamovitz-Moellendorff and the Orientalist Professor Menachem Milsom, who, at the time, was the Israeli governor of the West Bank. Thus, despite their opposition on almost every other issue, both Lewis and Said agreed on one fundamental point: the discipline of the Classics was the epitome of disinterested, objective scholarship.

My book, *The Fabrication of Ancient Greece 1785-1985*, which is the first of a four-volume series titled *Black Athena: The Afroasiatic Roots of Western Civilization*, is an attempt to challenge this assumption. Here I argue that, far from being neutral and peripheral, the German academic discipline of *Altertumswissenschaft*, transposed into England as "Classics," has been a central element of Northern European culture in the nineteenth and twentieth centuries and has performed a key political function: fostering the notion that Europe possesses a categorical superiority over all other continents, a claim that has been used to justify imperialism and neo-colonialism as *missions civilisatrices*. I maintain that it is to the work of the Classicists that we owe the construction of that cultural trajectory that has served to establish Greece as the sole birthplace of "Western Civilization" and the site of a unique, almost miraculous, spiritual development that supposedly elevates "Western Man" to humanity's pinnacle.

In *Black Athena*, I illustrate this thesis by examining the paradigms that have governed the Classicists' presentation of Greek culture, and the conceptual shifts that have characterized the historiographical approach to Greek history in the eighteenth and nineteenth centuries. In this context, I distinguish between two schemes of interpretation of the origins of Ancient Greece, which I have called the "Ancient" and the "Aryan" models.

The Ancient Model, simply defined, is the view the Greeks had of their history, beginning with the assumptions they made about both their origins and the debt they owed to other cultures. The Aryan Model—which is the paradigm in which most of us have been educated—is the nineteenth-century product of classical studies. Its main tenet is that the culture and people that made classical Greece originated from a Northern homeland. According to this model, Greek culture developed as a result of the mixing between an aboriginal "Pre-Hellenic" population and one or more invasions from the North by Indo-European speakers. Very little is known about these "Pre-Hellenes," apart from their having been "white" or "Caucasian," and definitely not Semitic or African. But the Aryan Model reconstructs their presence from what are supposedly the many linguistic traces of their culture in Greek language and proper names. Nobody disputes the fact that, although Greek is an Indo-European language, it contains an extraordinarily high proportion of non-Indo-European elements. The Aryan Model accounts for this pattern by attributing these non-Indo-European elements to the Pre-Hellenes. Thus, it admits that Greek is by no means a homogeneous language; however, it claims that, while there was ethnic and linguistic mixing, both invaders and natives were "racially pure," although the conquest was carried on by a "superior race." In this model, the Aryan conquest of Greece is contrasted to the Aryan conquest of India, as the latter occurred in a subcontinent where the aborigines were "dark." In the case of India, it could be argued, the conquest led, in the long run, to the "racial degradation" of the conquerors. By contrast, the conquest of Greece was likened to the Germanic destruction of the Roman Empire, in line with nineteenth-century ideology that pictured the Teutons as infusing new vigor into the Celtic and Latin-speaking European populations.

The Aryan Model had to confront one major problem, however. While the Germanic invasions are historical events, and there is strong linguistic and legendary evidence suggesting that there were Aryan conquests of India, such a tradition is completely lacking in the case of Greece. The solution was to appeal to oblivion. As the early twentieth-century Classicist J. B. Bury put it in *A History of Greece*, which is still a standard work: "The true home of the Greeks before they won dominion in Greece had passed clean out of their remembrance, and they looked to the east, and not the north, as the quarter from which some of their ancestors had migrated" (75). What Bury believed to be the product of the faulty memory of the Greeks I call the Ancient Model. This was the conventional view among the Greeks of the Classical and Hellenistic Age. It is the historical scheme referred to by the playwrights Aeschylus and Euripides, the historians Herodotus and Diodorous Siculus, the orator Isocrates, the guidebook writer Pausanias, and others. It was omitted by one or two writers who might have mentioned it, and it was denied only by Plutarch in what is generally seen as an outburst of spleen against Herodotus ("On the malice of Herodotus"). In other writings (*On Isis and Osiris*), Plutarch admitted Greece's deep cultural debt to the Near East, and he considered it axiomatic that Greek religion came from Egypt.

The Ancient Model acknowledged the central role played by the Egyptians and the Phoenicians in the formation of Greek culture. According to this model, Greece had once been inhabited by primitive tribes—Pelasgians and others. Then, around 1500 B.C., it had been colonized by Egyptians and Phoenicians, who built cities and civilized the natives. The Phoenicians had introduced the alphabet, while the Egyptians had taught the Pelasgians such things as irrigation and both the name and the worship of the gods (see, e.g., Herodotus, *The Histories*, Book II).

The Ancient Model did not need to postulate a Pre-Hellenic, non-Indo-European-speaking population on Greek soil, and it could satisfactorily account for the presence of non-Indo-European elements in Ancient Greek. Thus, it cannot be argued that it was overthrown because it lacked explanatory power, nor that it was superseded by a superior theory.

The Ancient Model was not seriously challenged until the end of the eighteenth century. It was overthrown only in the 1820s, when Northern European scholars began to deny that there had been colonizations in Greece from the East and the South, and began to downplay Egyptian and Phoenician influences on Greek culture. These historiographical developments cannot be linked to the appearance of any new evidence of the type that was later provided by the great discoveries of the nineteenth century. The first archaeological discoveries of Bronze Age Greece by Heinrich Schliemann, who in the 1870s excavated at Troy and Mycenae, and the gradual decipherment, in the 1840s and 1850s, of Cuneiform scripts took place decades after the change of model; Champollion's decipherment of Egyptian hieroglyphics was not accepted by most Classicists until the 1850s. Thus, we must look for the reasons for the demise of the Ancient Model not in developments internal to the disciplines, but in external factors, beginning with the early nineteenth-century *Zeitgeist* and its role in shaping the contemporary political and cultural milieu. In Europe, the years between 1815 to 1830 were oustanding for their political reaction and religious revival. In the aftermath of Napoleon's defeat at Waterloo, European governments strove to erase all traces of the French Revolution. They attempted to purge all ideas and theories which in their view had served to subvert the constituted order. One of the main outcomes of this process was the the devaluation of Egyptian culture.

The reaction against Ancient Egypt can be understood in light of Egypt's centrality to the creed of the Freemasons, whom the reactionaries believed to have been at the heart of the revolutionary project. Especially reviled was the Freemasons' anti-Christian "religion" (Deism). This doctrine denied the centrality of Christ and transcended what the high-ranking Masons saw as the limited religion or superstition of Christianity. Hellenism came to the rescue of the Christian order that was threatened by Freemasonry. In the long run, however, the Ancient Model was destroyed not because of any threat it posed to Christianity, but because of the pervasive impact of racism and the concomitant development in the nineteenth century of Romanticism and Progress Theory.

The growing importance of the American colonies, with their twin policy of enslavement of African Blacks and extermination of Native Americans, and later the growth of nationalism, is behind the tidal wave of racialism and the cult of ethnicity that swept Europe in the eighteenth and nineteenth centuries. Racism was reinforced by the development both of evolutionary theories, which looked at cultures as different stages in the progress of the human spirit, and of Romanticism, which in its anti-Enlightenment stance emphasized the importance of place and kinship in cultural formation.

Unlike the philosophers of the Enlightenment, who admired large empires (Egypt, China, and Rome), the Romantics favored small communities, for they believed that these were more conducive to the development not merely of virtue but of intellectual creativity. They also believed that these qualities best thrived in stimulating, cold, mountainous, Northern regions such as Scotland and Switzerland. Thus, the Ancient Greeks, who were beginning to be promoted as paragons of virtue, were proclaimed to be Northerners, whose values could not have derived from the luxurious and decadent South/East.

At the intersection of Romanticism and Progress Theory there is the assumption that cultures follow the same stages as biological organisms, developing in ascending cycles from youth to old age. By the late eighteenth century, this produced the concept and cult of childhood as a uniquely pure and creative period. Soon Ancient Greece came to represent the childhood of Europe. This notion was partially inspired by Plato's *Timaeus*, where the Athenian law-giver Solon is reminded by an aged Egyptian priest that "you

Greeks are always children . . . you are always young in soul, everyone of you. For . . . you possess not a single belief that is ancient" (Plato, *Timaeus* 22B: 33). From antiquity to the Renaissance, such an identification was a damning condemnation of Greek cultural shallowness. After the eighteenth century, the opposite was true. By the same token, the greater antiquity of the Egyptians and the Phoenicians, which previously had given them a reputation for cultural superiority, now became a liability. As later became better, the Greeks became the epitome of youthful dynamism and purity. Thus, the traditional view of Greece as the ethnic melting pot of the East Mediterranean became increasingly distasteful.

Even more unacceptable was the idea that the most significant conquerors of Greece might have been the Egyptians and the Phoenicians, who were beginning to be categorized as Africans and Semites. Such a picture was offensive in the climate of sweeping racism that prevailed at the turn of the nineteenth century.

As the century progressed, colonial expansion and the arrogant optimism that flowed from it sealed the fate of the Ancient Model. North Europeans needed to denigrate the people they were enslaving, exploiting, and exterminating in other continents. Less and less could they afford to acknowledge any debt to cultures rooted in Africa or the Middle East.

Accordingly, the image of the Greeks changed as well. They were no longer seen as intermediaries, who had transmitted the wisdom of the East to the West; they became absolute creators. Similarly, the essence of their contribution was redefined. At the beginning of the eighteenth century, the Ancient Greeks were admired because of Homer and the later poets. By the middle of the century, led by the German J. J. Winkelmann, the revered founder of art history, cultivated Europeans began to see Greek art as an expression of universal, transcendent values. Finally, in the 1780s, historians of philosophy agreed that there had been no philosophy before the Greeks. That Greece seemed to excel in poetry, art, and philosophy—that is, in two fields usually identified, respectively, with the youth and the maturity of a "race"— gave the Ancient Greeks a superhuman status as the models of a balanced and integrated humanity. The image of the "divine Greeks" was particularly strong in Germany, where Neo-Hellenism had become identified with a passionate quest for social regeneration.

In 1793, at the peak of the French Revolution, a young aristocrat and polymath, Wilhelm Von Humboldt, conceived a plan for a new education that would cure contemporary men and women, spiritually alienated by modernity, by putting them in contact with the most harmoniously integrated people of the past: the Ancient Greeks. Thirteen years later, in 1806, the Prussian government, in panic after its military humiliation by Napoleon at the battle of Jena, put Humboldt in charge of national education. Humboldt was thus able to implement many of his ideas, and through the institution of the *Gymnasium* and the University *Seminar*, he established a humanist education, focused on the science of antiquity (*Altertumswissenschaft*) and especially the study of the Greeks. He consciously aimed at providing an alternative to those who, being dissatisfied with the status quo, might look at political change for spiritual reintegration—a danger made all too real by the enthusiasm generated in Europe by Napoleon's armies. That the new education had meritocratic tendencies, and thus was seen as a threat to the aristocracy (who frequently opposed it), enhanced its sociocultural appeal. Similarly, its English offshoot, the "Classics," provided a middle way between reaction and revolution. From the beginning, the chief purpose of those advocating a humanistic education centered on the study of Ancient Greece was to forestall or avoid revolution. Indeed, the cult of the Classics served quite effectively to maintain the status quo, despite some minor trouble caused by the radicals associated with the Philhellenic movement that had been formed in support of the Greek War of Independence.

Considering the rise of popular and institutionalized Philhellenism, which naturally intensified after 1821, it is remarkable that the Ancient Model survived as long as it did. It was a very tough nut to crack, as Connop Thirlwall, the first writer of a history of Greece in the "new" way, wrote in the 1830s: "It required no little boldness to venture even to throw out a doubt as to the truth of an opinion sanctioned by such authority and by prescription of such a long and undisputed possession of the public mind" (Thirlwall, vol. 1, 1835–44: 63).

The man who accomplished this task was one of the first products of Humboldt's new educational system: Karl Ottfried Müller. Claiming a base in "science," which his predecessors had lacked, Müller maintained that the reports that we find in ancient Greek literature referring to settlements by Phoenicians and Egyptians, and the Egyptians' civilizing influence on Greece, were the result of liaisons between the Egyptian, Phoenician, and Greek priesthoods of later times and therefore were not to be trusted. Müller also insisted that, since none of the legends that made up the Ancient Model could be proven, they should not be believed (see *Introduction to a Scientific System of Mythology*, 1844).

There were two sleights of hand involved in these recommendations. The first was the requirement of "proof" in an area where the best that can be hoped for is competitive plausibility. The second was the fact that Müller was placing the onus of proof on those who accepted the massive ancient testimony rather than on those who challenged it. The unspoken assumption behind this move was apparently the new axiom that Europe was and had always been categorically separate from and superior to Asia and Africa. Thus, proof was required to justify something as "unnatural" as the Ancient Model. It is ironic, indeed, that the more the Ancient Greeks were admired, the less their views on their own history were trusted.

Müller's discrediting of the Egyptian colonization gained rapid acceptance, showing how well attuned he was to his times. Müller's denial of a Phoenician influence on Greece was less easily accepted. Thus, during most of the nineteenth century, the dominant image of the origins of Greece was what I call the "Broad Aryan Model." It rejected the Greek traditions concerning the Egyptians; it accepted, however, those concerning the Phoenicians, who, by the mid-nineteenth century, were the object of much interest and admiration in Britain. Men like William Gladstone, who wrote extensively on early Greece, felt a great sympathy for the upright, manufacturing, trading Phoenicians, who spread civilization while selling cloth and carried on a little bit of slaving on the side. Interestingly, the identification of the Phoenicians with the English was shared by the French and, somewhat later, the Germans, who therefore detested them. (It seems that the French image of *Perfide Albion* derived from the Roman stereotype of the "bad faith" Phoenician Carthago.) Nevertheless, the Phoenicians were then, as they had been at least since the Renaissance, chiefly associated with the Jews, with whom they shared a common language (Canaanite) and many religious and other customs. Thus, the peak of the Phoenician reputation in historical writing tallies well with the years of relative tolerance for the Jews, between the dwindling of the traditional Christian religious hatred and the development of "racial anti-Semitism."

With the rise of racial, as opposed to religious, anti-Semitism in the 1880s and 1890s, the belief in the Phoenicians' formative role in the creation of Greek civilization plummeted. At the peak of the imperial conquest, we have not only the Dreyfus case, but also the publication of very influential articles denying the existence of any significant extra-European influence in the formation of Greece. The Broad Aryan Model survived, however, until the period between 1925 and 1935, when ostracism of the "Semites"—now made responsible for the Russian Revolution and world communism—became almost universal, spreading not only among the "disreputable right," but also within regular academic circles in Europe and North America.

Although "external" forces provided the chief impetus for this shift of paradigms, an important impulse for the creation of the Aryan Model in the 1830s and 1940s came from developments "internal" to the field of linguistics —namely, the working out of the Indo-European language family and the consequent belief that, at some time, there must have been a single Proto-Indo-European language, spoken probably to the northeast of the Black Sea. The argument was that if Greek was an Indo-European language, then it must have been introduced, at some stage, from the North. On this basis, it was possible to postulate an Aryan invasion, despite the absence of any archaeological evidence for it or any ancient authority testifying to its occurrence.

The situation has changed sharply since 1945, when the moral revulsion at the consequences of anti-Semitism, now made visible by the genocide of the Jews, stimulated a revision of conceptual frameworks in all disciplines. Even more important have been the simultaneous rise of anticolonial liberation movements throughout the Third World and the building of Israel as a bastion of imperialism and "Western Civilization." All of these changes have led to the reacceptance of Jews as Europeans, while there has been a much smaller movement to restore the reputation of the Phoenicians.

Since the 1960s, a battle has raged about the restoration of the Broad Aryan Model. Resistance by the "extremists" seems to have come largely from inertia and respect for authority, which is naturally very high in such "traditional" disciplines as the Classics and Historical Linguistics. Still, the defenders of the Extreme Aryan Model have been weakened both by the changing intellectual climate and by the increasing evidence of Egyptian and Levantine influence in the Aegean during the Late Bronze and Early Iron Ages. The Broad Aryanists—led largely by Jewish scholars—are now gaining ground and will almost certainly succeed by the end of the century. The restoration of the Ancient Model will take somewhat longer.

It is important here to stress that, even if we accept the idea that the Aryan Model was conceived amidst the sins and errors of racialism and anti-Semitism, it does not follow that all of its assumptions have to be rejected. All that is necessary is to reopen the "competition" between the Aryan and Ancient models and to see which one has superior heuristic possibilities. This competition should be made not in terms of certainty, but in terms of competitive plausibility, and should be judged in light of the evidence provided by contemporary documents of the Late Bronze Age, by archaeological findings, linguistic materials (e.g., place names, divine and mythological names), and religious rituals. In some cases, documentary and archaeological evidence verifies the Ancient Model; in others, it supports the Aryan Model. We cannot doubt, for instance, the achievements of the early Indo-European linguists and the fact that, despite its many foreign aspects and elements, Greek is fundamentally an Indo-European language.

The framework for conceptualizing the relation between the Ancient and the Aryan models is presented in outline in the introduction to Volume I of *Black Athena*. However, the full arguments are developed only in Volume II, *The Archaeological and Documentary Evidence* (1991), and Volume III, *The Linguistic Evidence* (1997).

My work does not call for a complete restoration of the Ancient Model, but for a synthesis, incorporating the linguistic advances made in the nineteenth century and adjusting some traditional dates in the light of archaeological evidence from the twentieth. This "Revised Ancient Model" accepts the notion not only that there must, at some stage, have been substantial migrations or conquests from the North, but also that there were Egyptian and Phoenician settlements in Greece, and massive and fundamental cultural influences on the Aegean from the South and East. All in all, I see the need for a radical reassessment of the image of Ancient Greece. We must abandon the view that

Greek civilization sprang, like Athena, from the head of Zeus virgin and fully formed. We must recognize, instead, that Greece developed at the intersection of Europe, Egypt, and the Middle East. The greatness of Greek civilization, and the central role Greece played in the formation of European cultures, were the result not of isolation and cultural purity, but of frequent contacts between the many surrounding peoples of the Mediterranean Basin and the already heterogeneous natives of the Aegean.

REFERENCES

Bernal, Martin. (1987). *Black Athena: The Afroasiatic Roots of Western Civilization, Vol. I: The Fabrication of Ancient Greece, 1785–1985*. London: Free Association Books/New Brunswick: Rutgers University Press.

———. (1991). *Black Athena, Vol. II: The Archaeological and Documentary Evidence*. London: Free Association Books/New Brunswick: Rutgers University Press.

Bury, J. B. (1900). *A History of Greece to the Death of Alexander the Great*. London: Macmillan.

Gladstone, W. (1896). *Juventus Mundi: The Gods and Men of the Heroic Age*. London.

Müller, K. O. (1844). *Introduction to a Scientific System of Mythology*, trans. J. Leite. London.

Plato. (1975). *Timaeus*, trans. R. J. Bury. Loeb translation. Vol. XI. Cambridge, Mass.: Harvard University Press.

Plutarch. (1934–35). *De Iside et Osiride*, trans. F. C. Babbit, in *Plutarch's Moralia*, Vol. V (Loeb). Cambridge, Mass.: Harvard University Press/London: Heinemann (Vol. V).

———. (1934–35). *De Herodoti Malignitate*, trans. L. Pearson and F. H. Sandbach in *Plutarch's Moralia*, Vol. XI. Cambridge, Mass.: Harvard University Press/London: Heinemann.

Said, Edward. (1978). *Orientalism*. New York: Pantheon Books.

Thirlwall, C. (1835–44). *A History of Greece*, Vols. I–VIII. London.

von Humboldt, W. (1903–36). *Wilhelm von Humboldt gesammelte Schriften*, Vols. I–XVII. Berlin: Letzmann and Gebrhardt.

Winckelmann, J. J. (1764). *Geschichte der Kunst des Altertums*, ed. W. Senff. Weimar.

2

On the Scottish Origin of "Civilization"

George C. Caffentzis

> I have not consulted books; indeed I have not books to consult! But as well as my memory serves me, let us see, my lords, how the facts and the law stand. . . . It appears most clearly to me that not only every man may legally interfere to suppress a riot, much more to prevent acts of felony, treason, and rebellion, in his private capacity, but he is bound to do it as an act of duty.
>
> Lord Mansfield, 1780
(Quoted in Campbell, 1878)

The term "civilization" is commonly used in English to describe a set of positive, even ideal, social and historical values. "European Civilization," "Western Civilization," "Industrial Civilization": to most people, any use of the word signifies a positive achievement. Indeed, who would want to be labeled "uncivilized"? And who would not want to be a member of a "civilized" society?

There are scholars, however, who declare that they "have for some time rejected the notion of civilization" because of its discriminatory implications, as civilization is "by necessity defined by reference to the uncivilized" (White, 1987: 40).[1] Questions have also been raised concerning the ethical content of civilization, for it is apparent that the perpetration of horrid crimes is not sufficient to make an individual or a society uncivilized. If this were not the case, never, after the witch-hunt, the slave trade, Auschwitz, and Hiroshima, could we bring ourselves to speak of Western Civilization.

Many circumvent the problem by enclosing "civilization" within protective quotation marks, highlighting the distance between the ideal and its historical realizations. But this use of the term heightens the value of civilization, as it suggests that none of the peoples and countries defined as civilized are genuine embodiments of this ideal state. Indeed, that civilization is something to be aspired to is a "truth" few ever question, even among those prone to discard the term because of its exclusive meaning. This, I argue, is because the genesis of the concept is generally ignored, civilization being viewed as a timeless ideal, rather than a specific historical process. If the history of "civilization" were better known, we might be more cautious in granting this term our unquestioning seal of approval, even though we might still conclude that Europe, and "the West," are indeed civilized.

To investigate the development of the term "civilization" in the English vocabulary—that is, its trajectory from its origin to its final destination, as a term characterizing the highest form of social existence—is the purpose of this essay. As I will show, the development of "civilization" is genetically intertwined with that of the British financial system, with the subjugation of Scotland to the British Crown, and the eighteenth-century social struggles in and out of Scotland. Thus, "civilization" originally referred to three different but interconnected processes: the rationalization of intracapitalist relations (civilization *qua* reason); the disenfranchisement of the English workers from their "traditional" rights and liberties (civilization *qua* repression); and the destruction of communal relations in the Scottish Highlands, resulting in the integration of Scottish society into the orbit of Britain's imperial economy (civilization *qua* progress from barbarism). Fundamental to each of these processes was the assimilation of the English Common Law to the Scottish Civil Law,[2] the first meaning, in the English vocabulary, of the term "civilization."

ETYMOLOGICAL DEVELOPMENT OF "CIVILIZATION"

The word "civilization," with its roots in the Roman experience (from the Latin *civis*, citizen), is not to be found in Middle English. "Civilization" entered the language in the early eighteenth century, as a technical legal term possessing both a specific and a general meaning. In its more limited sense, it defined "A law, act of justice, or judgment, which renders a criminal process civil; which is performed by turning an information into an inquest, or the contrary" (*Oxford English Dictionary*, 1989). Generally, however, the word referred to the process of "assimilating common law to civil law" (Jowitt, 1959). So it stood in 1755 when Samuel Johnson, the author of the most famous eighteenth-century English dictionary, gave the term a specific legal definition. Up to this time "civilization" was cognate with "civilian," which meant a professor of Roman or Civil Law.

The term's definition changed in the last half of the eighteenth century. The 1828 edition of Noah Webster's *American Dictionary of the English Language* defined "civilization" as "The act of civilizing, or the state of being civilized, the state of being refined in manners, from the grossness of savage life, and improved in arts and learning." Webster made it clear that the legal definition was a secondary one, and he placed next to it a cautionary "not used." We catch sight of this semantic change in one of the entries of James Boswell's *Life of Johnson*:

On Monday, March 23 [1772], I found [Johnson] busy, preparing a fourth edition of his folio Dictionary. Mr. Peyton, one of his original amanuenses, was writing for him. I put him in mind of a meaning of the word side, which he had omitted, vis. relationship, as father's side, mother's side. He inserted it. I asked him if humiliating was a good word. He said he had seen it frequently used, but he did not know it to be legitimate English. *He would not admit civilization, but only civility. With great deference to him, I thought civilization, from to civilize, better in the sense opposed to barbarity, than civility,* as it is better to have a distinct word for each sense, than one word with two senses, which civility is, in his way of using it. (Boswell, 1953: 466. Italics mine.)

Why did "civilization," which originated as a legal term, become a synonym of "refinement" and "improvement" and the antonym of "barbarity" and "savage life"? An answer to this question will take us to that thin strip of Scotland bordering England called the "Lowlands," to that eighteenth-century flourishing of bourgeois thought that goes by the name of the Scottish Enlightenment,[3] and to that peculiar institution which is Scottish law.

The Scottish legal system has differed from that of England since the sixteenth century. Modern Scottish law came into existence with the introduction of the Calvinist *Institutes*, the pillar of the Presbyterian Kirk during the Reformation. This law was patterned on Roman Civil Law and incorporated the legal wisdom of the most successful empire Europe knew until the modern period. It relied on "principles," "reason," and "certainty," and thus stood in marked contrast to English Common Law, which was based on judicial precedent and was shaped by the indigenous struggles on the commons.

A sharp distinction between the Civil Law and the Common Law cannot be drawn on all grounds. "Those who contrast the Civil Law and the Common Law traditions, by a supposed non-use of judicial authority in the former and a binding doctrine of precedent in the latter, exaggerate on both sides" (Merryman, 1969: 48). But there was a significant difference in the way the two systems were viewed in the eighteenth century, North and South of the Scottish border. In England the Common Law was identified with the peculiarities of "English Liberty," while in Scotland it was taken as an example of English insularity, and contrasted to the universalizing Roman ethos of which Civil Law seemed to be the carrier. There was also a methodological difference between the Scottish and the English legal traditions: "[We have] a contrast between the two rival ways of constructing a legal system—the logical and deductive Scottish method formed upon Roman models, and the empirical and inductive English method built up by decided cases on native lines" (Holdsworth, 1938, XI: 16).

These contrasts were to have fatal consequences for the women of Scotland in the late sixteenth and early seventeenth centuries; for as we now know, the civilization of the Scottish legal system in the course of the Reformation was built on the stakes and gallows of the witch-hunt. The Scottish witch-hunt was notoriously much more intense and horrific than the English. Perhaps as many as three Scottish women were executed as witches for every English woman, even though England had a population four times that of Scotland (Levack, 1987: 184). In the past, the special severity of the witch-hunt in Scotland was attributed to the remoteness of the place, but the records show that the truly remote places in the Highlands and the Hebrides suffered no witch-hunt (Larner, 1981: 80; Smout, 1972: 189). The executed lived in Fife, Moray, Aberdeenshire, the Lothians, and the Borders, that is, in the Scottish Lowlands where the central government was in greater control (Larner, 1984: 72). In fact, the witch-hunt was due not to a lack but to a surfeit of civilization. There is now a scholarly consensus that explains the course of the witch-hunt in Scotland by pointing to the profound difference between the English and Scottish legal codes (Larner, 1981: 200; Levack, 1987: 184; Quaifee, 1987: 146). It is generally agreed that (1) Scottish law was inquisitorial, English law was not; (2) local, unsupervised magistrates often tried women as witches in Scotland, this did not happen in England; (3) judicial torture was rare in England, not in Scotland; (4) English juries required unanimity, Scottish juries required only a majority; (5) English law was flexible in sentencing, Scottish magistrates applied the stipulated capital sentence with few scruples. Christina Larner, who contributed to forging this consensus, summarized it in the following way: "The Scottish system was Roman, inquisitorial, and theoretical; the English based on statute law and pragmatic. A person accused of witchcraft under an inquisitorial system was tortured to confess and to name accomplices. The naming of accomplices produced the mass hunts characteristic of Scotland and parts of the Continent" (Larner, 1984: 77).

The witch-hunt in Scotland gave the English a graphic display of the differences between their legal systems, for tracts describing the Scottish witch-trials were popular with the English reading public throughout the seventeenth century. This perhaps accounts for the aura of severity that the Scottish law had in the English social imagination in the eighteenth century.

Even the 1707 Act of Union fell short of unifying England and Scotland with respect to the law.[4] Although Scotland at the time was underdeveloped economically and politically in comparison to England, the Scottish bourgeoisie prided itself in its older, imperially rooted legal institutions and strove to ensure their continuance. This was guaranteed by several provisions of the Union Treaty. The most crucial provision was Article XXII, which stipulated "that the laws which concern public right policy and civil government may be made the same throughout the whole United Kingdom; but that no alteration be made in laws which concern private right except for evident utility of the subjects within Scotland" (Walker, 1976: 125).

Allowing Scotland to retain its legal system was an important concession on the side of the English ruling class. It was an eloquent sign of its desire to win the support of the Lowland Scottish bourgeoisie who, it was hoped, would help them break the might of the Scottish Highlanders, whose military prowess England had learned to fear, after their invasions of England in 1715 and 1745, and their two aborted attempts of 1708 and 1719. The Scottish Highlanders posed a unique threat for the British Empire, which by the first quarter of the eighteenth century controlled parts of the Americas, India, and Africa. For they exposed its rear door to an uncolonized population who, in refusing English rule, refused integration in the expanding circuit of capitalist relations. The Act of Union showed that an alliance between the London rulers and the Lowland bourgeoisie was profitable to both parties. Thus, for the sake of the treaty, the English politicians bowed to the jewel of Scottish nationalist pride: the Civil Law tradition. In time, however, they themselves perceived the superior advantages of Scottish Civil Law as a principle of social organization. In view of the meaning the term was to acquire in this period, we could say that they themselves were "civilized."

SCOTTISH CIVIL LAW VERSUS ENGLISH COMMON LAW

The Civil Law was highly valued by the eighteenth-century Scottish ruling class, who believed it provided the foundations for social and political life. A legal career was a "must" among the bourgeoisie and the landed gentry alike, for anyone intending to participate in economic and political activity; it was a guarantee of prestige. When in the 1770s one of the first street directories was assembled in Edinburgh, the list of names placed the advocates first, then, in order, their clerks, the writers to the signant, their clerks, the nobility and gentry with town houses, and finally the remainder of the middle class, without much further distinction (Smout, 1972: 350). As late as the early nineteenth century, the dominant social and economic group in Edinburgh was the jurisprudential aristocracy, whose ranks produced the main figures of the Scottish Enlightenment. Lords Kames and Monboddo were eminent judges, John Millar and Adam Smith were legal scholars, and David Hume's only institutional position in Scotland was that of librarian at the Edinburgh Advocates' Library.

In the eighteenth century, the importance of mastering the Civil Law was so widely recognized among the upper class Scots that every year many directed their steps to the law schools of the continent, most often to Holland. Bowell did his legal studies at Utrecht, and in the seventeenth and eighteenth centuries about 1,600 Scottish lawyers studied in Leyden alone. Among the Advocates' Library's 1,500 law books, only about 100, in 1692, were not from continental presses (Holdsworth, 1938, XI: 15).

From their sojourn in Holland the aspirants to practice in the Parliament House brought back with them not only the principles they imbibed from the masters of the Roman-Dutch law, but also the treatises with which the law schools of the Dutch Universities were so prolific. No Scot lawyer's library was complete in those days which did not contain the works of Grotius, Vinnius, the Voets, Heineccius, and other learned civilians. (Walker, 1976: 134)

Such knowledge, Scottish law scholars believed, had much to contribute to the improvement of Britain's legal system, whose adherence to Common Law they viewed as perniciously flawed. English Common Law was too "peculiar" and was thus unfit for the management of international economic relations and too sensitive to pressure from popular struggles. In one word, it was too prone to "liberty." Why then, it was asked, had it prevailed in England over the rationally superior Civil Law? Two among the most eminent historians and legal philosophers of the Scottish Enlightenment, John Millar and David Hume, tackled this question.

In *An Historical View of the English Government* (1803), Millar argued that since the late Middle Ages Roman Civil Law had been associated with the institutional conflict between the universities and the court inns of Westminster (London), where (municipal) Common Law was taught. The tension between the nobility in Parliament and the clergy, who had run the universities, had reached a breaking point with the Reformation, when Civil Law had been improperly (in Millar's view) associated with Roman despotism, in both the ancient (imperial) and modern (catholic) sense of the word. The victory of the Reformation in England had sealed the fate of Civil Law (Millar, 1803: 316–40).[5]

The "unnecessary" association in the Middle Ages between the Civil Law and the Catholic Church is also the focus of Hume's account of its marginalization in England. Hume deplored that the English laity, covetous of the Church's possessions, should have rejected, together with the Catholic clergy, the Civil Law as well, viewing it as the tool of this discredited class. His objective was to remind the English of the immense social benefits Civil Law provided. In this process, he explicitly identified "civilization" with the principles of Civil Law. He argued that it had been the discovery of Justinian's *Pandects* that had restored Europe, after a centuries-long interruption, to its progressive path to civilization.[6] Civil Law had given "security to all other arts" and had acted as a "mild" but persistent historical force; for the judgments made on the basis of its "general and equitable maxims" had gradually improved not only the legal decisions, but the judges as well (Hume, n.d.: 510).

Hume and Millar did not despair of the possibility of civilizing the English legal system. Millar believed that it would soon be possible "for the enlightened judges of the present age to estimate the system of Roman jurisprudence, according to its intrinsic merits" (Millar, 1803: 338). Hume as well, despite his contempt for the English intellectuals and commoners, saw new possibilities in his age (Chisick, 1989). He admitted that "a great part of [Civil Law] was secretly transferred into the practice of the courts of justice," so that English law was rescued from "its original state of rudeness" (Hume, n.d.: 509).

"Secret transmission" is a major theme in Hume's social theory. Like other intellectuals of the Scottish Enlightenment, he considered "secrecy," "invisibility," "mildness," "custom," "habit," and "unintended consequences" as crucial tactics for social change, particularly when the interlocutors were the traditionalists in the English courts, who themselves were often besieged by the riotous English working classes.

The Scottish Enlightenment's "secret transmission" of civilization had three main objectives. The first was to turn English law into a more efficient vehicle for the management of exchange relations, through an injection of continental juridical wisdom. Scotland might be an underdeveloped country, but the best among its ruling class had been trained in the Netherlands, which at the time was *the* model of an advanced capitalist nation. It was in Amsterdam's banks and counting houses (as well as in Utrecht's law schools) that Scottish students learned how Civil Law was instrumental to the creation of a system of social exchange characterized by abstractness and regularity. Hume was confident that this knowledge would be valued by the English entrepreneurs (whether aristocrats or bourgeois), who frequently recognized their economic provincialism and turned to the Netherlands for inspiration.

The civilization of English law would also serve to thwart the English urban proletariat, who demanded a more egalitarian legal system, reflecting the "ancient rights of Englishmen"—that is, a system ensuring more popular control over the courts (through the extension of the right to trial by jury), over Parliament (through a widening of the electorate), and over the military (through restrictions on press-ganging and the use of martial law). Such demands were a challenge to the "thanatocratic" state England had become by the eighteenth century.[7] But the "civilization" of English law would void any appeal to traditional rights and to the judgment of sympathetic or pressurable jurymen. Under Civil Law, judgments would be shaped by "general and equitable maxims."

Finally, the aim of Scottish civilization was directed north of Edinburgh and Glasgow, at the Scottish Highlanders, who still lived under the law of the Celtic clan and constituted a threat to the commerce and government of the Scottish Lowlands and to the development of capitalism in Britain. They had to be defeated, possibly with the aid of the English army; but, most important, they had to be civilized.

CIVIL LAW AND THE RATIONALIZATION OF ENGLISH CAPITALISM

The "civilization" of English law was most urgently needed for the regulation of commercial international exchanges, where the application of Common Law proved disastrously inadequate. Based on precedents and drawn from the workings of a domestic economy, Common Law could not provide a legal framework for international trade, nor could it cope with the increasing sophistication and velocity of currency exchange. For example, the Common Law's preference for particularized contractual relations, that is, its tendency to understand contracts as occurring between concrete persons, and not abstract entities like corporations and the state, thwarted the creation of credit-based bank notes. In eighteenth-century England, the conflict between the Common Law and the development of finance and trade was escalating. The "financial revolution," launched after the "Glorious Revolution" of 1689, had led to the expansion of "symbolic" or "imaginary" forms of money (Caffentzis, 1989). But the invasion of the imaginary by the monetary sphere was not easily comprehended. As Sir Albert Feavearyear notes:

in the first half of the 18th century the customers of the London banks made use to about an equal extent of the notes of those banks and of drafts upon cash accounts kept with them. Between these two documents at the outset there was really very little difference. The notes were generally for large, and often for broken, amounts, were frequently made out, not to "bearer," but to "order," and in the latter case passed current by endorsement like a cheque. It is not surprising, therefore, to find that the early writers upon paper currency drew no distinction between the various forms in which they found it. They grouped them all together as "paper credit," and held that all of them drove out and took the place of metallic money. There was no important difference between the note signed by Francis Child, the banker, which said: "I promise to pay to Mr. John Smith or order, on demand the sum of £186. 14s. 2d.," and the draft signed by John Smith and addressed to Francis Child which said: "Pay to Robert Brown or order the sum of £186. 14s. 2d." No one regarded the former as in any way more entitled to be considered money than the latter. Davenant, Hume, and Sir James Steuart all spoke of notes, bills, drafts, bank credits, and even securities, as though they were a part of the circulating money of the country. (Feavearyear, 1963: 258–69)

In 1700, however, Chief Justice Sir John Holt declared that "promissory notes" were not negotiable. This meant that a John Smith would not be able to transfer his right to the payment of £186. 14s. 2d. to another person, and this in turn to another one. This measure provoked a crisis in the commercial and banking practice of England. Holt defended his decision, arguing that a note could not be a bill of exchange because "the maintaining of these actions upon such notes were innovations upon rules of the Common Law; and that it amounted to the setting up of a new sort of specialty, unknown to the Common Law, and invented in Lombard Street, which attempted in these matters of bills of exchange to give laws to Westminster Hall" (Holdsworth, 1926: 172).

In effect, Holt was claiming that the "promise" implied in a "promissory note" was legally valid only between identifiable individuals, and not between an individual and an abstract, interchangeable bearer of the note, as allowed by Civil Law (Rotman, 1987). "Lombard Street," however, did not appreciate Holt's defense of the Common Law's prejudice for nominalism, nor did it welcome his suspicion of continental innovations. Its spokesmen in Parliament overturned Holt's decision and confirmed as negotiable all notes payable to A simply, to A or order, to A or bearer. This is how Sir William Holdsworth, the twentieth-century legal historian, sums up this conflict between the defenders of Common Law and the spokesmen for the city's trading and financial interests: "This episode taught the courts that they could not wholly ignore approved mercantile custom; they must adapt the rules to such customs; that in fact there were cases in which 'Lombard Street must be allowed to give laws to Westminster Hall.' And the eighteenth century was to show that the courts had learned the lesson" (Holdsworth, 1926: 176).

In this context, the changes introduced by Scottish jurists, who frequently worked their way into English courts, gradually undermined the authority of Common Law. Evidence of this development can be found in some technical, but significant, points of law, such as the "doctrine of consideration" and that of "quasi-contract." Both areas show the mounting influence of capitalist relations on social life, and the growing dominance of abstract, general considerations in the regulation of social transactions.

The doctrine of "consideration" in Common Law served to distinguish two kinds of agreements: enforceable contracts and unenforceable "pacts." In the Common Law tradition, some "consideration" had to pass between two parties, in order for an enforceable contract to exist between them. (An unenforceable pact would be my promising to give my car to X simply because I like X, and without any "consideration" on X's part.)

In the course of the eighteenth century, this view was challenged by a new doctrine postulating that a "moral obligation," grounded on principles of equity, was a sufficient basis for the existence of a contract. Thus "consideration"—that is, the passing of values from one party to another, in the new Civil Law approach—became merely evidential, ceasing to be the criterion for the existence of a contract. As Sir F. Pollock pointed out, if this view had been accepted, the whole modern development of English contract law would have been changed,"and its principles might have been . . . assimilated to those of the law of Scotland" (Holdsworth, 1926: 34). More than that, had this view been accepted, then the question of who would decide what was a moral obligation would have become vital, and the distinction between moral reason and legality would have been in danger of collapsing.

A similar situation developed in the area of "quasi-contracts," these being obligations implied but not explicitly stipulated by law. The change here would have affected that increasingly grey area of contractual life, where one was under the obligation to pay, despite the lack of a contract (Harding, 1966: 285). Take the example of a merchant whose cargo was scattered in a storm, retrieved by another merchant's vessel, and returned to the first merchant. Was the first merchant obligated to pay the costs of retrieval? Not necessarily, since there was no explicit contract between the two merchants. But, under the rubric of "quasi-contract," one could argue that the first merchant had an implied obligation to pay the second. As Lord Mansfield, the leading theorist of such an extension of the law, put it, depending on the circumstances, "there are ties of natural justice and equity that compel one to pay or refund the money" (Holdsworth, 1926: 97).

As one can see from these encroachments of Common Law, the leading probe was the notion of "equity." "Equitable principles," "equitable maxims," abound in the writings of the Scottish Enlightenment. It was here that the Scottish "secret transmission" achieved its most "civilizing" impact on the English legal tradition.

From the Middle Ages to the eighteenth century, England had two courts and two legal systems: the King's courts with their highly developed Common Law, and the courts of Chancery, whose code of equity was historically rooted in the Civil Law. In the eighteenth century, the decision to go to the courts of Chancery was based on the possibility of having one's case judged outside the network of precedent. The courts of Chancery thrived in the marginal and undecidable aspects of the Common Law. But this practice generated a conflict between the two branches of the law, which Scottish jurists were quick to detect as the weak link in the English legal system. Thus, Lord Kames, in his *Principles of Equity* (1760), calling for the end of this division, stressed the superiority of Scottish law where principles of equity were fully integrated into the legal system. For "Equity, in the proper sense, comprehends every matter of law that by the Common Law is left without remedy" (quoted in Lehmann, 1971: 212). It is not insignificant that, as an example of the application of equitable principles, Kames mentions the suppression of workmen's combinations (MacCormick, 1982: 157-58).

CIVILIZATION AND THE REPRESSION OF POPULAR JUSTICE

For my part, my Passions are very warm for the Memory of King Alfred, who hang'd 44 Judges in one year, as Murthers of the Law.

North Briton Extraordinary, no. 83

While the British ruling class hailed the civilization of mercantile law, the civilization process was to find a formidable obstacle in the London "lower sorts," for whom the defense of Common Law was of prime importance. Being based on the trial by jury system, Common Law was more responsive to popular pressure, as the jury was almost independent of the judge.

It was for this very reason that Scottish jurists in England and their disciples labored to abolish this system, which was still used in both civil and criminal cases. In promoting this change, the Scottish jurists took the opposite path from that pursued by lawyers and philosophers on the continent. Here the "Enlightenment" inspired a juridical reform that was to eliminate the more inquisitorial aspects of Civil Law procedure, such as judicial torture, whose abolition was promoted by the Italian jurist Cesare Beccaria.[8] By contrast, the Scottish jurists strove to limit both the power of the jury and the right of the "populace" to interfere in matters concerning law and government.

What criteria inspired their work can be seen in a politically important libel case, *The Dean of St. Asaph's Case*, which was tried in 1783. The judge, Lord Mansfield, ruled that the jury only had the right to determine whether the accused wrote and published the document, and whether the document referred to the offended parties. Beyond that, it was the judge's prerogative to determine whether the publication was libelous. This refusal to grant the jury the right to make a "general verdict" well expresses the civilizing effort in England. "Civilization" meant that the juries would not be "intrusted with a power of blending law and fact, and following the prejudices of their affections or passions" (Holdsworth, 1938: 679). None fought more strenuously against jury trial than the same Scots-born Lord Mansfield who, in response to an effort to introduce the system in Scotland, wrote: "The partial introduction of trials by jury seems to me big with infinite mischief and will produce much litigation. . . . It is curious that fraud, which is always a complicated proposition of law and fact, was held in England as one of the reasons for a court of equity, to control the inconveniences of a jury trying it" (Campbell, 1878: 554).

Mansfield's words must be read in the context of the increasingly sharp confrontations between the state and the London proletariat which, year after year, led to a dramatic increase in the use of "summary proceedings" (i.e., trials without jury against offenders of parliamentary statutes, especially in the areas of taxation and "public peace"). "Of late," William Blackstone drily noted in his *Commentaries*, "[this procedure] has been so extended, as to threaten the disuse of trials by jury" (Blackstone, 1892: 676).

Born in the Scottish Lowlands in 1705, Lord Mansfield (originally William Murray) was the main agent of legal civilization in England. For more than fifty years, from the late 1720s to the mid-1780s, Mansfield worked at the civilization of English Common Law, and he nearly succeeded in "civilizing" the principles of commercial and mercantile law.

He met the consequences of his work, however, in the form of a riotous resistance by the London proletariat, which he helped to repress. This aspect of his work is often underplayed by the increasingly Thatcherite scholarship of our times. In a hagiographic biography, Edmund Heward concludes that "Lord Mansfield's greatest contribution to the law of England was establishing principle both as the mainspring of Common Law, and as a means of threading through the thickets of particularity" (Heward, 1979: 170). But Heward fails to inform us that many in the streets of London viewed Mansfield's "principle" as juridical despotism.

Resistance to Mansfield's civilizing efforts came from two sources. On the one side there was the "middling sort": the merchants and artisans, whose affairs were centered in London and the main provincial towns. On the other was "the inferior set of people," those whom Sir John Fielding described as "the infinite number of chairmen, porters, labourers and drunken mechanics" (Rude, 1962: 6). Both were excluded from the surplus generated by the system of slavery, extermination, and trade later known as the British Empire. Their confrontation with Mansfield intersected with a period of struggle that has passed into British history as the "Wilkes and Liberty" days (1763–74).

John Wilkes was a leading organizer of the "Society of Supporters of the Bill of Rights." He was a flamboyant politico who embodied the resistance to the threat civilization posed to English law. The Wilkites demanded the total accountability of magistrates, from the king to the local J.P., before the law; the elimination of class-based discrimination in legal practices; the institution of trial by jury in almost all legal proceedings; and the gaining of public consent before military force could be used in controlling social crises (Brewer, 1980: 140). William Moore, a contemporary of Wilkes, thus summarized the Wilkite position: "the greatest happiness any nation can enjoy, is being governed by laws by the consent of the people, either collectively or representatively, and of having a right to call the principal magistrates intrusted with the execution of those laws to an account for maladministration" (Brewer, 1980: 142).

Naturally, the Wilkites found their nemesis in Lord Mansfield. *The North Briton*, the major organ of the Wilkites, continually countered Mansfield's assault on public accountability, equality, jury trial, and deference to public consent in times of crisis:

the judge has little more to do than to superintend the trial, and to preserve inviolate the forms of justice. . . . But can this compliment be paid to a judge, who confounds, controuls and browbeats a jury? Who changes, garbles and packs a jury? Who in all his speeches, is perpetually talking of supporting the measures of the government, that is the prerogative of the crown, but never once of supporting the privileges of the people. (Brewer, 1980: 158)

At the peak of the Wilkite campaign against Mansfield, an anonymous letter writer appeared on the London scene to challenge the chief justice. Under the pseudonym "Junius" in November 1770, he published a public letter "To The Right Honourable Lord Mansfield," whose beginning reflected the anti-Scot sentiment pervasive in London and the major provincial towns at the time:

"I own I am not apt to confide in the professions of gentlemen of that country, and when they smile, I feel an involuntary emotion to guard myself from mischief" (Junius, 1978: 207). The letter points to the struggle between Common and Civil Law, which had reached a climax during the reign of James I, the Scottish king (Levack, 1973: 122-23):

In contempt or ignorance of the common law of England, you have made it your study to introduce into the court, where you preside, maxims of jurisprudence unknown to Englishmen. The Roman code, the law of nations, and the opinion of foreign civilians, are your perpetual theme; but whoever heard you mention Magna Carta or the Bill of Rights with approbation or respect? (Junius, 1812: 162-63)

Junius bemoaned the introduction of the rules of equity:

Instead of those certain, positive rules, by which the judgement of a court of law should invariably be determined, you have fondly introduced your own unsettled notions of equity and substantial justice. Decisions given upon such principles do not alarm the public so much as they ought, because the consequence and tendency of each particular instance, is not observed or regarded. In the mean time the practice gains ground; the court of King's Bench [Mansfield's court] becomes a court of equity, and the judge, instead of consulting strictly the law of the land, refers only to the wisdom of the court, and to the purity of his own conscience (Junius 1812: 164). . . . But what kind of conscience is it that is "making the trial by jury useless and ridiculous" and would like "to introduce a bill into parliament for enlarging the jurisdiction of the court, and extending your favorite trial by interrogatories to every question, in which the life or liberty of an Englishman is concerned"? (Junius, 1812: 174)

The letter, which Horace Walpole called "the most outrageous I suppose ever published against so high a magistrate by name" (quoted in Junius 1978: 206), ended with a warning concerning the possible consequences of Mansfield's civilizing project: "It is remarkable enough . . . that the laws you understand best, and the judges you affect to admire most, flourished in the decline of a great empire, and are supposed to have contributed to its fall" (Junius, 1812: 181).

Junius's defense of the "traditional rights of Englishmen" undoubtedly appealed to the "middling sort," who feared the advance of civilization on the level of property transactions. But Mansfield's work was known in a more carnal way by the London proletariat and those who appeared at the sites of the provincial assizes.

Judicial hanging, as a means of class intimidation, was an essential element of the restructuring of mercantile law that Lord Mansfield was responsible for (Hay, 1975). In his twenty-nine Sessions at the Old Bailey, Mansfield personally ordered 29 people for branding, 448 for transportation, and 102 for hanging (Linebaugh, 1993: 360). He was also for twenty-two years on assize (the court sessions periodically held outside of London), where he treated the provincials to the same terror he meted out in London (Heward, 1979: 66–70). Thus, Mansfield was popularly considered a reincarnation of Judge Jenkins, the hanging judge of the first period of judicial thanatocracy; and "the *cheveux de frise* [the eighteenth-century equivalent of barbed wire], atop the wall of King's Bench prison, was known as 'Lord Mansfield's teeth'" (Linebaugh, 1993: 360). Mansfield's principles of equity stopped at the debtors and thieves. Even in his seventy-sixth year (1781), he demanded in the House of Lords that both the families of imprisoned debtors and spiritous liquors be kept out of prison, so that "imprisonment should in future be more rigid" (Heward, 1979: 61). His request was likely stimulated by the events of the previous year, which were crucial for the fate of civilization in England.

In June 1780 the London proletarians took to the streets in what became known as the Gordon Riots. Their main objects were juridical: the "delivery of Newgate," the freeing of the debtors, the attack on the Old Bailey, and, last but not least, the destruction of Lord Mansfield's house.[9]

In the days after June, the "savagery" of the London poor was much decried, by poets and politicians alike, as an ominous sign of imperial fall. The crowd left a burning Newgate Prison reinforced by the liberated prisoners, and Lord Mansfield heard that

an immense multitude, carrying torches and combustibles, were marching down Holborn, and entering Bloomsbury Square . . . when they began to batter his outer door, he retreated by a back passage with the Countess; and he had hardly escaped from their fury when their leaders were seen at the upper windows, tearing down and throwing over furniture, curtains, hangings, pictures, books, papers, and every thing they could lay their hands on, likely to serve as fuel for the fire that was already blazing below. In this instance resembling a Paris mob, they declared that there was to be no pillage, and that they were acting on principle. Pilfers were punished; and one ragged incendiary, to show his disinterestednesss, threw into the burning pile a valuable piece of silver plate and a large sum of money in gold, which he swore should not "go in payment of masses." (Campbell, 1878: 524)

Two opposing principles of justice met in Bloomsbury Square on that day. On the one side was Mansfield's transmission of the Civil Law of Rome into the sinews of the emerging global empire, and on the other was a proletariat who demanded a justice beyond and against the universalization of mercantile law. This conflagration of civilization is thus described by Campbell: "Flames were speedily vomited from every window; and, as no attempt was or could be made to arrest their progress, long before morning nothing of the stately structure remained but the bare and blackened skeleton of the walls" (Campbell, 1878: 524).

The lawyer-poet, William Cowper, thus lamented over the burning books of civilization:

So then—the Vandals of our isle,
Sworn foes to sense and law,
Have burnt to dust a nobler pile
Than ever Roman saw! (Quoted in Campbell, 1878: 525)

None lamented, however, those shot by the soldiers who came on the scene two hours after Mansfield's books began to burn. Nor, until recently, have John Gray, Leititia Holland, and Mary Gardiner been mourned, who were sentenced to death for taking part in the assault on "the noble pile" (Linebaugh, 1985). Their notion of "right" was not included under Blackstone's categories, and their "wit and genius" have not been inscribed in well-purchased pages. Yet their power was decisive. The Gordon Riots put an end to the civilization of English law. Within a decade, Mansfield's innovations began to be rejected in the areas of contract and punishment by the very lawyers and judges who had stood before him in awe. This contraction from the Civil Law was done in the style of jurisprudence. But behind the rejection of Mansfield's civilization of law lay the "bare and blackened skeleton" of his home. His library was not strong enough.

SCOTLAND AND THE CIVILIZATION OF THE HIGHLANDS

Somebody observing that the Scotch Highlanders, in the year 1745, had made surprising efforts, considering their numerous wants and disadvantages: "Yes, Sir, [said he] their wants were numerous; but you have not mentioned the greatest of them all—the want of law." (Boswell, 1934: 126)

Johnson's joking remark pointed to a contradiction that plagued the lawyers and philosophers of the Scottish Enlightenment. At the very time when they were striving to civilize the courts and streets of London, their own countrymen, if not blood relations, were the most "barbarous," "lawless" people in eighteenth-century Britain. Johnson, however, was wrong. The Scottish Highlanders had laws. They were the law of the clan, pivoted on communal identity and communal land property, and administered by the clan chief and the heads of the septs, the chieftains, who governed without the blessing of a king, archbishop, or chief justice. The chiefs were "a law unto themselves"; they were also owners of clan land, as land tenure in the eighteenth century was becoming increasingly privatized.[10] But although they rented to "tacksmen," who in turn sublet to clansman tenants, clannish obligations still subsisted. The chief was expected, in times of collective or personal crisis, to extend his surplus to his clansfolk. And the rents the chiefs exacted were tempered by a sort of "war communism," as the chiefs saw in their clansmen not only a source of labor but also a source of military strength.

This unstable combination of tribal communalism, feudalism, and private ownership called for a military loyalty that was no longer known to the press-ganging English. Chieftains, tenants, and subtenants all were expected to join in military enterprises, whether they involved cattle-rustling, interclan feuds, or the attempt to seize state power in the world's largest empire. Such an attempt was made in 1745, the year referred to in Johnson's joke, when the Scottish clansmen marched from Inverness to put "Bonny Prince Charlie" on the English throne.[11]

Their gestures became the marvel of the age, inspiring much reflection on the civilization process. But the spectacle of the 1745 invasion of the Lowlands and England (like the one in 1715 and the aborted ones in 1708 and 1719) was as distressing to the Scottish civilizers as to the English. "How could they have done it?" More crucially, "How could they be stopped from trying again?" was a question on everyone's mind in Edinburgh and Glasgow (as well as in London) decades after the event. This is how Adam Smith answered the first question in his 1766 Lectures on Jurisprudence:

Another bad effect of commerce is that it sinks the courage of mankind, and tends to extinguish martial spirit. In all commercial countries the division of labour is infinite, and every ones thoughts are employed about one particular thing. . . . Each of them is in a great measure unaquainted with the business of his neighbour. In the same manner war comes to be a trade also. . . . The defense of the country is therefore committed to a certain sett of men who have nothing else ado; and among the bulk of people military courage diminishes. . . . This is confirmed by universal experience. In the year 1745 four or five thousand naked unarmed Highlanders took possession of the improved parts of this country without any opposition from the unwarlike inhabitants. They penetrated into England and alarmed the whole nation, and had they not been opposed by a standing army they would have seized the throne with little difficulty. (Adam Smith, 1978: 540–41)

The invasion was blamed on civilization, that is, on the increasing "refinement," "luxury," and "effeminacy" brought about by the commercial spirit whereby "The minds of men are contracted and rendered incapable of elevation, education is despised or at least neglected, and heroic spirit is almost utterly extinguished. To remedy these defects would be an object worthy of serious attention" (Adam Smith, 1978: 541).

The task was either to strengthen the heroic spirit of the civilized Lowlanders, or to "refine" and "effeminize" the Highlanders. The Scottish intellectuals realistically opted for the latter course. Their first task was to create the conditions whereby the Highlanders could become civilized. This posed the problematic of historical stages—Savagery, Barbarism, and Civilization—which, not surprisingly, became a major theme in the thought of the Scottish Enlightenment.[12] Adam Ferguson, David Hume, Lord James Burnett Monboddo, Lord Kames and Adam Smith were among a host of chronographers who expatiated on "how from being a savage, man rose to be a

Scotsman," as Walter Bagehot later quipped (quoted in Bryson, 1968: 89). While their approach differed, they agreed that these clannish "Irish" roaming the Highlands were a model of barbarism. (The Lowlanders were frequently unwilling to admit that the Highlanders were Scots.)

In the anthropological scheme of the Scottish Enlightenment, "barbarism" was an intermediate stage between "civilization"—whose essence was law and convention, providing order and stability for the protection of property—and "savagery," which was characterized by the absence of property. Savages were hunters and fishermen. Barbarians came into being with movable property (they were herders living in small clans), while only with unmovable property could "civilization" take off. As Ferguson put it (echoing Rousseau): "He who first said 'I will appropriate this field; I will leave it to my heirs'; did not perceive, that he was laying the foundation of civil laws and political establishments" (Bryson, 1968: 48).

How could one transform these "Irish" Highlanders from barbarians into civilized "Scots"? A social "contract" struck with the clan leaders, or among the Highlanders themselves, would be unthinkable. To Locke's assumption of an "original contract" Scottish philosophers unanimously objected that this would first require the formation of individuals capable of contracting. Smith rejected John Locke's theory with sarcasm: "Ask a common porter or a day-labourer why he obeys the civil magistrate, he will tell you that it is right to do so, that he sees others do it, that he would be punished if he refused to do it, or perhaps that it is a sin against God not to do it. But you will never hear him mention a contract as the foundation of his obedience" (Smith, 1978: 402-3).

For Adam Smith, civilization originates not from the private consent of independent individuals, but from the principles of authority and utility. Hume's rejection of contract theory was even more decisive. He wrote in 1752: "'Tis vain to say, that all governments are, or should be, at first, founded on popular consent, as much as the necessity of human afairs will admit . . . I maintain . . . that conquest or usurpation, that is, in plain terms, force, by dissolving antient governments, is the origin of almost all the new ones, which ever were established in the world" (Hume, 1768: 499).

Here in essence was a strategy for the civilization of the Highlanders. Its premise was that it would be impossible to negotiate with them, for no agreement would be binding on them. Another plan was necessary, grounded on a healthy dose of Humean force and followed by measured injections of Smithian authority and utility. The plan called for a military defeat of the Highlanders, the cooptation of the remaining leaders, and the application of "utility" for the transition to civilized life. The first part of the plan was put into place with the defeat of the clans at the battle of Culloden in 1746.

Some five thousand men had risen under their chiefs for the Pretender: they were physically smashed as fighting units by the battle and by the atrocities which followed it. Legislation then consolidated the work of the army throughout the Highlands. No one anywhere in the Highlands was allowed to carry firearms (a significant exemption was made for cattle drovers), or to wear Highland dress or to play the pipes which were associated by the Government with barbarous habits and martial deeds. . . . A committee of Edinburgh lawyers was constituted to administer the estates forfeited from rebel leaders in all parts of the Highlands. Though not in any way vindictive, they worked on the assumption that Highland peasants were ignorant, idle and culturally savage, and they therefore strove to do all they could to eliminate the mores of the clan. (Smout, 1972: 321)

On this committee sat Lord Kames and others familiar with Hume's writings and Smith's lectures. They were in a position to transform the Highlands because the forfeited estates would only be sold to chiefs who supported the government. In 1752, legislation annexed thirteen forfeited estates "unalienably" to the Crown. All rents and profits were to be used for "Civilising the Inhabitants upon the said Estates and other Parts of the Highlands and Islands of Scotland," and for promoting among them "the Protestant religion, good Government, Industry and Manufactures and the Principles of Duty and Loyalty to his Majesty, his Heirs and Successors" (Youngson, 1973: 27).

The task of "civilizing" the Highlands thus fell to Scottish lawyers. Now other aspects of Hume's and Smith's concept of civilization came to the fore. "Utility," that is, the cultivation of self-interest, commerce and the division of labor, would undermine, once and for all, clannish communalism and martial spirit. The financing of an extensive education system and the construction of roads in the post–1745 era further tamed the Highlands. Later, a combined policy of enclosures, transportation, and factory work drove the Scots out of the Highlands into the capitalistic world. Through these processes, precapitalist Scotland ceased to exist, and a new "civilized" society took its place. How quickly this civilization process occurred can be seen by Johnson's description of the Highlands forty years after Culloden:

There was perhaps never any change of national manners so quick so great and so general, as that which has operated in the Highlands by the last conquest and the subsequent laws. We came hither too late to see what we expected—a people of peculiar appearance and a system of antiquated life. The clans retain little now of their original character: their ferocity of temper is softened, their military ardour is extinguished, their dignity of independence is depressed, their contempt of government subdued, and their reverance for their chiefs abated. Of what they had before the late conquest of their country there remains only their language and their [rural] poverty. (Johnson, 1971: 57)

Those too were lost with the Clearances, the land enclosures that took place in Scotland in the 1790s and early nineteenth century. Indeed, famines and clearances were the final result of the civilization of the Highlands.

CONCLUSION

Although the Scottish civilians and their allies made much progress in the eighteenth century on the path to civilization, Hume and Millar's hopes were never fulfilled. Commercial law in England proved to be the one area where civilization was most successful. Demands arising from England's domination of world trade and the increasing commodification of everyday life were a powerful propellant to the rationalistic ideology of Roman law. But in the post–1789 period anything Roman began to smack of subversion. Suddenly "theories," "reason," and "equality" became symptoms of revolution, and the credit of the Ancient Romans (along with their legal system) began to diminish. Thus, in his *Reflections on the Revolution in France*, Edmund Burke depicted the Romans as the "harshest of that harsh race" of conquerors, who modeled for the French revolutionaries the use of rationalistic terror (Burke, 1961: 199).

In such a changed climate, the vaunted universalistic, rationalist Civil Law lost its luster. The civilization of the criminal law in England was even less successful. The great political tumults of the Wilkites and the premonitory rumble of the Gordon Riots stopped the efforts to eliminate jury trials and to introduce inquisitorial methods in criminal proceedings in England. The ideological winds were changing. The implicit premise of Edward Gibbon's *Decline and Fall of the Roman Empire* (1776) was that the Roman state, although equipped with the most severe and equitable legal system, had not been able to defeat the insurrectionary movement of Christianity in its midst (Gibbon, 1952: 204). Thus, a refined skepticism as to the value of Civil Law as a defense of property and the state undermined the keystone of the civilian's argument.

Finally, the extirpation of the Highlanders succeeded beyond the expectations of Edinburgh legal aristocracy. The Highlanders were more decimated than civilized. The communal and feudal power of the clan chiefs was broken and the population scattered, but the legal structure of the Scottish land law did not undergo a complete civilization. In early nineteenth-century Scotland, Bell could write that "A double system of jurisprudence in relation to the subjects of property, has arisen in Scotland, as in most European nations—the one regulating land and its accessories according to the spirit of Roman jurisprudence which prevailed before the establishment of feus" (quoted by T. B. Smith, 1961: 38). And Smith could echo him in the mid-twentieth century: "the land law of Scotland remains the most feudal in the world" (T. B. Smith, 1961: 181–82). Although feudal obligations attached to land tenure were monetarized after Culloden, resistance to absolute ownership of land won the day and in the Scottish lawyers' own backyard.

These failures sealed the fate of legal civilization. Roman law, after a period of renaissance in the mid-eighteenth century, after the Gordon Riots began to lose its social and ideological power in Britain. This decline was never again reversed. The Civil Law's separate institutional existence ended in 1867 with the reform of the ecclesiastical and Admiralty courts and the destruction of the Doctors' Common (Levack, 1973: 201). However, 1867 was only the time of the burial, the project of civilization had died long before.

It appears in conclusion that the other definition of "civilization" which Boswell had urged Samuel Johnson to introduce in his Dictionary in 1772—in the sense of "opposed to barbarity"—was prescient. As a Scotsman trained in Civil Law, Boswell perhaps sensed that the time for legal definitions was passing, but nevertheless the transformation of the Scots from clanspeople and cattle rustlers to bankers and merchants (a transformation that was congruent with his life) needed a name. "Civilization" was a most appropriate term, as it blended the French concern for manners (Civility) with the Scottish commitment to Civil Law, and it suggested a strategy that combined military terror with economic development, a strategy indeed that would be used again and again at the service of the British Empire. We will not investigate here what motivated Johnson to refuse the term. Whatever his motives, it is sufficient to recognize that the collapse of the Civil Law tradition in the nineteenth century gave the Boswellian version of "civilization" the power to expand and dominate the linguistic and ideological field.

NOTES

1. E. Frances White quotes Graham Connah on this point: "The term 'civilization' has been quietly abandoned by many writers, it is too vague a concept and too subjective to be useful. It also has unpleasant connotations that are at best ethnocentric and at worst egocentric. It implies an 'us' and 'them' situation: we are 'civilized,' they are 'primitive'" (White, 1987).

2. There are two senses of "Civil Law" in English: one in contrast to Criminal Law and the other in contrast to Common Law. In the former sense, Civil Law regulates the conduct of exchange relations between private persons, while Criminal Law deals with conduct that implies liability to prosecution and punishment by the state. In the latter sense, Civil Law is a legal system based on Roman law, whereas Common Law is based on the body of law developed in the English King's courts. Thus, there are two senses of legal "civilization," that is, the transformation of Criminal into Civil Law and the transformation of Common into Civil (or Roman) Law. In this essay, we deal exclusively with the second transformation.

3. The Scottish Enlightenment refers to a period roughly from the 1730s to the 1780s, and to a set of persons (from Hutcheson to Millar) that includes philosophers, engineers, chemists, lawyers, and other intellectuals working in the narrow strip between Glasgow and Edinburgh. These Scottish intellectuals organized the "hardware" (the steam engine) and the "software" (theories of human nature) appropriate for the original exemplar of industrial capitalism. A sociological account of their circle can be found in Camic (1983).

4. A most unusual situation resulted from the Act of Union from the point of view of the "law of property, which nature herself has written upon the hearts of all mankind" (Edward Christian, quoted in Hay, 1975: 19). The most basic property rights and their adjudication were determined by a border, as English Common Law was not truly sovereign north of Dumfries (Walker, 1976).

5. The course of the Protestant Reformation in England was quite different from that of its Scottish version, a difference that had consequences for the tension between the Common and Civil Law. In England, Protestantism was driven by the Church of England, whose main interest was the destruction of the power of papal agents in England, and was therefore concerned with placing limits on Canon Law which was derived from Roman models. In Scotland, the driving force was Calvinism which demanded the generalizable Roman law.

6. The *Pandects* was the last major compilation of Roman law commissioned by Justinian in A.D. 530. It consists of fifty books, divided into laws, of selections from juridical writings from the republican period. It was meant to be the first complete legal code since pre-imperial times.

7. "Thanatocracy" is the term Linebaugh has coined to describe the expanded use of capital punishment to regulate class conflict in eighteenth-century Britain (Linebaugh, 1993).

8. Cesare Beccaria's *On Crimes and Punishments* (1764) not only criticized judicial torture but also argued for "a fixed code of laws, which must be observed to the letter," quite uncharacteristic of the Common Law.

9. For another account of the Gordon Riots emphasizing its class sentiments ("a groping desire to settle accounts with the rich, if only for a day, and to achieve some rough kind of social justice"), see Rude (1973: 289).

10. The elaborate division of agricultural labor that prevailed in the pre-Clearances Highlands is thus described by Smout: "The arable was divided runrig, and the organization of the whole joint farm was a cooperative one between eight or a dozen tenants, who contributed something to the common plough and obeyed communal rules for the grazing. They were everywhere assisted in husbandry by a large class of subtenants . . . normally these men held no more than a diminutive strip of arable and the right to graze a cow or a couple of goats on the pastures. They paid the tenant rent by working without wages upon his land for a certain time each week: the rest of the time they devoted to winning their own subsistence from the ground" (Smout, 1972: 317).

11. The 1745 invasion was a major effort by the "crofters in the Highlands and the small craftsmen in the Lowlands" to overturn the increasing, encroaching pressure on their form of life emanating out of London, Edinburgh, and Glasgow (Plumb, 1950: 107).

12. Social science, Marxist and non-Marxist, has not transcended this schema, although refinements are always available. Nineteenth-century theorists of civilization integrated racial determinants; early twentieth-century variants included disquisitions on parallel stages of rationality and prelogicality, while even postmodernists like Michel Foucault, Jean-François Lyotard, and Jean Baudrillard depend on it for their ironies (Baudrillard, 1983). Only by acknowledging that intellectual transmission is not simply a matter of diffusion from center to periphery can the stages metaphor be transcended.

REFERENCES

Ankarloo, Bengt, and Gustav Henningsen, eds. (1993). *Early Modern European Witchcraft: Centers and Peripheries*. Oxford: Clarendon Press.
Bagehot, Walter. (1965). *Collected Works*, Vols. I-VIII. Cambridge, Mass.: Harvard University Press.
Barstow, Anne Llewellyn. (1994). *Witchcraze: A New History of the European Witchhunts*. San Francisco: Pandora.
Baudrillard, Jean. (1983). *Simulations*. New York: Semiotext(e).
Blackstone, William. (1892). *Commentaries on the Laws of England*. New York: Strouse and Co.
Boswell, James. (1934). *Boswell's Life of Johnson*. George Birbeck Hill, ed., revised and enlarged by C. F. Powell, Vol. II. Oxford: Clarendon Press.
———. (1953). *Life of Johnson*. London: Oxford University Press.
Brewer, John. (1980). "The Wilkites and the Law, 1763–74." In John Brewer and John Styles, *An Ungovernable People: The English and Their Law in the Seventeenth and Eighteenth Centuries*. New Brunswick, N.J.: Rutgers University Press.
Bryson, Gladys. (1968). *Man and Society: The Scottish Inquiry of the Eighteenth Century*. New York: Augustus M. Kelley.
Burke, Edmund. (1961). *Reflections on the French Revolution*. Garden City, N.Y.: Doubleday.
Caffentzis, George C. (1989). *Clipped Coins, Abused Words, and Civil Government: John Locke's Philosophy of Money*. New York: Autonomedia.
Camic, Charles. (1983). *Experience and Enlightenment: Socialization for Cultural Change in Eighteenth-Century Scotland*. Chicago: University of Chicago Press.
Campbell, John. (1878). *The Lives of the Chief Justices of England*, Vol. III. New York: Cockcroft and Co.
Chisick, Harvey. (1989). "David Hume and the Common People." In Peter Jones, ed., *The "Science of Man" in the Scottish Enlightenment: Hume, Reid, and Their Contemporaries*. Edinburgh: Edinburgh University Press.
Connah, Graham. (1987). *African Civilization: Precolonial Cities and States in Tropical Africa, An Archeological Perspective*. Cambridge: Cambridge University Press.
Feavearyear, Sir Albert. (1963). *The Pound Sterling: A History of English Money* (2nd ed.). Oxford: Clarendon Press.
Forbes, Duncan. (1975). *Hume's Philosophical Politics*. Cambridge: Cambridge University Press.
Gibbon, Edward. (1952). *The Decline and Fall of the Roman Empire*, Vol. I. Chicago: Encyclopedia Britannica.
Harding, Alan. (1966). *A Social History of English Law*. Harmondsworth: Penguin.
Hay, Douglas. (1975). "Property, Authority and the Criminal Law." In Douglas Hay et al., *Albion's Fatal Tree*. New York: Pantheon Books.
Heward, Edmund. (1979). *Lord Mansfield*. Chichester and London: Barry Rose.
Holdsworth, Sir William. (1926). *A History of English Law*, Vol. VIII. Boston: Little, Brown.
———. (1938). *A History of English Law*, Vols. X, XI. London: Methuen and Co.
———. (1966). *Some Makers of English Law*. Cambridge: Cambridge University Press.

Hume, David. (1768). *Essays and Treatises on Several Subjects in Two Volumes.* London and Edinburgh: Millar.
———. (n.d.). *History of England,* Vol. II. Philadelphia: Claxton, Remsen and Haffelfinger.
Johnson, Samuel. (1971). *A Journey to the Western Islands of Scotland.* Mary Lascelles, ed. New Haven, Conn.: Yale University Press.
Jowitt, Earl. (1959). *The Dictionary of English Law.* London: Sweet and Maxwell.
Junius. (1812). *Junius,* including the letters by the same author, Vol. II. London: F., C. and J. Rivington.
———. (1978). *The Letters of Junius.* John Cannon, ed. Oxford: Clarendon Press.
Larner, Christina. (1981). *Enemies of God: The Witch-hunt in Scotland.* Baltimore: Johns Hopkins University Press.
———. (1984). *Witchcraft and Religion: The Politics of Popular Belief.* Oxford: Basil Blackwell.
Lehmann, C. (1971). *Henry Home, Lord Kames, and the Scottish Enlightenment.* The Hague: Martinus Nijhof.
Lenman, Bruce. (1977). *An Economic History of Modern Scotland: 1660–1976.* Hamden, Conn.: Archon Books.
Levack, Brian. (1973). *The Civil Lawyers in England 1603–1641: A Political Study.* Oxford: Clarendon Press.
———. (1987). *The Witch-hunt in Early Modern Europe.* London: Longman.
Linebaugh, Peter. (1993). *The London Hanged.* New York: Cambridge University Press.
———. (1985). "The Delivery of Newgate, 6 June 1780." *Midnight Notes* 8.
MacCormick, Neil. (1982). "Law and Enlightment." In R. H. Campbell and Andrew S. Skinner, *The Origins and Nature of the Scottish Enlightenment.* Edinburgh: John Donald Publishers.
Manchester, Anthony Hugh. (1966). "The Reformation of the Ecclesiastical Courts." *American Journal of Legal History* 10: 51–75.
Mann, F. A. (1982). *The Legal Aspect of Money* (4th ed.). Oxford: Clarendon Press.
Lord Mansfield, Ashburton and Thurlow. (1797). *A Treatise on the Study of the Law.* London: Harrison, Cluse and Co.
Marx, Karl. (1963). *The Eighteenth Brumaire of Louis Napoleon.* New York: International Publishers.
Merryman, John Henry. (1969). *The Civil Law Tradition.* Stanford, Calif.: Stanford University Press.
Millar, John. (1803). *An Historical View of the English Government,* Vol. II. London.
Oxford English Dictionary, 2nd ed. (1989). Oxford University Press.
Plumb, J. H. (1950). *England in the Eighteenth Century.* Harmondsworth: Penguin.
Quaifee, G. R. (1987). *Godly Zeal and Furious Rage: The Witch in Early Modern Europe.* New York: St. Martin's Press.
Rotman, Brian. (1987). *Signifying Nothing: The Semiotics of Zero.* New York: St. Martin's Press.
Rude, George. (1962). *Wilkes and Liberty: A Social Study of 1763 to 1774.* Oxford: Clarendon Press.
———. (1973). *Paris and London in the Eighteenth Century: Studies in Popular Protest.* New York: Viking Press.
Smith, Adam. (1978). *Lectures on Jurisprudence.* R. L. Meek, D. D. Raphael, and P. G.

Stein, eds. Oxford: Clarendon Press.
Smith, T. B. (1961). *British Justice: The Scottish Contribution*. London: Stevens and Sons.
———. (1962). *Scotland: The Development of Its Laws and Constitution*. London: Stevens and Sons.
Smout, T. C. (1972). *A History of the Scottish People: 1560–1830*. London: Fontana.
Walker, David M. (1976). *The Scottish Legal System: An Introduction to the Study of Scots Law*. Edinburgh: W. Green and Son.
White, E. Frances. (1987, Fall/Winter). "Civilization Denied: Questions on Black Athena." *Radical America*, 21(5): 38–40.
Youngson, A. J. (1973). *After the Forty-five: The Economic Impact on the Scottish Highlands*. Edinburgh: Edinburgh University Press.

3

True West: The Changing Idea of the West from the 1880s to the 1920s

Chris GoGwilt

There is no "true West" in a sense that is analogous to "true North," the term used to distinguish the pole of magnetic north from the real position of the earth's northern pole. However, as the Italian Marxist Antonio Gramsci argued in the 1930s, citing the authority of English philosopher Bertrand Russell, "because of the historical content that has become attached to the geographical terms, the expressions East and West have finished up indicating specific relations between different cultural complexes" (Gramsci, 1985: 447). My present concern is the recent history usually masked by that "historical content" which has come to be attached to the term "the West" and its cognates—"Western Civilization," "Western history," or "Western culture." Everyday usage in such diverse formulations as "Western diplomats," "Western philosophy," and "Western food" suggests that there is something essentially "Western," of long-standing historical continuity, linking all these things from diplomacy to philosophy to food. I argue, however, that it was only between the 1880s and the 1920s that "the West" entered the English language as a term linking a contemporary political bloc, a discrete historical development within world history, and a lived sense of cultural identity.[1]

Two contexts help show how the idea of the West, in a remarkably short period of time, came to appear an age-old idea. The first is that of British imperial rhetoric during the 1890s, at the height of the jingoism, propaganda, and politics of the "new imperialism." The second is that of Russian intellectual debates from the 1860s, which exercised a profound influence over the main currents of Western European culture and politics over the turn of the century. In both cases, it is apparent that the term gained currency in response to major social and political upheavals: in response to revolutions in Russia in 1905 and 1917; and in response to increasing resistance to colonialism. Behind the new rhetorical force attached to the term "the West" over the turn of the century, then, lies a far-reaching contestation of history and tradition—over contending versions of Europe's cultural heritage, and over the significance of Europe's colonial entanglement with the rest of the world. In the convergence of British and Russian influences on the term, an idea of "the West" emerged which has since served to reconstitute historical discontinuity as the continuity of "Western history."

Highlighting the recent emergence of the idea of the West cannot merely be a disinterested contribution to cultural history. It provides, however, an opportunity to reconceive debates about "Western Civilization." Both in the recent polemics concerning the teaching of "Western Civilization" courses, and in more theoretical debates such as those concerning the philosophical critique of "Western metaphysics," the seemingly descriptive term "the West" has perpetuated deep-rooted confusions over those "relations between different cultural complexes" it is used to designate. Most important of all is the misconception that the idea of "the West" is a coherent, intelligible idea, an idea whose historical referent is readily available to the users of the term. Such a "true West," I propose, is a myth; and to recognize it as such is to pose new challenges for academic study, teaching, and research.

Significant antecedents to the twentieth-century idea of the West may certainly be found. Hegel's *Philosophy of History* makes use of a contrast between East and West that sets a precedent for subsuming European history within a larger, single, self-contained historical evolution (Hegel, 1975: 196–97). In a very different vein, Marx's occasional pragmatic use of the term "the West" to distinguish levels of industrialization between Britain and India anticipates the way capitalism becomes virtually synonymous with "the West" (Marx, 1975: 320–21). Between Hegel and Marx it is possible to recognize two key elements in the twentieth-century idea of "the West": from Hegel, an intellectual historical evolution essentially linked to, but not synonymous with, European history; and from Marx, a historical evolution grasped in terms of the development of capitalism. Yet in neither case could "the West" constitute what Arnold Toynbee, in *A Study of History* (1935–61), would elaborate as "an intelligible field of study." What was occurring in the West (for Marx) or what was to be realized in the movement from East to West (for Hegel) was, for both, a process of universal human history. The idea of "Western" history that was to emerge between the 1880s and the 1920s, from one perspective, developed a more realistic assessment of the relation between world history and the European history that both Hegel and Marx made their privileged point of reference. Yet this new sense of historical proportion also eclipsed the imperative to realize European history as part of a single unfolding history of humanity. "The West"—as historical and political expression—became insulated from the world and world history.

It was not, however, around the term "the West" that such debates were articulated during the period of Europe's consolidation of worldwide hegemony in the nineteenth century. As Edward Said has shown, it was the term "the

East" that dominated almost every area of nineteenth-century European culture. Summarizing his point early in the study of what he calls the discourse of Orientalism, he writes:

Orientalism is never far from what Denys Hay has called the idea of Europe, a collective notion identifying "us" Europeans against all "those" non-Europeans, and indeed it can be argued that the major component in European culture is precisely what made that culture hegemonic both in and outside Europe: the idea of European identity as a superior one in comparison with all the non-European peoples and cultures. (Said, 1979: 7)

It is revealing that almost all of the examples of this sort of Orientalist discourse depend on a contrast between *Europe* and "the East." The increasing shift from the use of the term "Europe" to that of "the West," from around the turn of the century, tells of an important change in the fundamental shape of the idea of European identity. Increasing use of the term "the West" by no means uniformly indicates a diminishing sense of the superiority of a European identity. Nonetheless, a new awareness of global proportions radically unsettled ideas about what that European identity was.

There is one famous formulation of a "Western" perspective which helps measure the gap between nineteenth-century Orientalist assumptions about Europe's cultural and political superiority and those connected with the twentieth-century idea of the West. Thomas Babington Macaulay's report on Indian education, the famous Minute of 1835, helped shape British policies toward India by arguing for the promotion of European literature and science against the "Oriental system of education" supported by an earlier generation of English administrators. Macaulay's argument rests on the notorious claim that "a single shelf of a good European library was worth the whole native literature of India and Arabia." And he adds: "The intrinsic superiority of the Western literature is, indeed, fully admitted by those members of the Committee who support the Oriental plan of education" (Macaulay, 1970: 722). Marking a decisive change in Britain's administration of India, Macaulay's report brings together under the banner of education the fundamental tenets of the Liberal attitude toward Empire. What gives its reference to "the Western literature" a contemporary ring is the assumption of a set of values intrinsic to "Western" history, culture, and society, which forms the basis for modernizing "non-Western" societies.

To the extent that Macaulay's report provides a matrix for the set of concerns that will crystallize around the twentieth-century idea of the West, it outlines a set of conflicting claims about culture that lie at the heart of the contemporary term. When Macaulay identifies the key question facing administrators, it is to emphasize the question of how best to teach—whether in Arabic and Sanskrit or in English—over the question of *what* to teach. This enables him to link two different strains of his argument—first, that there is more useful knowledge contained in "the Western literature" than in the Arabic and Sanskrit literature; second, that this knowledge makes the English language the most worth learning. On the first point, knowledge and science are not directly linked to European societies and languages—indeed, Macaulay insists on the importance of Renaissance Europe having turned away from its vernacular as well as its indigenous myths and historical chronicles. On the second point, not only is such a link essential, but also it is made with respect to a particular European language, namely, English. Here we have an underlying contradiction that also informs contemporary formulations of the values of "Western Civilization," particularly as they are used within academic contexts: their universal applicability, on the one hand; and their rootedness in particular languages, societies, and cultures, on the other.

Yet, while Macaulay's famous Minute anticipates these guiding contradictions, Macaulay does not use the term "the West" in a contemporaneous a way. The term is simply descriptive, by contrast to the "Eastern" tongues of Arabic and Sanskrit. For Macaulay, there is nothing intrinsically "Western" about the knowledge contained in the shelf of a good European library. Precisely because the superiority of European knowledge remained unquestioned, there was no need for an idea of "the West." The need for such an idea only developed when it was no longer clear (to writers and administrators like Macaulay) what the intrinsic superiority of Europe's knowledge had to do with Europe and with what Europeans were doing administering societies outside Europe.

The significance of this shift from an idea of Europe to an idea of the West is further indicated by the diversity of uses of the term "the West" in the development of the political rhetoric of English imperialism through the nineteenth century. Benjamin Disraeli's *Tancred, or The New Crusade* (1847) and Charles Kingsley's *Westward Ho!* (1855) provide interesting mid-Victorian reference points, since each develops contrasting views of Britain's imperial destiny. Different though each novel is politically and in historical setting, both orient their historical subjects in relation to the medieval Crusades, which provide a historical grounding-point for constructing an opposition between East and West, between the "East" of Islam and the "West" of Christendom. Disraeli's *Tancred* does so explicitly in drawing a contrast between the way Europe's identity was shaped by the Crusades and the way nineteenth-century England might be regenerated by a new crusading spirit. Despite the idiosyncrasies of Disraeli's novel, one characteristic feature of what Said has called Orientalism emerges: the connection between the view that the origins of civilization lay in "the East" (which is to say, the Middle East), and militarist projects to conquer and control that "East" as part of a civilizing mission. Despite one or two references to "Western dress" or the philosophy and knowledge of "the West," it is striking that Disraeli, in a novel whose aim is to examine ways to renew European culture, never formulates his key ideas either in terms of, or in opposition to, a presumed continuity of "Western" history.

Charles Kingsley's *Westward Ho!* looks for the spirit of England's regeneration in a very different historical model. England's historic defeat of the Spanish Armada serves as an example for the spirit Kingsley proposes for nineteenth-century England. Kingsley's novel, by contrast to Disraeli's, is saturated with references to "Western" motifs, and most particularly to the key motif of the "westward course of Empire." In drawing, above all, on the rhetoric of Elizabethan England, Kingsley deliberately attempts to recapture a spirit of travel, adventure, and imperialist expansion; but what is notable in the novel's elaboration of the spirit of "westward" movement is the lack of any sense of Europe as the place of "the West." "The West" is not the place of civilization, let alone the reference point for a distinct "Western Civilization." Rather "the boundless west," in the most characteristic formulation of the novel, is the scene of maritime travel and adventure that will prove the English character to be more enduring than that of the Spanish rivals.

Taken together as two very different sources for the emergence of the "new imperialism" of the 1890s, Disraeli's *Tancred* and Kingsley's *Westward Ho!* illustrate that the political force of the term "the West" and its cognates remained diffuse and inconsistent within the dominant discourses of Empire in Victorian England. In neither Kingsley's archaic use of the term nor in the few modern usages that surface in Disraeli's work does "the West" emerge as a contemporaneous political identity assumed to connect whoever (or whatever) it qualifies with a history of cultural development both distinct from and superior to other cultures. Thus, the term "the West" in nineteenth-century usage, though often synonymous with Europe and particularly in contrasts between Asia and Europe, lacked the full social, political, and cultural associations embedded in the idea of "Europe."

The relatively sudden emergence of "the West" to replace nineteenth-century assumptions about Europe's cultural and historical identity involves an important rearrangement of associations. The archaic associations of "westering" motifs that Kingsley uses are emptied out to give new political value to the merely descriptive and relative term of Disraeli's novel. This process of remotivating earlier ideas of the West is registered in the poetic imagery of English Romantic poetry. From Percy Bysshe Shelley's "Ode to the West Wind" to patterns of sunset imagery found in lines like Wordsworth's "Thy sun hath had elsewhere its setting" (from "Ode: Intimations of Immortality"), poetic allusions to "Western" motifs constitute a distinctive mark of Romanticism. By contrast to Macaulay's prosaic use of the descriptive term "Western" in a political document, such poetic imagery involves a complex echoing of those Renaissance "westering" motifs that surface in the "boundless west" of Kingsley's *Westward Ho!*. The political impulse informing Romantic imagery of the early nineteenth century may be explained, however, as a repudiation of the political forms of Empire of the past and as an attempt to articulate a new universalism for the present. The metaphor of "the West" is used but deliberately disengaged from its temporary moorings in any real place.

A well-known sonnet by John Keats offers an instructive example. "On First Looking into Chapman's Homer," Keats's first published poem, explores the continuity of the spirit of poetry from Homer to the present (1816). The extended metaphor of the sonnet compares the act of reading Homer to travel and exploration. The octave works through a dense network of allusions to mythological places in Homer's work until the turn from the octave to the sestet clarifies the force of the extended metaphor in order to emphasize the poet's discovery of Homer through Chapman's translation. There, the poem shifts to describe, in the sestet, discoveries of new worlds—Herschel's discovery of Uranus and Bilbao's discovery of the Pacific Ocean. The overall argument of the poem seems to exemplify, and certainly anticipates, that contemporary idea of Western Civilization which traces a continuity of literary, scientific, and political history from classical Greece to modern times. Yet in the third line Keats draws on a complex poetic image that gives an interesting perspective on the way the term "western" functions in giving coherence to a perceived continuity of historical development. The opening reads:

> Much have I travell'd in the realms of gold,
> And many goodly states and kingdoms seen;
> Round many western islands have I been
> Which bards in fealty to Apollo hold.

The phrase "western islands" artfully links allusion to the Greek myth of the Hesperides to a specific, real geographical place, the British Isles, in order to consolidate the metaphorical connection between geographical travel and reading of the Classics. The emphasis on "many western islands" establishes at once that the poet is well read and well traveled. But, syntactically, it also belongs to the extended argument of the sonnet, which we might paraphrase—"I have traveled and read a great deal; but the experience of Chapman's translation changed my sense of both travel and literature." The internal dynamic of the poem might suggest, then, that the power of Chapman's translation of Homer—and the power of poetry in general—brings together into a single lyrical vision all the "many western islands" of the world.

What is revealing in this poetic achievement, however, is that the poem's use of the rich resources of diverse associations in the adjective "western" are legible only if one assumes the absence of the twentieth-century concept of "the West" as cultural history, political identity, or literary tradition. This point emerges precisely from the rich variety of cultural, political, and literary associations embedded or resonating in Keats's phrase, which we might amplify to include, besides the Homeric allusions—Virgil's use of the westward motif in *The Aeneid*, Dante's references both to Virgil and to Homer's Ulysses; the ambiguity of reference to the idea of the British Isles as the "western isles" and the Scottish and Irish "western isles" associated but having accrued a distinct geographical and political register of their own. Finally, since the phrase anticipates the concluding comparison between reading Chapman's Homer and Cortez's discovery of the New World, there is an allusion also to the "West" of the Americas, geographically lying to the West of Europe and imaginatively offering the hope of realizing the El Dorado myth in terms of the older Blessed Isles of Greek myth. The unifying vision of all these "western islands" can ever appear only as a momentary, if not mistaken, identity of myth and history.

This poetic use of the term "western" is radically different from the twentieth-century commonplace usage, both in the relation it posits between a multiplicity of "wests" and a singularity of lyrical experience, and in the sort of coincidence it crafts between mythological and geographical references. Today the rhetorical force of "western" culture depends on assumptions almost uncannily applicable to Keats's linking of Greek culture, literary tradition, translation, scientific discovery, and Europe's imperial expansion. But there is a great gulf separating Keats's use of the term "western" as a buried and allusive metaphor (one among others) for the possibilities of realizing universal human history from the contemporary sense of "the West" as a specific history—and most specifically, to paraphrase Theodor Adorno's famous statement about philosophy, as one that missed the opportunity of realizing itself as the horizon of all human history (Adorno, 1973: 3).

All these examples serve to illustrate the variety of different registers of meaning surrounding nineteenth-century English literary borrowings of older ideas of a mythic land to the west, of a westward movement ascribed to history or poetry, and of different cultural-geographical constructions of an opposition between East and West. On the one hand, they show the relative absence in English of that idea of the West that would become consolidated over the turn from the nineteenth to the twentieth century. On the other hand, when Keats's poem is linked to a whole set of English Romantic usages of "westering" metaphors, the example of English Romanticism suggests that the rhetorical force of earlier motifs of a "westering spirit" diminished politically through the nineteenth century (Hartman, 1970).

What, then, suddenly gave wide currency to an idea of "the West" as a coherent social, political, and cultural reality at the end of the nineteenth century? And what prompted the urgency with which the coherence of such a "reality" was argued? The rise in usage of "the West" and "Western Civilization" from the 1880s to the 1920s calls attention to a radical shift in the writing of world history from Herder's *Ideas on the Philosophy of the History of Mankind* (1784–91) to Spengler's *The Decline of the West* (1918–22) and (most notably in the context of our focus on English usages) Arnold Toynbee's *A Study of History*, conceived in the early 1920s and executed in twelve volumes between 1934 and 1961. Entirely absent in Herder, the term "the

West" becomes the organizing principle for Spengler and Toynbee.

With both Toynbee and Spengler, there is good reason to emphasize, as Roberto Retamar has done, the deciding factor of the Bolshevik Revolution of 1917 in determining the boundaries—both political and historical—of the twentieth-century idea of "the West" (Retamar, 1986: 1–25). However, what the reaction to the Bolshevik Revolution crystallized was an idea of the West that had already begun to emerge from responses to Russian ideas since the 1880s. The extreme conservative reaction against communist Russia consolidated a process whereby an evolving Russian debate about Europe helped redefine European culture and history in terms of an opposition between "Western" Civilization and the Russian, or Slavic peoples.

In 1883 we find an article in the French periodical, *La revue des deux mondes*, attempting to explain the significance of the term "Occidental" in Russian polemical debate: "'Occidental' can signify, depending on which camp you belong to, a path of light or a cursed trait" (Melchior, 1883: 793). Eugene Melchior, the Count de Vogüé, the author of the article and an influential commentator on Russian literature and culture, was writing about the novelist Ivan Turgenev, explaining the significance of his admission to feeling "Occidental": "It is necessary to be up to date with Russian polemics and with the jargon of contending parties to understand what storms this inoffensive word can unleash, what floods of ink and bile it lets loose each day" (793).

The two camps were those of the "Slavophiles" on the one hand and the "Westerners" on the other, both terms being pejorative inventions of the other side. The Slavophiles advocated a return to the purely Slavonic principles of pre-Petrine Russia (in other words, before Peter the Great's modernizing reforms on European models), while the Westerners espoused social and political reform according to European democratic models.

The significance of this Russian inflection to the idea of "the West" emerges in the literature on "nihilism," the phenomenon associated with the social and political movement of the 1860s that touched virtually every Russian intellectual. By the final decades of the nineteenth century, "nihilism" had come to signify a multiplicity of interrelated things: a broad social movement of the 1860s; a philosophical principle; and extremist violence of Russian revolutionaries (*Nuttal Encyclopedia*, 1900). Linked to a whole range of momentous social upheavals—the assassination of the Tsar Alexander II in 1881; the rise of Panslavism throughout Eastern Europe; the Japanese defeat of Russia in 1905; the revolution of the same year—the specter of Russian nihilism had haunted Europe in the years leading up to the First World War. By 1917, the contrast between Russia and "the West" had established a constellation of associations around which "Western civilization" could be constructed as the historical heritage to be defended against the assault of Russian nihilism.

The fact that Russian nihilism should come to stand for the assault on

Western traditions and values is particularly curious, given that the defining feature of the nihilism of the 1860s was its extreme reliance on rationality and science. Scientific positivism is the hallmark of Turgenev's portrait of a nihilist, Bazarov, in *Fathers and Sons*, the novel that made the term "nihilism" the rallying cry both for and against the new generation of Russian intellectuals Turgenev had sought to represent. Neither side of the polemical divide was content with the spirit in which Turgenev had presented his nihilist. Not in dispute, however, was the rationalist basis on which the "nihilist" sought to reform Russian society. The nihilist was a man who "looks at everything critically," according to one of Turgenev's characters. He was, as Kropotkin explained in 1899, "a positivist, an agnostic, a Spencerian evolutionist, or a scientific materialist" (Kropotkin, 1988: 195).

In this respect, the nihilists were more extreme "Westerners" than the so-called "Westerners" of the Slavophile controversy, as is amply illustrated by the novel that became a virtual handbook for nihilists, N. G. Chernyshevsky's *What Is to Be Done?* (1863). Its heroic nihilist is the new feminist woman, Vera Pavlovna, in whom the spirit of Russia's future is portrayed. Chernyshevsky's optimistic views of the perfectibility of humankind are embodied in her vision of a huge crystal house, obviously modeled on that mid-nineteenth-century emblem of industrial progress, Paxton's Crystal Palace, built for the Great Exhibition of 1851.

But the nihilism of the 1860s dramatically altered the nature of the earlier, tamer polemic between Slavophiles and Westerners. This change is evident in the work of Fyodor Dostoyevsky, whose reaction against the crude materialism and revolutionary spirit of the 1860s is notoriously embodied in his novel, *The Possessed* (1871). One of the most vehement and powerful of a whole set of antinihilist novels spawned in the wake of Turgenev and Chernyshevsky, it illustrates the psychological intensity with which the debates of the 1860s had uprooted the old camps of the Slavophile-Westerner debate. For his reactionary politics and his religious mysticism, Dostoyevsky has often been classed a Slavophile. But his works bring together Slavophile and Westerner principles in a way that captures the psychological complexity of the cultural identity of Russian intellectuals after the 1860s. Peter Christoff, discussing the transformation of Slavophile ideas in this period, notes the importance of the exchange in the 1860s between the early Dostoyevsky (then more sympathetic to "Westerner" positions) and the Slavophile K. S. Aksakov. Responding to Aksakov's extreme rejection of European literary models, Dostoyevsky had argued: "But of course the European ideals . . . views and . . . influence have been, and still are . . . of great importance to our literature. . . . But have we imitated them slavishly? *Have we not experienced them as part of our own lives?* Have we not worked on our own Russian view from those foreign facts?" (cited in Christoff, 1979: 350; emphasis in the original).

Dostoyevsky's emphasis—"Have we not experienced them as part of our own lives"—points to a complexity of cultural identification captured with psychological intensity in his fiction. It is this simultaneous clash of cultural contrasts—Western versus Russian—that gives the cue to the construction of a new concept of "the West." The suggestion that "our Russian view" can transform those imitated models clearly has a political dimension, which, in terms of Dostoyevsky's influence, accounts for much of the fascination for Dostoyevsky among Western European readers. This messianic Panslavism is perhaps most explicit in the famous "Pushkin" speech:

Yes, the Russian's destiny is incontestably all-European and universal. To become a genuine and all-round Russian means, perhaps (and this you should remember), to become brother of all men, *a universal man*, if you please. Oh, all this Slavophilism and this Westernism is a great, although historically inevitable, misunderstanding. . . . Oh the peoples of Europe have no idea how dear they are to us! And later—in this I believe—we, well, not we but the future Russians, to the last man, will comprehend that to become a genuine Russian means to seek finally to reconcile all European controversies, to show the solution of European anguish in our all-humanitarian and all-unifying Russian soul . . . and finally, perhaps to utter the ultimate word of great, universal harmony. (Dostoyevsky, *Diary of a Writer*, 1985: 979)

The rhetoric of the "Russian soul" had an immense impact over the period of European fascination for things Russian. Whether as political threat or intellectual excitement, this challenge was read in Dostoyevsky's fiction as a far-reaching imaginative unsettling of European cultural and historical identity.

Dostoyevsky's *Notes from Underground*, a repudiation of Chernyshevsky's *What Is to Be Done?*, succinctly captures a new attitude toward European examples of progress that had long marked Russian views of "the West." The new attitude to emerge from the nihilist challenge of the 1860s may be read in the "underground man's" attitude toward Chernyshevsky's Crystal Palace:

You believe in the Palace of Crystal, eternally inviolable, that is in something at which one couldn't furtively put out one's tongue or make concealed gestures of derision. But perhaps I fear this edifice just because it is made of crystal and eternally inviolable, and it will not be possible even to put out one's tongue at it in secret. (Dostoyevsky, *Notes*, 1972: 42)

Dominick LaCapra, placing *Notes from Underground* at the turning point in Dostoyevsky's attitudes, argues that

What Dostoyevsky came to see more forcefully in time—and to oppose vehemently—was the possibility that Russia faced its greatest threat of disruption from its Westernized intellectuals. . . . The apparent and apparently decisive difference between the young and the later Dostoyevsky was the difference between support of, and opposition to, this possibility. But in his novels . . . the will to believe does not simply and complacently culminate in belief, and the "Westernized" other is within as well as without. One name for this "Westernized" other is the Underground Man. (LaCapra, 1987: 38)

LaCapra's description captures one crucial element of the problem of cultural identification which comes to mark the idea of the West over the turn of the century—that it is primarily an identity one learns, in the specific Russian sense of becoming Westernized. The problem of the "Westernized" other crystallized the idea of a history of thought or intellectual heritage that may be assumed by anyone, but whose very features are threatened by the "underground" roots (historical or racial) of the peoples who assume it. This problem of the "Westernized" other was also posed by British colonialism, where, as a result of Macaulay's style of colonial education, a new type of "native" intellectual was forming, educated to become at once Western and other than Western. In each case, reaction to this experience of the "Westernized other" precipitated a cultural reversal whereby "culture" or "civilization" was redefined against the presumption of its universality. What is striking about this production of "Western Civilization" as a unique form of culture is the priority of that non-Western intellectual experience in defining the very terms of a "Western" cultural identity.

The translation, appropriation, and reversal of Russian attitudes toward Europe may be seen emerging in Melchior's studies on Russian novelists. In the completed study based on his essays in *Le revue des deux mondes*, "nihilism" becomes the key term for interpreting Russian novelists and Russian culture in general: "The Russian people are afflicted with a national, a historical malady, which is partly hereditary, partly contracted during the course of its existence. The hereditary part is that proclivity of the Slavonic mind towards that negative doctrine which today we call Nihilism, and which the Hindu fathers called *Nirvana*. In fact, if we would understand Russia well, we must recall to our minds what she has learned from ancient India" (Melchior, 1974: 20).

The racial stereotype of the "Slavonic mind" reproduces those Orientalist assumptions that Edward Said has shown to be so important for European self-definitions, and it is interesting to note that this influential translator of Russian ideas was in fact, by profession, an Orientalist. Yet in the very authority of reference to Orientalist knowledge, one may see a crucial transformation in the assumptions of European Orientalism. Melchior draws on the authority of one of the most important nineteenth-century Orientalists, Max Müller, to offer a revealing definition of the "malady" of Russian nihilism: "Max Müller says that the Sanskrit word [Nirvana] really means 'the action of extinguishing a light by blowing it out.' Will not this definition explain Russian Nihilism, which would extinguish the light of civilization by stifling it, then plunge back into chaos" (Melchior, 1974: 22). As this image confirms, response to Russian ideas helped give cultural and political shape to a perceived threat to enlightened civilization. Between the 1880s when Melchior was writing on the Russian novel and the 1910s when Spengler was beginning *The Decline*, "the West" emerged as the cultural, political, and historical entity threatened by Russian nihilism.

Melchior's emphasis on the linguistic roots of the term "nihilism" also specifies the way the philosophical concept becomes entangled with cultural and racial stereotypes. The term "nihilism" had previously been leveled pejoratively against philosophical trends in the first half of the nineteenth century. The term came to Russia along with the ideas of Comte, Feuerbach, Mill, and Spencer, although the Russian nihilists of the 1860s succeeded in turning it, momentarily, into an affirmative label. Not only does Melchior's linguistic-racial etymology give greater cultural-historical depth to the Russian sense of the term. It also attributes a deeper logic to Russian nihilism, whereby extreme rationalism inevitably turns into mysticism and is directed against reason itself.

Melchior's formulation of Russian nihilism reflects that complex process whereby principles from the Enlightenment were redefined in terms of a new cultural and political identity. "Nihilism," associated with Russian thought, allows for a (confused) cultural identification between Western Europe and Enlightenment *against* Russia. Defined all at once by contrast to Russian thought and in the very terms of Russian debates (most notably in the term "Western"), this consolidation of "Western" philosophy coincides with the new social and political currency of the term "the West" in mapping new political divisions within Europe onto old imperial and Orientalist divisions of the world.

The complexity of this mixing of social and political associations with the more specifically philosophical concept is vividly demonstrated in the case of Friedrich Nietzsche, for whom the concept of nihilism—as the conceptual riddle of reason directed against reason itself—became a guiding term for his critique of philosophy and his revaluation of all values. Nietzsche began to use the term at precisely the same time that Russian nihilism was attracting widespread interest and causing widespread misunderstanding. As Johann Goudsblom points out: "The very first time he uses the term he dissociates himself emphatically from 'nihilism cast in the Petersburg mould'" (Goudsblom, 1980: 11). As always, however, Nietzsche emphasizes the problematic entanglement of social and political concerns with philosophical ideas, not only making use of stereotypes of Russian nihilism and nihilists, but also alluding to French and English variations. Indeed, these allusions to the various manifestations of nihilism are quite in keeping with his diagnosis of nihilism as the defining problem of the Europe of his time. What is most revealing for our current argument, however, is the absence of an idea of "the West" in Nietzsche's work. For Nietzsche, nihilism can figure neither as an outside threat to "Western civilization" nor as the inherent dynamic of disintegration of "Western culture."

This point takes on considerable historical interest in light of later appraisals of Nietzsche's philosophy and his discussions of nihilism in particular. In lectures on Friedrich Nietzsche, Martin Heidegger makes a distinction between Russian nihilism and the "classical nihilism" of Nietzsche. Having first explained the origins of the usage of the term "nihilism" in Turgenev's novel, and within Russian social and political thinking generally, Heidegger cites Dostoyevsky's famous Pushkin speech concerning the "type of our negative Russian person." He then insists on a different usage of nihilism by Nietzsche:

For Nietzsche, however, the term "Nihilism" means something substantially "more." Nietzsche speaks of "European nihilism." He means by this not that positivism that emerged around the middle of the nineteenth century and spread throughout Europe, but rather "European" has here a historical significance, signifying "Western" [abendländisch] in the sense of Western history [abendländischen Geschichte]. (Heidegger, 1986: 2–3; my translation)

Lecturing in Nazi Germany, Heidegger was addressing an audience for whom Nietzsche, nihilism, and Western history had all been inflected by Nazi appropriations. Yet the distance between Nietzsche's "European" and Heidegger's "Western" registers a reactive borrowing of the Russian stereotype by European intellectuals, filtered through successive versions of the Slavophile-Westerner controversy and informed by contemporary political events.

The complex echo-effect of Russian nihilism throughout Europe belongs to a widespread social and political upheaval that was dramatically transforming the shape of Europe over the turn of the century. Far from a mere change of names—from "Europe" to "the West"—the adoption of a specifically Russian idea of the West shows a reaction to the breakup of the old political formations of Central and Eastern Europe. The nihilist condenses into a single-figure racial stereotype of the "Slav," religious stereotypes of the "Russian soul" and political stereotypes of the bomb-throwing anarchist. Thus, nihilism harbored the hopes, anxieties and fears regarding the new social formations emerging from the collapsing empires of Tsarist Russia and Austro-Hungary. This gives particular resonance to the stereotype of "the Slav" (as the flip-side of the Westerner), which condensed an immense range of newly articulated political identities, from the Panslav imperialism of Russian reactionaries to the diversity of nationalist aspirations in the Balkan States.

The social and historical significance of a newly defined Eastern Europe over the turn of the century is a matter of considerable importance. For example, as Steven Aschheim has discussed, the changing definition of Eastern Europe is closely connected to the sharp rise of anti-Semitism over the turn of the century (Aschheim, 1982: 31, 79, 185–214). In a recent article, Robin Okey writes:

The term "eastern," or even "oriental," had often been attached by English and French writers to places in the Balkans, Romania, Transylvania, or the Russo-Polish borderlands. Its increasing application to an entire regional state system, observed by Lhéritier in 1935, broadened the area of its use and inevitably had a distancing effect. The institutes and reviews which were now set up—*Le monde slave*, the London School of Slavonic and East European Studies, the Breslau *Osteuropa* Institute, and the Polish West Slavonic, Baltic and Silesian Institutes, reflected scholarly concern for newly important entities, but also the degree to which these were bones of contention. (Okey, 1922: 120–21)

Okey's argument in general sheds light on the contentious changes in definitions of Central Europe and Eastern Europe from the 1840s to 1945, providing an important counterpoint to the changing definition of "the West." For, although Okey's argument is focused for the most part on the fate of the concept of "Mitteleuropa," the term "the West" emerged from the same set of contentious debates over definitions.

Perhaps the most influential person to articulate an idea of "the West" as the conceptual lever for redefining Europe was Oswald Spengler. In the introduction to *The Decline of the West* (1917), Spengler wrote:

The word "Europe" ought to be struck out of history. There is historically no "European" type. . . . It is thanks to this word "Europe" alone, and the complex of ideas resulting from it, that our historical consciousness has come to link Russia with the West in an utterly baseless unity—a mere abstraction derived from the reading of books—that has led to immense real consequences. In the shape of Peter the Great, this word has falsified the historical tendencies of a primitive human mass for two centuries, whereas the Russian *instinct* has very truly and fundamentally divided "Europe" from "Mother Russia" with the hostility that we can see embodied in Tolstoi, Aksakov, or Dostoyevsky. "East" and "West" are notions that contain real history, whereas "Europe" is an empty sound. (Spengler, 1918: 16)

By naming Russian authors to establish the "real history" of the terms "East" and "West," Spengler shows an indebtedness to the Slavophile-Westerner debate. Particularly interesting is his attraction to the Slavophile strain of Russian thinking which he uses, among other things, to quarantine the revolutionary example of recent Russian history from the definition of Western Civilization, which is the key element of his vast orchestration of world history. Spengler's distinction between "Europe" and "the West" might be characterized as the classical case of a reaction against the Bolshevik Revolution which paradoxically redefined the nineteenth-century idea of Europe in the distorted image of Russian intellectual debates.

Spengler's distinction between "Europe" and "the West" is revealing also for his attempt to overcome the crisis in philosophies of history over the turn of the century. His insistence on striking the word "Europe" from history surfaces in an attack on the provincialism of nineteenth-century historical perspectives:

"Thanks to the subdivision of history into 'Ancient,' 'Medieval,' and 'Modern'—an incredibly jejune and meaningless scheme, which has, however, entirely dominated our historical thinking—we have failed to perceive the true position in the general history of higher mankind, of the little part-world which has developed on West-European soil from the time of the German-Roman Empire, to judge of its relative importance and above all to estimate its direction" (Spengler, I: 16). More might be said about the contradictory combination of an evolutionary model—"the general history of higher mankind"—and the attempt to place European history in the relative perspective of world civilizations. If there is nothing new about the general shape of this contradiction, what is distinct about Spengler's attempt to overcome the limitations of historical relativism is the key idea of the West as a term that can set one fraction of world history in a determined relation to world history. In this methodological maneuver, which in itself carries a certain truth, we might grasp how the insistence on striking the word "Europe" out of history creates a new historical fiction: "the West"—a "true West" that can measure historical process as accurately as a compass may be used to judge "true North."

Heidegger's echo of Spengler's reaction against the influence of Russian nihilism offers perhaps a more consistent grasp of the crisis at the heart of philosophies of history. If Spengler's response to the Hegelian philosophy of history is to reject the philosophical problems of dialectical reason in order to build a grander world-historical scheme, Heidegger insists on the problems of dialectical reason to the virtual exclusion of any historical grounding. Heidegger's distinction between Europe and "Western history" serves not as the lever for a fuller historical perspective, but rather as a means to accentuate the crisis of historical perspective that may then be understood to inhere in all philosophical enterprise. Thus, distinct though Heidegger's response to the problem of history is from Spengler's, what is striking is the new accentuation on an idea of "the West" that becomes for Spengler a discrete historical development—"Western Civilization"—and for Heidegger the limit to thinking history—which is to say, "Western philosophy." It is in this way that the historical shift at the turn of the century may be understood not as a crisis in Western traditions thinking (not even a crisis of European intellectual history), but as a crisis that produced an idea of "the West" projected back onto history as the limit to historical thinking: for Spengler a positive limit, by which one might demarcate the unfolding of all history; and a categorical limit for Heidegger, which imposes a condition of silence on thinking about world history. The implications of this point, I believe, are that there is no reason to assume that the philosophical problems of modernity are peculiar to a "Western" tradition; or to assume that it makes sense to group historical processes under the category of "Western" history.

Arnold Toynbee's surveys of world history, published between 1934 and 1961, constitute perhaps the most sustained attempt to make "Western

Civilization" "an intelligible field of historical study" (Toynbee, 1934: 36; 1961: 162). Though criticized for its spiritual interpretation of history and marginalized from mainstream historical work, *A Study of History* reveals much more about the problematic paradigm of "the West" than the less programmatic, seemingly pragmatic uses of the term "the West" among mainstream historians. It is notable that Toynbee's idea of "the West" bears the influence not only of Spengler's *The Decline of the West* but also of Toynbee's experiences as foreign policy analyst before and during the First World War. Conceived in the early 1920s, Toynbee's *A Study of History* emerged from the crucible of the First World War. Yet its leitmotif of "Western Civilization" reflects the contours of changing ideology and policy in British imperialism from the 1890s to 1920s.

An influential, if also eccentric, precursor to Toynbee's historiographic agenda can be found in the work of the now little-known sociologist Benjamin Kidd, an obscure civil servant, largely self-educated, who rose to instant fame with the publication in 1894 of *Social Evolution*. Written during the "new imperialist" fever of the 1890s, *Social Evolution* transposes the Social Darwinism of Herbert Spencer's "struggle for existence" from the struggle between individuals within society to the struggle between biopolitical entities within world history. Anticipating Spengler's life-cycles of civilizations and Toynbee's justifications of "Western Civilization" as an intelligible field of study, Kidd argued that "to obtain a just conception of our Western Civilization, it is necessary to regard it from the beginning as a single continuous growth, endowed with a definite principle of life, subject to law, and passing, like any other organism, through certain orderly stages of development" (Kidd, 1894: 147).

Kidd's blend of popular Darwinism, sociology, and idealist philosophy produced a fascinating fit between political enthusiasm for the "new imperialism" and fin-de-siècle anxieties about racial and cultural degeneration. The title of his second book, *The Control of the Tropics* (1898), published as the United States embarked on its war for colonial possessions (the Spanish-American War of 1898), captures the spirit in which Kidd rationalized the organic development of "Western Civilization" in terms of the territorial politics of the "new imperialism." As he had argued in the conclusion to *Social Evolution*: "Now it would appear probable that we have, in the present peculiar relationship of the Western peoples to the coloured races, the features of a transition of great interest and importance, the nature of which is, as yet, hardly understood. . . . [T]here can be no question as to the absolute ascendancy in the world today of the Western peoples and of Western civilisation" (Kidd, 1894: 312). The centrality of racism is clear, too, in his formulation of "the struggle of the Western races for the larger inheritance of the future" (Kidd, 1898: 2).

Kidd's influence is difficult to determine. The wide dissemination of *Social Evolution*, which ran to many editions and was translated into many languages, gives pause for thought as to the increasing currency it might have given the catchphrase "our Western Civilization." Kidd's "bio-political defense of Empire," moreover, was eagerly read by Joseph Chamberlain and urged on President McKinley by expansionist advisers (Crook, 1984: 3). Yet the idiosyncrasy of Kidd's emphasis on the possessive pronoun in "*our* Western Civilisation"—a characteristic formulation—is a revealing feature of this early popularization of the term. It speaks to the quality of Kidd's writing as a whole, within which this particular term might well have sounded like a crude generalization (particularly to the established elite), of a piece with that "bad" literary style that made the *Dictionary of National Biography* comment, "No wonder that academic circles always refused to take his books seriously" (305–6).

Whatever the exact nature of Kidd's influence, his idea of "the West" as a contemporary political entity, racially defined and expressing a common historical heritage, sheds light on the increasing importance of the term "the West" in the changing shape of British imperial ideology and policy over the first two decades of the twentieth century, as politicians and policy advisers sought to articulate Britain's new role in world politics. These changes might for convenience be divided into three stages. The first is marked by the disillusionment with the "new imperialism" of the 1890s following the protracted South African Boer War from 1899 to 1902, won by the British at the cost of humiliating defeats. The second stage begins with the end of Britain's "splendid isolation" from European alliances, marked by the 1902 *entente cordiale* with France which prefigured the battlefronts of the First World War when Britain and France constituted the "Western allies" engaged with Russia on the Eastern front against Germany. The third stage, in the aftermath of the First World War, is marked by the effort to establish new international alliances, at such conferences as the Peace Conference, the League of Nations Conference, and the Imperial Conference where the formal structure of the British Empire was refashioned to produce the British Commonwealth. Between the Boer War and 1919, as the administrative structure of formal Empire dissolved, the idea of the West emerged to re-tailor imperialist assumptions to suit a new politics of neo-colonialism.

One figure who exemplifies the changing ideology of British imperialism over this period is Arthur J. Balfour, prime minister from 1902 to 1905 and leader of the conservative "Unionist" party until 1913, during a period when it was split apart between adherents of free trade (the mainstay of nineteenth-century imperialist policy) and tariff reformers (who envisioned a new protectionist imperial federation of white dominions). Not only did Balfour preside over a period in which British imperialist ideology was compelled to adjust to the challenges of decolonization, but also it was during his administration that the new alliance with France (the *entente cordiale* of 1902) radically altered Britain's isolation from the balance of power within Europe. In a lecture delivered in 1908 on that favorite conservative fear of the "decadence" of society, morals, and empire, Balfour sought to overcome such anxieties by arguing: "Progress is with the West: with communities of the European type. And if *their* energy of development is some day to be exhausted, who can believe that there remains any external source from which it can be renewed? Where are the untried races competent to construct out of the ruined fragments of our civilisation a new and better habitation for the spirit of man?" (Balfour, 1908: 42).

In many respects, Balfour's "West" is the heir to Kidd's. The fundamental racism in Kidd's formulation of cultural heritage and "the struggle of the Western races for the larger inheritance of the future" is duplicated in Balfour. It is modulated, moreover, into an argument to be tirelessly rehearsed about the perils of decolonization: "The influence which a superior civilisation, whether acting by example or imposed by force, may have in advancing an inferior one, though often beneficent, is not likely to be self supporting; its withdrawal will be followed by decadence, unless the character of the civilisation be in harmony both with the acquired temperament and the innate capacities of those who have been induced to accept it" (Balfour, 1908: 58–59).

Balfour, still leader of the Unionist party, formulates an idea of "the West" which gives rhetorical leverage to a crucial shift in imperialist ideology. The key building block of British imperial superiority—"race"—is used to rationalize an idea of "the West" that is strangely at odds with Empire. Drawing on the classical analogy for decline-and-fall arguments—that of the Roman Empire—Balfour remotivates the geographical contrast between Eastern and Western parts of the Roman Empire to define "the West" in terms of a racial ethos—and against the political structure of Empire. Considering "the long agony and final destruction of Roman Imperialism in the West" (14), Balfour conjectures that, among other causes for the decline of the Empire, there existed "some obscure disharmony between the Imperial system and the temperament of the West" (40).

This rhetorical emphasis on the "temperament of the West" conveniently displaces the peculiar difficulties facing official imperial ideology between 1902 and 1919, as it sought to differentiate between England's relation to such colonial territories as Canada and Australia, on the one hand, and India, Malaysia, and British-controlled Africa, on the other. These difficulties are exemplified in the speeches of Alfred Milner, South African governor during the Boer War, and a proponent of Joseph Chamberlain's vision of a protectionist imperial federation. Milner tirelessly proclaimed an idea of imperial unity based on an idea of "Empire citizenship." When Milner spoke of membership in "this world-wide state, this Empire," his emphasis on the bond of race by which he imagined his citizens of Empire to be "equal sharers in a common heritage" (Milner, 1909: 88–89) provides an instance of what Benedict Anderson shows to be "the fundamental contradiction of English official nationalism, i.e., the inner incompatibility of empire and nation" (Anderson, 1991: 93): "I have emphasised the importance of the racial bond. From my point of view this is fundamental. It is the British race which built the Empire, and it is the undivided British race which can uphold it. . . . But what do I mean by the British race? I mean all the peoples of the United Kingdom and their descendants in other countries under the British flag. The expression may not be ethnologically accurate" (Milner, 1909: xxxv). What Milner's phantom "Empire citizenship" reveals is the attempt to consolidate Empire along newly articulated racial lines—as a federation of essentially white dominions. Where Milner's "Empire citizenship" foregrounds the "inner incompatibility of nation and empire," Balfour's idea of "the West" provides a more successful imaginary resolution to that ideological contradiction.

With Balfour's "West" we find a very different form of imperialist ideology from that of Thomas Babington Macaulay in the early nineteenth century. For Macaulay, the ideals of universal human enlightenment matched the task of colonial governance—a European education would produce "a class who may be interpreters between us and the millions whom we govern; a class of persons, Indian in blood and colour, but English in taste, in opinion, in morals and in intellect" (Macaulay, 1970: 729). It was this confidence and power that enabled him to write, in an address to Parliament on the government of India, of "an empire exempt from all natural causes of decay . . . the imperishable empire of our arts and our morals, our literature and our laws" (718). In the opening section of "Decadence," Balfour explicitly refers to Macaulay's Liberal vision of Empire. It is worth citing because it shows how Balfour's formulation of the "West" is based on a reversal of older imperial motifs: "To Macaulay . . . it seemed natural that ages hence a young country like New Zealand should be flourishing, but not less natural that an old country like England should have decayed. Berkeley, in a well-known stanza, tells how the drama of civilisation has slowly travelled westward to find its loftiest development, but also its final catastrophe, in the New World. . . . But why *should* civilisation thus wear out and great communities decay?" (Balfour, 1908: 1). Balfour arrests the "westward" movement of Empire to produce a culturally, historically, and politically bounded "West." In this reversal of imperial rhetoric, moreover, Balfour constructs his West against Macaulay's "empire exempt from all causes of decay" and against his educational ideal. Education has an important place in Balfour's vision (his lecture was delivered at Newnham College Cambridge), but his "West" is primarily defined by that element of historical, racial, and political "temperament" that cannot be taught.

It is no coincidence that education plays so important a role in determining the contradictions and peculiar power of the twentieth-century idea of the West. If the notion of "Western Civilization" seems premised on an ideal of universal education, what the examples of Kidd and Balfour help show is how "the West" comes to be defined precisely in opposition to that ideal. This general problem became one of the defining features of Arnold Toynbee's efforts to make "Western Civilization" an "intelligible" field of historical study. As Toynbee himself elaborated it, there was a double threat to the stability of the very notion of "Western Civilization": a threat from within and without which Toynbee defined through the categories of the "internal" and "external" "proletariat." Toynbee's anti-Marxist appropriation and redefinition of the "proletariat" makes the term stand neither for an economic class nor for the privileged consciousness of society transforming itself: "The true hallmark of the proletarian is neither poverty nor humble birth but a consciousness—and the resentment which this consciousness inspires—of being disinherited from his ancestral place in Society and being unwanted in a community which is his rightful home" (Toynbee, 1939, V: 63). For Toynbee, the masses of Europe and North America, though linguistically and racially related to "the creative minorities" responsible for the achievements of "Western Civilization," represented an "internal" threat to the survival of "the West" matched by the "external" proletariat of the non-Western masses.

These inner and outer limits of "Western Civilization" rest, however, on a peculiar but highly revealing definition of "an 'intellectual proletariat'" (Toynbee, 1939: 157). Toynbee argues:

In any community that is attempting to solve the problem of adapting its life to the rhythm of an exotic civilization to which it has been either forcibly annexed or freely converted, there is need of a special social class to serve as a human counterpart of the "transformer" which changes an electric current from one voltage to another; and the class which is called into existence—often quite abruptly and artificially—in response to this demand has come to be known generically, from the special Russian name for it, as the intelligentsia (a word whose meaning is expressed in its very formation, in which a Latin root and a Western idea are acclimatized in Russian by being given a Slavonic termination). The intelligentsia is a class of liaison-officers who have learnt the tricks of an intrusive civilization's trade so far as may be necessary to enable their own community, through this agency, just to hold its own in a social environment in which life is ceasing to be lived in accordance with the local tradition. (Toynbee, 1939: 154)

Since members of an "intelligentsia" exist by Toynbee's definition between two civilizations—suffering "from the congenital unhappiness of the bastard and the hybrid" (155)—their case serves as an exemplary problem in examining the coherence or disintegration of civilizations. In general, their example provides the key definition for Toynbee's formulation of the double threat facing a civilization from an "internal" and "external" proletariat, precisely because the definition of an intelligentsia makes it all at once "internal" and "external": "wherever we find an intelligentsia in existence, we may infer, not only that two civilizations have been in contact, but that one of the two is now in process of being absorbed into the other's internal proletariat" (155); and thus "the intelligentsia complies in double measure with our fundamental definition of a proletariat by being 'in' but not 'of' two societies and not merely one" (156–57).

Toynbee's prime examples are drawn, significantly, from imperial Russia and the British Raj:

> The process of manufacturing an intelligentsia is still more difficult to stop than it is to start . . .; the competition becomes so keen that the number of candidates rapidly increases out of all proportion to the number of opportunities for employing them. When this stage is reached, the original nucleus of an intelligentsia which is consoled by being employed becomes swamped by the adventitious mass of an "intellectual proletariat" which is idle and destitute as well as outcast. The handful of chinovniks is reinforced by a legion of "Nihilists," the handful of babus who thankfully drive their quills, or resignedly tap their typewriters, by a legion of "failed B.A.s." (Toynbee, 1939: 157)

These particular examples of an "intellectual proletariat" are revealing because, in providing the exemplary model for the disintegration of civilizations in general, they also provide the key examples of a challenge to Toynbee's explicit agenda to demonstrate the intelligibility of "Western Civilization." Simultaneously internal and external to "Western Civilization," this "intelligentsia" and their conflicted cultural experience (we might recall the experience of the "Westernized other" within and without) paradoxically threaten and define the "intelligibility" of Toynbee's "Western Civilization."

Arnold Toynbee's survey of world history echoes Spengler's attempt to strike the word "Europe" out of history and to give "real historical content" to the term "the West." Alongside the direct influence of *The Decline of the West*, Toynbee's experience as Foreign Office adviser during the 1914–18 war decisively shaped the agenda of his surveys of history around a conscious effort to reconceive Europe historically, in the spirit of postwar European reconstruction. In his collection of essays, *The New Europe: Some Essays in Reconstruction* (1915), he had sought to articulate a European political and historical identity more deeply rooted than the nationalisms he took to be the cause of the war. As with Spengler, the impact of the Russian Revolution was decisive in this effort of historical reconstruction, sharpening a division between Eastern and Western Europe already important in his earlier work. Yet Toynbee's "apocalyptic vision of what was at stake" in the Bolshevik Revolution illustrates a key dimension of the paradoxical redefinition of Europe in the distorted image of Russian intellectual debates. What preoccupied Toynbee, as intelligence officer responsible for covering the Ottoman Empire, was, as William McNeill puts it, "the notion of a confrontation between insurgent Islam and a decadent British Empire, doomed to reenact in the twentieth century the nineteenth century role of the Habsburgs with respect to east European nationalisms." Toynbee's "key insight"—that "the right of self-determination could not be confined to European and Christian nations"—illustrates how his vision of "Western Civilization" was the counter-idea not only to the Bolshevik communist model, but also to the shape of "self-determination" as applied to

British colonial territories (McNeill, 1989: 75–76). In this, for all his exaggerations, idiosyncrasies, and historical insights, Toynbee captures the spirit in which the idea of the West was formulated at the beginning of the twentieth century to resist decolonization.

While the full significance of Toynbee's historiographic project properly belongs to a later stage in the consolidation of "the West" than the historical frame of the present essay, the logic of Toynbee's argument, and of his use of the particular historical examples of the Russian and Bengali "intelligentsias," reiterates the contours of that turn-of-the-century formation of "the West" which we have traced in this essay. Toynbee's need to repudiate the cultural, political, and existential predicament of this "Westernized" intelligentsia is revealing because it is those conflicted cultural experiences that give the term "the West" its cultural and historical depth of perspective. Thus, what Toynbee demonstrates is the manner in which the opposition between Russia and the West served not only to quarantine the example of the Bolshevik Revolution, but also to repudiate the cultural complexity of an emerging postcolonial world.

Ultimately, a critical grasp of the recent rhetorical emergence of the term "the West" can provide the basis for recognizing the multiplicity of historical traditions that give shape to what is called "Western history." There are, indeed, many instances in which the seemingly monolithic idea of "Western history" may be shown to rest on a variety of different, often contending meanings of "the West." One thinks, for example, of the American "West," which coexists without too much apparent confusion with the rather different sense of "the West" of "Western Civilization." Another example is the difference over terms used to describe the Maghreb region of Northern Africa. While the term "Maghreb" in Arabic means "the West," in so-called "Western" countries the whole Maghreb region is commonly designated as "Eastern."

This last example recalls Antonio Gramsci's argument concerning the historical constructedness of geographical terms. Indeed, Gramsci uses a version of that example to make his point, when he writes: "Italians often, when speaking of Morocco, call it an 'Eastern' country, to refer to its Moslem and Arab civilisation" (Gramsci, 1985: 447). The force of Gramsci's example does not depend on identifying, by contrast to the "East" of Islam, a "West" of Christendom. Rather, it is to call attention to "specific relations between different cultural complexes"—and these happen to concern the place of Italian history within capitalist historical formations. Thus, Gramsci is by no means attempting to produce a philosophy of history that might serve as a scientific gauge of "true West" in universal history. At the same time, however, to abandon this seemingly fixed measure of human history is not to succumb to a mere relativism of culture and history. As Partha Chatterjee puts it, in his recent examination of discourses of nationalism, "'Western universalism' no less than 'Oriental exceptionalism' can be shown to be only a particular form of a richer, more diverse, and differentiated conceptualization of a new universal idea" (Chatterjee, 1993: 13). It is to enable a richer, a more diverse, and a more historically accurate conceptualization of human history, that I argue for dislodging the paradigm of "Western Civilization." There are, in Keats's phrase, "many western islands," but there is no "true West."

NOTE

1. This argument is explored at length in my study of Joseph Conrad, *The Invention of the West: Joseph Conrad and the Double-Mapping of Europe and Empire* (Stanford, Calif.: Stanford University Press, 1995). The current essay is a revised and expanded version of the Epilogue to that book.

REFERENCES

Adorno, Theodor. (1973). *Negative Dialectics*. Trans. E. B. Ashton. New York: Continuum Books.
Anderson, Benedict. (1991). *Imagined Communities: Reflections on the Origin and Spread of Nationalism*. Rev. ed. London: Verso.
Aschheim, Steven E. (1982). *Brothers and Strangers: The East European Jew in German Jewish Consciousness, 1800–1923*. Madison: University of Wisconsin Press.
Balfour, Arthur James. (1908). *Decadence*. Henry Sidgwick Memorial Lecture. Delivered on January 25, 1908, at Newnham College. Cambridge: Cambridge University Press.
Baritz, Loren. (1960–61). "The Idea of the West." *American Historical Review* 66: 618-40.
Berkeley, George (Bishop of Cloyne). (1752). *A Miscellany Containing Several Tracts on Various Subjects*. London.
Billington, James H. (1970). *The Icon and the Axe: An Interpretive History of Russian Culture*. New York: Vintage.
Chatterjee, Partha. (1993). *The Nation and Its Fragments: Colonial and Postcolonial Histories*. Princeton, N.J.: Princeton University Press.
Chernyschevsky, Nikolai. (1983). *What Is to Be Done? Tales of New People*. Trans. Laura Beraha. Moscow: Raduga.
Christoff, Peter K. (1979). *K. S. Aksakov: A Study in Ideas*. Princeton, N.J.: Princeton University Press.
Crook, D. P. (1984). *Benjamin Kidd: Portrait of a Social Darwinist*. Cambridge: Cambridge University Press.
Davis, H.W.C., and J.R.H. Weaver, eds. (1927). *Dictionary of National Biography: 1912–1921*. London: Oxford University Press.
Derrida, Jacques. (1976). *Of Grammatology*. Trans. Gayatri Chakravorty Spivak. Baltimore, Md.: Johns Hopkins University Press.
———. (1978). *Writing and Difference*. Trans. Alan Bass. Chicago: University of Chicago Press.

———. (1982). *Margins of Philosophy*. Trans. Alan Bass. Chicago: University of Chicago Press.
Dostoyevsky, Fyodor. (1951). *Crime and Punishment*. Trans. Constance Garnett. New York: Harper.
———. (1962). *The Possessed*. Trans. Andrew MacAndrew. New York: Signet.
———. (1972). *Notes from Underground and The Double*. Trans. Jessie Coulson. Harmondsworth: Penguin.
———. (1985). *The Diary of a Writer*. Trans. Boris Brasol. Salt Lake City, Utah: Gibbs M. Smith.
Goudsblom, Johann. (1980). *Nihilism and Culture*. London: Blackwell.
Gramsci, Antonio. (1985). *Selections from the Prison Notebooks*. Ed. and trans. Quinton Hoare and Geoffrey Nowell Smith. New York: International Publishers.
Hartman, Geoffrey H. (1970). *Beyond Formalism: Literary Essays 1958–1970*. New Haven, Conn.: Yale University Press.
Hegel, Georg Wilhelm Friedrich. (1900). *The Philosophy of History*. Trans. J. Sibree (1857). New York: Colonial Press.
———. (1970). *Vorlesungen uber die Philosophie der Geschichte*. Frankfurt: Suhrkamp.
———. (1975). *Lectures on the Philosophy of World History. Introduction: Reason in History*. Trans. H. B. Nisbet (from the German edition of Johannes Hoffmeister). Cambridge: Cambridge University Press.
Heidegger, Martin. (1986). *Nietzsche: Der Europaische Nihilismus. Gesamtausgabe*. Band 48. Frankfurt: Klostermann.
Herder, Johann Gottfried. (1803). *Ideas on the Philosophy of the History of Mankind*. Trans. T. Churchill. London.
Herzen, Alexander. (1924). *My Past and Thoughts. The Memoirs of Alexander Herzen*. Trans. Constance Garnett. London: Chatto.
Hobsbawm, Eric, and Terence Ranger, eds. (1983). *The Invention of Tradition*. Cambridge: Cambridge University Press.
Judd, Denis. (1968). *Balfour and the British Empire: A Study in Imperial Evolution, 1874–1932*. London: Macmillan.
Keats, John. (1959). *Selected Poems and Letters*. Ed. Douglas Bush. Boston: Houghton Mifflin.
Kidd, Benjamin. (1894). *Social Evolution*. London: Macmillan.
———. (1898). *The Control of the Tropics*. New York: Macmillan.
———. (1902). *Principles of Western Civilization*. London: Macmillan.
Kipling, Rudyard. (1954). *Barrack-Room Ballads and Other Verses*. Garden City, N.Y.: Doubleday.
Kropotkin, Peter. (1988; 1899). *Memoirs of a Revolutionist*. Ed. James Allen Rogers. London: Cresset Library.
LaCapra, Dominick. (1987). *History, Politics, and the Novel*. Ithaca, N.Y.: Cornell University Press.
Macaulay, Thomas Babington. (1970). *Prose and Poetry*. Cambridge, Mass.: Harvard University Press.
Magris, Claudio. (1991–92). "Mitteleuropa: Reality and Myth of a Word." *Edinburgh Review* 87 (Winter): 141–53.
McIntire, C. T., and Marvin Perry, eds. (1989). *Toynbee Reappraisals*. Toronto:

University of Toronto Press.
McNeill, William H. (1989). *Arnold J. Toynbee: A Life*. Oxford: Oxford University Press.
Melchior, Eugene (Comte de Vogüé). (1974). *The Russian Novelists*. New York: Haskell.
Milner, Alfred. (1909). *Imperial Unity: Speeches Delivered in Canada in the Autumn of 1908*. London: Hodder and Stoughton.
Nietzsche, Friedrich. (1968). *The Will to Power*. Trans. Walter Kaufmann and R. J. Hollingdale. New York: Vintage.
———. (1969). *On the Genealogy of Morals and Ecce Homo*. Ed. and trans. Walter Kaufmann. New York: Vintage Books.
———. (1990). *Beyond Good and Evil*. Trans. R. J. Hollingdale. London: Penguin.
Okey, Robin. (1992). "Central Europe/Eastern Europe: Behind the Definitions." *Past and Present: A Journal of Historical Studies* 137 (November): 102–33.
Retamar, Roberto. (1986). "Our America and the West." *Social Text* 15 (Fall): 1–25.
Said, Edward W. (1979). *Orientalism*. New York: Vintage Books.
Spengler, Oswald. (1980; 1918, 1922). *The Decline of the West*. Vols. I, II. New York: Alfred A. Knopf.
Suleri, Sara. (1992). *The Rhetoric of English India*. Chicago: University of Chicago Press.
Toynbee, Arnold. (1914). "The Slav Peoples." *Political Quarterly* 4 (December): 33–68.
———. (1915). *The New Europe: Some Essays in Reconstruction*. London: Dent.
———. (1934). *A Study of History*. Vol. I. London: Oxford University Press.
———. (1939). *A Study of History*. Vol. V. London: Oxford University Press.
———. (1961). *A Study of History*. Vol. XII. London: Oxford University Press.
Turgenev, Ivan. (1895). *Fathers and Children*. Trans. Constance Garnett. London: Heinemann.
Viswanathan, Gauri. (1989). *Masks of Conquest: Literary Study and British Rule in India*. New York: Columbia University Press.
Walicki, Andrzej. (1975). *The Slavophile Controversy: History of a Conservative Utopia in the Nineteenth Century Russian Thought*. Trans. Hilda Andrews-Rusiecka. Oxford: Clarendon Press.
———. (1979). *A History of Russian Thought From the Enlightenment to Marxism*. Trans. Hilda Andrews-Rusiecka. Stanford, Calif.: Stanford University Press.
———. (1982). *Philosophy and Romantic Nationalism: The Case of Poland*. Oxford: Clarendon Press.
Williams, Raymond. (1985). *Keywords: A Vocabulary of Culture and Society*. Rev. ed. New York: Oxford University Press.
Wood, James, ed. (1900). *The Nuttal Encyclopedia*. London and New York: Frederick Warne.
Young, Robert. (1990). *White Mythologies: Writing History and the West*. London: Routledge.

4

The God That Never Failed: The Origins and Crises of Western Civilization

Silvia Federici

It's August 1944. . . . Nothing yet has been discovered about the Nazi atrocities. . . . We're still living in the first age of humanity, pure, virginal, for another few months. Nothing has been revealed about the Human Race.

Marguerite Duras, The War

We can no longer afford to take that which is good in the past and simply call it our heritage, to discard the bad and simply think of it as a dead load which by itself time will bury in oblivion. The subterranean stream of Western history has finally come to the surface and usurped the dream of our tradition.

Hannah Arendt, Origins of Totalitarianism

That the impossible should be asked of me, good, what else could be asked of me? But the absurd! Of me whom they have reduced to reason.

Samuel Beckett, The Unnamable

The contemporary debates on multicultural education have underscored the limits of the Western Civilization courses, which in some universities form the core of the undergraduate curriculum. Criticism has focused on the Eurocentric bias that is perpetuated by the enthronement of "Western Civilization" as the pillar of introductory college education. As an alternative, advocates of multiculturalism have proposed that we integrate "non-Western" cultures into the core curriculum, so as to give our students an education more reflective of American cultural diversity.[1] Few, however, have questioned whether "Western Civilization" can provide a pedagogically defensible framework even for the student of countries and cultures usually grouped under the name of "the West." It is in fact assumed that "Western Civilization" represents a European viewpoint or the viewpoint of people who trace the ancestry back to Europe. Thus, the main failure of this paradigm is always taken to be its limited capacity for inclusion. In this essay, however, I dispute this view and argue that the Western Civilization framework cannot be defended on any pedagogical ground. First, its "will to unify" requires that what contradicts its continuity postulate be censored or marginalized. Western Civilization, in this sense, is a classic example of those totalizing perspectives, portraying history as the product of a single, undifferentiated subject, which have been contested by feminists and afrocentrists as exclusive of their experience and bound to represent the master's viewpoint.

Second, we can very well appreciate Greek philosophy or learn about the fall of the Roman Empire without hypothesizing a 2,000-year long "Western tradition," spanning in at least two continents. Indeed, it can be argued that only when freed from the Procustean bed to which the Western Civilization framework submits them can the histories of Greece, Rome, Europe, and America be meaningfully introduced to the classroom.

A further reason for questioning the validity of "Western Civilization" is the tradition of cultural chauvinism associated with this concept, and the political use that still is made of it in the highest spheres of power. This is not to suggest that any competing perspective may be ideologically neutral. A plethora of deconstructive analyses have alerted us to the artificial character of seemingly neutral geographical terms (e.g., Africa, Europe). However, none can compare in its ideological potential with "Western Civilization," both because the latter's shifting contours undermine its cognitive accountability and because of its enduring institutional backing. Undoubtedly, changing labels may not be more than a formal exercise. But if transcending the Western Civilization paradigm is not a sufficient condition for creating a more historically conscious curriculum, it is still a necessary one.

In support of this thesis, I will first examine the concept of Western Civilization in its historical function and theoretical premises. A tome of genealogical semiotics would be needed to trace this term's complex synonymy relations, shifting hierarchies of usage, semantic tensions, and referential transformations. But even a sketchy excursus through the nodal points of its constitution indicates that accepting the notion of Western Civilization is to accept a historical fiction. It is to accept a concept that (like the "eternal feminine") is a-prioristically constructed, has no historical referent, and can be legitimized only by political *fiat* or by the specious postulate of a transhistorical Western Mind.

I will then show, using the example of Nazism, that the Western Civilization framework can be maintained only through a set of adjustments that violate the very principles of truthfulness and rationality that Western Civilization allegedly promotes. One such adjustment is the exclusion from the history of Europe and its empires of those who did not identify with the political ideology of "the West," of those who struggled against it, or, in J. P. Sartre's words, knew Western Civilization only through their scars.

WESTERN CIVILIZATION: ORIGINS AND DEVELOPMENT

[Civilization] sums up everything in which Western Society of the last two or three centuries believes itself superior to earlier societies or "more primitive" contemporary ones. By this term Western society seeks to describe what constitutes its special character.

Norbert Elias, 1978

In an era that has alerted us to the constructed character of meaning, it may appear futile to criticize a concept such as "Western Civilization" on the basis of what an older terminology would have defined as its ideological character. No term, we are reminded, is generated through an act of immaculate conception; each implies theoretical choices. Thus, a more complex process may be required prior to invalidating any meaning "in use," particularly one that has enjoyed such currency throughout this century. Special considerations, however, are in order in the case of intellectual frameworks that claim to have a pedagogical (explanatory, heuristic) value. We should ask, for example, what methodology they teach; what assumptions they encourage us to make about history; to what social values they commit us; and, first of all, what merits they can claim as preferential schemes of historical interpretation.

From this viewpoint, we have to recognize that the concept of "the West" is highly problematic, since it pretends to be constructed by reference to conventional geographical coordinates and yet maps the world in ways that defy "common sense," leaving entire regions in limbo. Moreover, it does not specify from whose viewpoint the partition is made, which in the case of a relative term is generally considered a violation of logical norms. Worse yet, a genealogy of "Western Civilization" demonstrates that this concept has historically developed in the context of military and ideological warfare, as the label for a political reality that could be conceived as unified only by reference to perceived enemies and contenders. Thus, to continue to use this term is not only to validate a view of the world as constituted by opposite blocks, but also to adopt an adversarial self-definition.

The notion of "the West" as a political designation dates back to the sixteenth century, originating from the two major crises Christianity faced during this period, the Protestant Reformation and the expansion of the Ottoman Empire, which called for the invention of a secular term to replace the now contentious Christendom. "West," "Europe," and "Occident" were for a time used interchangeably. One of the first appearances of "West" was in Edward Fairfax's translation of Tasso's *Jerusalem Delivered* (1600), an allegorical celebration of the anti-Ottoman League formed by Phillip II, the pope, and the Venetian rulers, which was to defeat the Turkish navy at the battle of Lepanto in 1571. Tasso used the Crusades as the setting for his allegory, which had the League standing for the Crusaders and the Turks playing the Saracens. In stanza 16 of canto 4, the Devil appears as the commander of a vast underground army moving against the Crusaders. In Fairfax's translation, the Devil's rallying call introduces us to the first political usage of "Western":

> The Western rebels, with your power withstand
> Pluck up these weeds, before they overgroe
> The gentle garden of the Hebrewes land . . .

In the seventeenth and eighteenth centuries, however, "the West" performed primarily a geographical function, differentiating the eastern from the western Church, the eastern from the western Empire, the eastern from the western world. It was a synonym with "Occident," as in the English divine Thomas Becon's 1553 expression, "The occidentall or weast churches thorow out all Europe" (*Oxford English Dictionary*, 1989, Vol. XX: 162). But it never succeeded in replacing "Christendom." This was to be the fate of "Europe," a geographical term, already used in Ancient Greek and Latin, which, until the eighteenth century (witness the works of Rousseau and Kant, among others), was the preferred political term for transnational self-reference, while "Christendom" became increasingly obsolescent,[2] and "West" and "Occident" were left to play subordinate roles, being introduced mainly to refer to the Americas, as in Berkeley's famous "Westward Ho!" (Hay, 1957: 94, 116).

Only in the aftermath of the nineteenth-century colonial penetration of India, China, and the Middle East did "the West" take on a more prominent political role, as the signifier of Europe's imperial project. It was at this time that it began to include the United States, previously referred to as the "New World," and to merge with the concept of "civilization," the term coined by Enlightenment philosophers to describe the aim of social evolution, which they identified with the processes and institutions marking the development of private property, the family, and monetary relations (Stocking, 1987; Caffentzis, in this volume).[3]

As a synonym for social progress, "civilization" remained throughout the nineteenth century the prime signifier in the anthropological self-presentation of the European elites. Thus, the "civilized"/"savage" ("primitive," "backward") contrast became a standard element in European literature. But "civilization" and "the civilized world" were for a time used without further qualification, as if it were self-evident that no other contender existed for this title. Only when Europe's expansionary drive reached Egypt, India, and China, countries densely populated and with a long commercial and literary tradition, did the Europeans concede that theirs was one among different, though inferior, civilizations.

Evidence of this recognition is the complex social mapping performed by Hegel in his lectures on the "Philosophy of History," delivered in 1820 to a Berlin audience of future civil servants. Arguing that history moves "from East to West, for Europe is the absolute end of History" (Hegel, 1956: 103), Hegel forged a hierarchical scheme to describe the place of the Western world in historical development that remained standard for most of the century. He excluded Africa from the civilized world (Hegel: 99), a main condition for his reconstruction of world history along an East/West axis; he traced the "proper Emergence" of the Absolute Spirit back to Greece—the first society, he claimed, based on the "free individual" and sufficiently "dynamic" to transmit its cultural acquisitions (Hegel: 223). And he declared India and China "stationary" cultures, overcome by history's progressive westward move, which he modeled on the westward migrations of the Aryan tribes, with the Germanic people playing a special role, as the carriers of the highest manifestations of the divine spirit.

As Stocking points out, the hypothesis of an origination of European languages from an Aryan homeland, developed by nineteenth-century German philologists, provided a major intellectual buttress for the German tendency, from Herder through Schlegel to Hegel (and beyond), to visualize the progress of civilization as a movement from East to West across Asia, conceived in racial terms. This racialist tendency in nineteenth-century German cultural thought was to have a considerable impact on Anglo-French thinking about the question of civilization, at a time when German scholarship commanded international respect (Stocking, 1987: 24–25). However, it was the advent of Darwinian evolutionary theory and the expansion of colonial conquest, in the second part of the century, that codified the spousal of "civilization" with "Western" and the racialization of this term.[4]

In becoming "Western," "civilization," which had previously been considered (by Enlightenment philosophers) a universal stage in humanity's "growth," began to signify a culturally relative state, characterized by unique norms, attitudes, and mentalities. Ironically, however, its exclusionary connotations were only intensified, as "Western" became now an explicit mark of superiority to others.

The exclusionary meaning of "Western Civilization" was consolidated in the post–World War I period, when "the East" began to appear in the eyes of the European bourgeoisie as a rising tide of forces, threatening to destroy its world hegemony. The 1920s were the years when the East/West conflict came to dominate the thinking of the *bienpensants* in Europe, as reflected by the proliferation of books dedicated to this topic—for example, Henry Massis's *Defense de l'Occident* (1921) and Rene Guenon's *Òrient et Occident* (1924) (Michaud, 1977: 1436ff). Several factors contributed to this development. First, the rise of nationalism and anticolonial striving in Asia raised the specter of the decline of Europe's colonial power, metaphorically expressed by the obsession with the demographic growth of the "yellow races" and the claim that Europe rushed toward "racial suicide." The fear of "the East" was also fueled by events in Europe. Both in defeated and victorious nations, in Germany above all, the devastations caused by World War I provoked a widespread revulsion against "Western values"—against a science, technology, and Reason that so readily had put their powers at the service of carnage—leading many to turn to Bolshevism or to cultivate Oriental philosophies (Taoism, Hinduism, Buddhism) (Cadwallader, 1981).[5] Thus, while the Dadaists celebrated the end of "the West," refusing to shore up its ruins with cultural shards, while Romain Rolland and Herman Hesse studied Buddhism and dreamed of an East-West syncretism, in France, a motley crowd of royalists, right-wing Catholics, industrialists, and conservative intellectuals, who made no mystery of their sympathies for fascism and later very often became Nazi collaborators, rose to defend "Western Civilization" from the "yellow peril" and "Asiatism,"[6] terms that merged the triple menace of Bolshevik Revolution, anticolonial revolt, and mystical rejection of Western economic striving (Cadwallader: 28–42). In this context, "Western Civilization" stood as a defense of individualism against Bolshevik collectivism and Buddhist transcendence of self, of work-oriented activism against the "Eastern" ascetic withdrawal from material pursuits, of "Western" scientific rationalism against "Oriental" mysticism. Most important, "Western Civilization" stood as an explicit defense of capitalism and Europe's "civilizing mission" in the colonies (Cadwallader: 66–68), while "the East" became the signifier for a formidable double threat: the yogi and the commissar (Koestler, 1945).

World War I also consecrated the ascendance of the United States as the leading capitalist power and opened the way to the disengagement of an increasingly international capitalism from territorial Europe, which further undermined the bourgeois identification of the goals of "civilization" with those of European culture. Thus, "Western Civilization," which until the war had primarily thrived on European soil, became the official ideology of the United States, where it "[became] the answer to international and political struggle" (Kaplan, 1982: 5), and the centerpiece of college education.[7]

In American hands, "Western Civilization" has served a variety of political objectives, as a prop used at different times to bolster the animal spirits of the capitalist class, to guide the newly independent "Third World" nations onto the path of "modernization," to reaffirm Europe's commitment to NATO against centrifugal tendencies, to deflect the danger of the "welfare state," and, pivotal to all, to rally anticommunist crusaders to the defense of the "Free World." At each turn, the appeal to "Western Civilization" has served to dress the mundane objectives connected with the expansion of capitalist relations with a spiritual mantle, playing a role similar to that of Christianity in the political life of the Middle Ages. The vehicles of this cultural politics were innumerable tracts, lecture series, and seminars, produced in the shadows of power, which form a genre of their own, mixing historical overviews, moral considerations, and policy analyses in a standardized format, tailored to American needs. For while in Europe "Western Civilization" had been vindicated as a Latin or Germanic offspring, stress was now placed on its North Atlantic roots, even though this required attributing a more composite essence to "the ethos of the West," and devising a long train of steps to establish a credible connection between such hardly compatible phenomena as twentieth-century American industrialism and Hellenism, Judeo-Christian monotheism, Roman law, and Protestant individualism.[8] What would Plato have thought in finding himself anachronistically identified as a forerunner of Luther or as one of the forefathers of NATO, as it became common to suggest in the political language of the 1950s, was a question never asked. Indeed, such rhetorical license would not claim special notice, so accustomed have we become to hearing Western Civilization defended in the language of *Realpolitik*, were not "Western Civilization" still being considered a worthwhile object of study and a cultural norm aspiring to have a canonic value.

In reality, today as well the notion of "Western Civilization" depends for its content on the dicta of the dominant capitalist nations, and the annual reports of the U.S. State Department are generally more useful in deciding what the West is and who belongs to it than any cultural map. So instrumentally defined is "Western Civ" that the same countries or ideologies could become "Eastern" or "Western" depending on the context and the shift of political alliances. Marxism, for example, while generally pictured as an offspring of the despotic "East," has often been vindicated as a "Western" product when the interlocutors were Third World nationalists, who had to be reminded that even for their struggles they were in debt to "the West," since presumably never would they have rebelled against colonialism had not Marx and other Western revolutionaries equipped them with the idea of human rights. "Western" in this process has acquired both a denotative and connotative character. To this day, it denotes those abiding by the principles of private enterprise, and, in one stroke, it sets up a cultural norm, in the same way as "German," during the Third Reich, became a qualification of goodness and superiority, and an indication not only of ethnic origin but also of moral resolve (Glaser, 1978: 171).

"WESTERN CIVILIZATION" AND THE "WESTERN MIND"

A genealogy of the concept of Western Civilization indicates that for several decades this has been one of the most value-laden concepts in the American vocabulary, and we cannot use it without making a tacit pledge to a political stance. But even if we could divorce the ideological "West" from "the West" of the classroom, we would still confront the problem that the concept cannot be methodologically grounded except on the basis of an idealist philosophy that has long been discredited in every intellectual quarter.

The first methodological problem in the way of any account of "Western Civilization" is deciding what criteria should be used toward its definition. The birth of "Western Civilization," in fact, was the demise of what had been, until the late nineteenth century, a crucial distinction between "civilization" and "culture." As it is well known, the civilization/culture dichotomy originated in post–Napoleonic Germany, when, in the aftermath of the nation's defeat, German culture (defined as a spiritual entity) was opposed to the (external, material, exteriorized) French civilization.[9] In the traditional dichotomy, culture stood for (intangible) spiritual qualities possessed by a people (or race), while civilization was identified with observable, quantifiable elements, and thus was taken to be more reliable scientific evidence of a people's achievements.

With the advent of "*Western* Civilization," the difficulty of establishing any methodologhical criteria for the definition of the term has only intensified, as any distinction between "civilization" and "culture" has inevitably dissolved. Thus, in political and scholarly parlance, the two terms are usually merged, and it is generally assumed that the institutions of "the West" are the product of a specific intellectual and moral propensity. This means that "Western Civilization" is simultaneously treated as an historical and a philosophical concept, constructed both by reference to an alleged historical continuity (between the institutions of classical Greece and Rome, those of medieval Europe, and those of modern/post–Reformation Europe and America), and by the identification of specific values presumably responsible for the uniqueness of "the West." This implies imputing a qualitative uniformity, or at the very least a spiritual kinship, to the historical periods, countries, and institutions the concept identifies. However, as George Barraclough has shown (already in 1955), the existence of a continuous "Western tradition" is not supported by the scholarship in the field. As he put it, noting with concern the novel popularity of the term: "It is noteworthy that it has emerged as a dogmatic assertion precisely at the moment when . . . the interpretation of history upon which it is based has been shattered by historical criticism and discarded by historical scholarship" (Barraclough, 1955: 32).

Barraclough argues, for instance, that the Roman Empire (one of the pillars of "the West," together with Christianity and the "classical tradition") could hardly provide the basis for Western/European coherence, being itself increasingly sustained from Eastern, non-European lands (34). He adds that the direct heir of Rome was not "the West," but Byzantium, where Roman civilization and the very structure of the Roman state continued down to the fall of Constantinople (35). By contrast, "classical civilization" was extinct in Rome; as shown by Christian art, whose anti-classical character gives evidence against the continuity of the classical tradition (36). Barraclough adds that, far from seizing on what was vital in the Roman world, the Church was hostile to the Roman tradition; and that the places that really mattered in the early Christian centuries were not in Europe but in Africa or Asia Minor (37). Most important, he warns that "Much of the apparent unity of thought—presumably characterising 'the west'—is due primarily to the fact that the Catholic Church extirpated its opponents (e.g., the heretics), burned their literature, and had the monopoly of writing" (38).

Furthermore, justifying the idea of Western Civilization on the basis of a presumed continuity of values—as it is done when "Western Civilization" is identified with a unique predisposition to defend individual liberties, scientific objectivity, moral and cognitive universalism—obscures the fact that much of the history of the West contradicts its moral and intellectual pretensions, and postulates a teleological view of history, which inevitably is permeated by idealist and racialist connotations.

It is significant, in this context, that the only philosophers who have tried to ground methodologically the idea of "Western Civilization" have come from the German idealist tradition, from Hegel to the Neo-Kantians. For only through an a-prioristic, teleological notion of *form*, such as German Idealism in all its varieties developed, can the existence of any such cultural totality be argued.

Neo-Kantianism developed in pre–World War I Germany in response to the crisis of Hegelian historicism that confronted the German intellectuals with the need to find a new methodology for the social sciences. Forced to abandon the assumption of a universal historical subject, the Neo-Kantians resorted to regional totalities presumably common to specific sociocultural groups and formations. In so doing, they embraced the Kantian tenet that our apprehension of reality is structured by a-priori schemata, but they denied that these have a universal extension or are exclusively of a cognitive nature. The Neo-Kantian forms are culturally relative psychic schemes, which structure both our knowing and doing, in such a way that the actions and productions resulting from them are characterized by a unitary qualitative configuration. Exemplary of such forms are Wilhelm Dilthey's "worldviews" (*Weltanschauungen*), Max Weber's ideal types (e.g., "the Protestant Ethics"), Ernst Cassirer's symbolic forms, and (most crucial to our topic) Oswald Spengler's "morphology of history," which patterns historical "forms" on the model of living organisms.

Spengler's *Decline of the West* (1918) was a milestone in the attempt to apply the concept of "form" to an understanding of world history, which he interpreted as the product of diverse, incommensurable "mentalities," each being the carrier of a particular type of consciousness and "destiny." His work, however, shows the limits of this approach. It shows that apprehending the historical process through historical forms—each characterized by one all-pervasive quality—leads us necessarily to ontologize the historical process and to read it as a manifestation of transhistorical subjectivities, patterned still on the Hegelian logos. Indeed, the language adopted by Spengler (as well as by other Neo-Kantians) is one that constantly personifies historical forces, moving unproblematically from the concept of Western Civilization to that of a "Western Soul" or "Western Mind." Such qualitative forms, moreover, can only be apprehended through an intuitive act (*Verstehen*), performed by intentionally predisposed subjects; consequently, they are open to any interpretation. For Spengler, for instance, the uniqueness of Western Civilization consisted in its "world-historical consciousness," that is, its ability to project itself on a temporal dimension and conceive of its being as constituted in time. On this basis, he rejected any identification between "Western Culture" and the "Classical Culture" of Greece and Rome, which he considered ahistorical and ruled by "mythological thinking" (Spengler, 1926, I: 10). As is well known, he also proclaimed that Western Civilization was the last phase of Western Culture, that stage when, having exhausted its metaphysical soil, "the West" would consummate its historic decline. By contrast, Max Weber, Edmund Husserl, and, later, Ernst Cassirer identified the essence of "the West" with a unique rationalistic disposition and insisted on its linear development from Greece (Husserl, 1970: 274ff). But no less than Spengler, they treated it as a cultural a-priori—that is, a transhistorical condition of historical becoming that (in Husserl's words) can never be deduced from the visible history to be read through facts and events.

The Neo-Kantian framework enjoyed an immense popularity in the post–World War II period in U.S. academic circles where, through Cassirer's work, it became one of the dominant influences in linguistics and anthropology (Redfield, 1953: 735). However, the totality presumed by the form/structure framework has undergone a devastating criticism in the last generation of scholarship. In the 1960s, philosophers like W. O. Quine, Thomas Kuhn, Michel Foucault, and Jacques Derrida challenged the scientific status of the intentional totalities that the Western Civilization framework presumes. Quine demonstrated the existence of a deep "indeterminacy," which makes the attribution of the same intent to different human beings in different social settings problematic (Quine, 1962). Kuhn, in turn, has argued that the continuities found in the history of science and societies put in question the assumption of cultural progress and accumulation which "Western Civilization" relies on, for discontinuous conceptual paradigms are incommensurable. Poststructuralist and feminist philosophers have also stressed the contested and imposed character of any social regularity.

Nevertheless, the terminology that characterizes the Western Civilization discourse shows that Western Civilization is still conceptualized as an organic form. We hear of the "Western Mind," or "the genius of the West," as if the West were an individual organism; it is asked whether Western Civilization "must decline," or will continue to "grow." Western Civilization, we are told, can at times abscond, lie in wait for a more propitious environment, then it resurfaces invigorated in a new soil, it suffers setbacks, occasionally it fails to stand up to its principles, changes its abode, is cross-fertilized, and so forth.

The operational effects of this conceptual machinery, which starting in the 1940s became fairly standardized in its metaphors and topoi, can be seen in some of the texts which, at different historical junctions, sketched out the discourse, later transposed to the classroom in the form of the required "Western Civilization" courses.

Ernst Cassirer's *The Myth of the State* (1946) and Louis Rougier's *The Genius of the West* (1971) are proper examples of this genre. These works differ in important respects. *The Myth of State*, written in 1943–44 and published originally in *Fortune* magazine by one of Europe's most eminent scholars, is as expected more learned and pessimistic in tone. *The Genius of the West*, by contrast, is such an unrestrained paean to the progress of "Western Reason" that even Professor v. Hayek, one of the founders of the Principles of Freedom Committee who sponsored the book, found it "unduly optimistic" (Rougier, 1971: xviii). Yet, their reading of the history of "Western Civilization" is essentially the same. We have the ritual origination in Greece, as the cradle of rational thought and democracy; Western Civilization then leaps to Rome to acquire the principle of law; in the Christian Middle Ages it discovers the value of human life, and, from then on, its genetic pool being firmly established, we witness a constant ripening of its fruits. The scientific and industrial revolutions become a fulfillment of Greece's penchant for deductive reasoning and scientific inquiry, the Anglo-American liberal tradition brings to fruition the lessons of the Athenian Agora and of Rome's universalizing legislation, and so forth.

In Rougier, this cavalcade through the achievements of Western Civilization touches the absurd, as when we are informed that the greatness of Greece stemmed not solely from the rigors of its axiomatic thinking and its discovery of democratic institutions, but was predominantly due to the "scrupulous respect given to private property" (Rougier, 1971: 16), its "monetary discipline," and its well-organized import-export exchange structure. "In brief, Athens in the period of her greatness had what we call today a free-market economy. And it was this which gave her undisputed leadership in wealth and culture" (Rougier, 1971: 18).

In this balance sheet, slavery is either not mentioned, or, in Rougier's case, it is only *post factum*, in order to explain why Greece did not have an industrial revolution (Rougier, 1971: 34). Slavery (for Rougier) is a "handicap" soon to be remedied by the Christian discovery of the value of work. Not a word is uttered about the Catholic Church's legendary corruption, its centuries-long blessing of slavery and conquest, its *autos-da-fé* and torture chambers. Most important, in both authors we find a staunch commitment not only to present Western Civilization as the highest stage reached by the human spirit, but also to devalue "the other." In Rougier the intelligent, dynamic West is contrasted to the submissive, superstitious, magical Orient which, even when it practices mathematics, can never transcend a narrow, pragmatic empiricism. In Cassirer the "serenity" of Western thinking is counterposed to the dangerously instinctual, mythical world of the "savage." Finally, both authors have an irrepressible impulse to ontologize: for both authors, it is self-evident that the greatness of the West is the product of a unique attitude and mentality; in the pre-Nazi era one would have said a "race."

WESTERN CIVILIZATION IN THE CLASSROOM

It is easy to criticize the biases that transpire from Rougier's and Cassirer's works. Yet, apologies and distortions are inevitable once we attempt to subsume complex historical processes under a single unifying principle, and we identify ourselves and the students we teach as the heirs of the history thus reconstructed. There are strategic consequences to this move. When we teach history as one enterprise, and an enterprise by which "we" are identified, we cannot acknowledge the existence of conflicting interests operating in the historical scenarios we discuss, nor can we give serious consideration to counter-examples; and to the extent that we pass value judgments, we have to opt for either wholesale glorification or wholesale condemnation.

These constraints are evident in the last generation of textbooks, which are written in an intellectual milieu averse to the totalizing approach implicit in the idea of "Western Civilization." The impact of poststructuralist, feminist, and afrocentrist critiques has not been lost to the compilers of the latest accounts of "Western Civilization." It is significant that, in their opening pages, most shun any attempt to define their object of study or to circumvent the problem of specifying the criteria for unity by means of cosmetic devices, such as that adopted by Greaves, Zaller, and Roberts, who suggest that "the West" embraces a variety of civilizations (*Civilizations of the West: The Human Adventure*, 1992). However, to the extent that the framework is de facto maintained, its compelling logic asserts itself, even if driven only by inertia. Thus, aspects of "Western History" that might call for a reassessment of its merits are introduced with justificatory clauses, whose function is not to explain but to exculpate. We are told, for example, that the Spanish Inquisition was "the dark side of Spanish Genius" (Perry et al., 1992: 359); that colonial conquest was the unintended result of legitimate desires—witness the case of Spain that "stumbled onto its overseas empires" (332), or of Britain that "picked up a whole subcontinent [India] without half trying" (Hughes, 1991: 62). Again, it is asserted that it was not unnatural for the European elites, in the sixteenth and seventeenth centuries, to make their fortunes "by plunder and conquest," since "their ancestors had done the same thing for centuries" (Perry et al., 1992: 329).

The lesson to be drawn from these statements is that we cannot maintain the "Western Civilization" framework as a matter of convenience, if we want to teach history in a coherent and nonapologetic manner. Moreover, as a tool of historical and cultural interpretation, "Western Civilization" constantly confronts us with contradictions and unsoluble aporias. How, for example, can we successfully insert Plato in the history of "Western Civilization"? For there are arguably two Platos. We have Plato the "civilized" philosopher, expert in mathematical reasoning, who, but for the existence of slavery (and, perhaps, his ambivalence with regard to free enterprise), could have placed Greece on the technological map. But we also have Plato the oriental despot, the defender of castes, of whom it is rumored that he learned his wisdom from Egyptian priests, the Plato against whom Karl Popper, in his *Open Society and Its Enemies*, warned us, as the instigator of totalitarian thinking (Popper, 1945). Which Plato will the "Western Civilization" framework demand we present to the classroom, and which should we suppress? How shall we justify the heterodox dimensions of his thought? Shall we grant him limited citizenship in the "Western" Olympus? And at what cost shall we say that he "belongs to the West"?

We encounter the same plethora of difficult cases when we pass to the study of countries and cultures. First and foremost, we confront the still unresolved "German Problem." From the viewpoint of "Western Civilization," Germany cannot be disowned. What would "Western Civilization" be without Mozart, Bach, Beethoven, Goethe, Hegel, Nietzsche, and even Marx? Truly, can "the West" afford not to claim as its own the most popular political theorist since the advent of Christianity? Yet, Germany is a "troubled nation," to use a euphemism that became popular in the post–World War II period. Less scandalous but still puzzling is the case of France, which is the reputed source of many values "the West" wishes to claim as its own, but has all too often been dangerously on the edge. How to forget that France was the country where "the mob," donning the red caps of the liberated slaves, brought the "better sort" to the guillotine? Were these red-capped *sans-coulotte* Parisians also "Western" citizens? Or should we decide that the Parisian masses abdicated their "Western" heritage at the very moment in history when their country presumably embodied this heritage at its best? Another paradox is Greece, which was an essential part of "the West"—in fact, it "gave rise to the West"— six centuries before Christ, but soon apparently lost its "Western" vocation, to the point that no account of "the West" would nowadays strive to include its more than 2,000-year-old history.

Italy as well, Rome notwithstanding, is not seen as consistently "Western." Not only does its fascist past make its credentials less than immaculate, but also its substantial leftist movement has repeatedly challenged the solidity of the country's commitment to "Western" values. Indeed, in the heyday of the cold war, intellectuals like Hans Kohn took it upon themselves to expel Italy,

Germany, and Spain from "Western Civilization." Kohn also proceeded to put France on probation as a potential member and to attach the word "modern" to "Western Civilization" in order to argue that only England and America should be granted this title. As he wrote: "In our modern Western society with its almost unbroken growth from the late seventeenth century to World War I, it is Britain that is the point of origin and the model. The United States . . . is the purest expression of that society's political ideals and strength and thereby its most 'Western' member" (Kohn, 1957: 17). As for France, here—Kohn claimed —"the Western democratic revolution is forever being fought, without ever being finally resolved" (16–18).

The Western Civilization paradigm forces us to approach selectively the history we teach. It also requires that we employ artificial props to support the thesis of its continuous propagation through space and time. Among the most common devices are the notions of "legacy" and "heritage," which take the transmission of property as the model for historical development and, through an act of temporal conquest, enable "Western Civilization" to appropriate as its own all that is valuable in the past. These metaphors hide the fact, however, that many of "Western Civilization's" alleged achievements—for instance, the conquest of political liberties—were not handed down to us, as if through a legal transaction, by qualified representatives of the "Western Spirit." Far from it, most of "the West's" celebrated gains, particularly at the level of political rights, were worked and fought for by many who were not considered "Westerners." Indeed, many of our political rights were wrenched into existence against the resistance of the most typical "Westerners." The "Western Civilization" "legacy" metaphor also hides the role European and non-European workers have played in building the wealth and culture of Europe and America. Typically, credit for technological development is laid at the doorstep of Greek Rationalism or is presented as the logical unfolding of a Promethean inner "Western" predisposition; rarely is it asked, in a Brechtian mode, "Who built the factories?" In a similar vein, Greece is made to account for the development of democratic ideals. This assumption, repeated for over two centuries, has channeled the path of historical research. Only to the extent that the Grand Narrative of "Western Civilization" has been challenged, and new voices have been heard, has it been possible to question its validity and to discover that such a peculiarly "Western" ideal as the concept of freedom as self-determination is a gift that the Europeans and Americans received from the "uncivilized" (Brandon, 1986; Linebaugh, 1991).

All these difficulties place "Western Civilization" in the same conceptual predicament as Ptolemaic astronomy was in the seventeenth century. By that time, Ptolemaic theory, which had developed in the second century A.D. as a crystalline model of circular perfection, had become, in Copernicus's words, a conceptual "monster," crushed under the burden of major epicycles, eccentrics, equants, and other ad hoc devices, which astronomers employed to rescue it in front of increasingly recalcitrant celestial appearances. Although its place in the university curriculum was guaranteed throughout most of Europe by the power of state and church, in the seventeenth century Ptolemaic theory was kept alive only by intellectual inertia and political intimidation.

We are in a similar situation now with respect to "Western Civilization." Today "Western Civ" serves at best as an abbreviation for a series of "required" historical facts to be "covered" between the first and last day of the semester. But the bundles of supplements and ad hoc devices that are found in the recent texts remind us of Tycho Brahe's last-ditch attempt to revise Ptolemy's theory by integrating Copernicus's view while still keeping the earth still. Everything in these texts has the quality of a qualification and a supplement. Here we have a section on "The West and the World" that "explores the West's changing perception of the rest of the world"; there we have an account of "The Role of Women in Western Civilization," or a description of "Gladiatorial Contests in Ancient Rome" and "Greek Geriatrics." But since the principles of inclusion are not revealed, each new addition appears as arbitrary as an item in a shopping list. Such a conceptual situation, however, is not stable, as the anomalies continue to accumulate. In fact, the "Western Civilization" scaffold would have collapsed under the weight of its contradictions except for the formidable institutional power that has been mobilized in its support whenever its crises have reached unacceptable levels. Exemplary was the complex operation undertaken in the postwar period to rescue "Western Civilization" from the crisis opened by Nazism. All the theoretical energies of the paradigm were taxed then, and in the process strategies were devised that became standard in dealing with future difficulties. These devices have made it possible to continue the "Western Civilization" genre without utter embarrassment. But they have also demonstrated the inadequacies of this framework. To the extent that historians have been unwilling to question "Western Civilization's" alleged commitment to universalistic, humanitarian values, they have also been forced either to declare Nazism unintelligible or to resort to psychologistic categories that in fact abdicate historical analysis.

THE CASE OF NAZISM

The advent of Nazism opened a major crisis in the conceptual scaffold of "Western Civilization." We can question Hannah Arendt's claim that this was "perhaps the most profound crisis in Western history since the downfall of the Roman Empire" (Arendt, 1951: 9). But there is no doubt that decades of self-complacent praises of Western humanism stood on trial when the death camps were revealed to the eyes of the world. Few in 1945 could have listened without embarrassment to the words with which, only ten years before, in a lecture delivered in Vienna, Edmund Husserl had characterized Europe's unique teleology: "No matter how hostile they may be toward one another, the European nations nevertheless have a peculiar inner kinship of spirit which runs through them all, transcending national differences. There is something like a sibling relationship which gives all of us in this sphere the consciousness of homeland" (Husserl, 1970: 274).

A sense of epochal crisis was also pervasive in American intellectual circles in the 1940s. As W. T. Stace rather disparagingly acknowledged in *The Destiny of Western Man* (1942): "This despair of reason, this profound unfaith in the rationality of our ideals, this deep defeatism in regard to our values, is, in the most up to date intellectual circles, the fashion of the moment" (Stace, 1942: viii).

Every crisis opens new possibilities. The confrontation with Nazism was an opportunity for the European intelligentsia to dissociate itself from an ideology that had proved compatible with, if not instrumental to, conquest and enslavement. Indeed, for many among the new generations, Nazism was a point of no return. But strong institutional forces worked against such reckoning. The postwar economic order, shaped by the ascending American hegemony and the onset of the cold war, needed a "West" morally triumphant. It was feared that the debacle of "Western Civilization" could promote the advance of communism. As C. H. Wendel stated in his "Foreword" to Cassirer's *The Myth of the State* (1946): "Most people talked easily about the fact that we were going through a crisis of world history. It was natural to expect a confused welter of ideas in the public mind about the philosophy of history or about the nature of our civilization. All sorts of quasi-philosophies were likely to spring up in such conditions, inspired by some ideology or the political interests of those who enunciated them" (x).

The task of dispelling the sense of doom prevailing on both sides of the ocean was taken on by the American elites who, as the heirs of Europe's colonial empires, most stood to profit from a rehabilitation of "the West." The restoration of "Western Civilization" was, within U.S. geopolitics, the cultural equivalent of the Marshall Plan. As the Marshall Plan solidified Europe's economy by bringing it into the circuit of American capitalism, so did the reconstruction of "Western Civilization" call for its moorings on North Atlantic shores. Thus, the accounts of "our Western tradition" produced in U.S. political circles in the 1950s introduced new qualifiers (the "free West," "modern Western society") that stressed its filiation from Britain and its special rootedness in Anglo-American soil (Kohn, 1957: 18). At the same time, while the politicians were readjusting the map of "the West," a more complex rescue operation was carried on in intellectual circles, which was to turn the lesson of "Western Civilization," as taught by Nazism, into a critique of communism.

A key role in this process was played by *Partisan Review*, a magazine founded in 1937 by a circle of self-styled "dissident Marxists," who brought to the task the credibility attached to their experience as insiders of the communist movement and their knowledge of the latest political debates and philosophical trends. Through a mixture of literary and political commentaries, the editors of *Partisan Review* crafted strategies that reconstructed "Western Civilization" for a post–Nazi, anticommunist world, creating new paradigms that were later promoted in academia, through Western Civilization, philosophy, and literature courses, up until the 1960s. In this task they were so successful that, in an unprecedented move in the history of American literary journals, soon after its formation, *Partisan Review* also began publication in England.

Two tendencies emerged in the response to the crisis of "Western Civilization." The first was to argue that Nazism was a completely alien phenomenon, an unaccountable break with "Western Civilization's" humanitarian and democratic teleology. Among the supporters of this theory was Hannah Arendt, who later expanded upon it in one of the foundational tomes of cold war thought, *The Origins of Totalitarianism* (1951). Here Arendt considered the possibility that Nazism derived from imperialism, noting the fundamental similarity between the two phenomena (Arendt, 1951: 123). But, unlike Aimé Cesaire (1955), she dismissed this hypothesis, indulging in quite a few nostalgic sighs on the virtues of the imperial venture. "[For] we must . . . admit a certain nostalgia for what can still be called a golden age of security" (123).

In order to radically differentiate imperialism from Nazism, however, Arendt had to admit that "Western Reason" is compatible even with extermination, provided it finds its utility in it. Thus, imperialism—which she labeled "an entirely new concept" of "suprising originality," for "without imperialism the world might never have become one" (125)—was consistent with "Western Civilization" because it was economically rational, fully within the logic of capitalism (142), while Nazism, by contrast, had abandoned all utilitarian considerations (31). Arendt had to rationalize colonial racism as well. She argued that, as a political principle, racism was a reaction to the traumas the Europeans suffered in the "Dark Continent," where, "Under a merciless sun, surrounded by an entirely hostile nature," they had been faced with human beings who lived without any purposes and accomplishments and were, therefore, for them "as incomprehensible as the inmates of a madhouse" (190). In an empathic mood, Arendt speculated that the Boers never overcame the humiliation they had experienced in front of beings "whom human pride and the sense of human dignity could not allow them to accept as fellow men" (192). "Race [then] was the Boers' answer to the overwhelming monstrosity of Africa." "[It was] an explanation of the madness which grasped them . . . like a flash of lightning . . . [demanding] 'Exterminate all the brutes'" (192).

Arendt's excursus into the psychology of the Boers has at times been found "undigestible" even by her admirers (Kateb, 1984: 61–63). It demonstrates, however, the conclusions we must reach if we are committed to expelling Nazism from "the West." As such, it is a caveat to the scholars who still adopt this position (e.g., R. A. Pois, 1986).

While the inexplicability theory placed Nazism outside of "Western Civilization," a more radical solution consisted in postulating the existence of internal dangers besieging "Western rationality" from within, and calling, therefore, for a more cautious evaluation of its powers. The lesson that was drawn from Nazism was that "Reason" cannot provide a reliable guide in social and political action. Thus, any attempt to bring about social change is necessarily doomed to failure.

Existentialism, in its American version, forged by William Barrett, gave a theoretical justification to the fear of political engagement. With its discourse of anguish, guilt, and life-unto-death, its emphasis on the ambivalence of human behavior, and the impossibility of reducing the human experience to categorical schemes, American existentialism served to project a world where any hope for social improvement could automatically be suspected of totalitarian aspirations. It served to demonstrate that to act is to fall into dogmatism, to prematurely put an end to questioning, and that any step we may take to improve the human condition is necessarily a first step into the gulag.

To underscore this lesson, throughout the 1940s, the *Partisan Review* alternated articles on existentialism and anticommunism as part of one narrative, mixing George Orwell, Arthur Koestler, and Arthur Schlesinger with Carl Jaspers and, above all, Albert Camus. No existentialist philosopher, in fact, was for a time more influential than the author of *The Plague*, whose warning that we all carry the germs of the pestilence, and by our attempts to improve humanity we only spread the disease, won for it general acclaim. Soon, even Heidegger was quoted as an authority on the pitfalls of "Western Reason," rehabilitated by William Barrett, who devoted his career (from *Irrational Man* [1958] to *What Is Existentialism?* [1964]) to launch his views in America. As with many Nazi scientists who, being considered useful to the objectives of the cold war, were given a political facelift, similarly, intellectuals who had paved the way for Nazism were recruited in the crusade against political activism. Cast in the socratic role of the Questioner, Heidegger became the prophet who had warned against the dangers of technology and scolded "the West" because of its "will to reason" and domination of nature. Among those reintegrated into the "Western" fold was also Ernst Junger, the author of *Fire and Blood, The Battle as an Inner Experience, Thunder of Steel*, and an early supporter of Nazism. Of him, Louis Clair was to say that "he perhaps probed more deeply into the perplexities of modern civilization than any of his contemporaries" (Clair, 1947: 453, 464).

Old warriors too were rediscovered, each with a specific function: Kierkegaard to exalt the virtues of individualism and the sins of schematism; Dostoyevsky to attack "utilitarian reason" and the dream of human perfectibility. As in pre-Nazi Germany, so in post–World War II United States, Dostoyevsky was invoked, time and time again, as a witness to the fundamental irrationality of "man" (Stern, 1965: 262). His main contribution, however, was the tale of the "Grand Inquisitor" which, in the 1950s, became one of the literary manifestos of the anticommunist crusade. Turned into a small book, to facilitate its diffusion, *The Grand Inquisitor* (1947) taught that "man does not live on bread alone," and it instructed the new generation to set up an unsurmountable contradiction between "freedom" and "happiness," a code for "materialism." (Later, *The Grand Inquisitor* was used against the supporters of the "welfare state" which, in the post–1970 defenses of Western Civilization, was portrayed, together with the "population explosion," as one of the major threats to "Western values.")

An excessive trust in reason, it was claimed, had blinded "the liberal mind" to the existence of evil in the heart of "man." The imperative was now to recognize (as Arthur Schlesinger put it in 1947) that "man is not essentially good" (Schlesinger, 1947: 235, 236). In support of this view, Freud was called upon to conjure the specter of uncontrollable, instinctual drives, lurking beneath the veneer of "civilization," while Hitchcock's movies drove home the lesson for the broader public, instilling a Hobbesian fear of thy neighbor, under whose benevolent appearance, they suggested, a murderer could hide.

But the proof for the basic irrationality and evil of "man" was also sought for in a more tested intellectual tradition. The salvaging of "Western Civilization," in fact, brought together, demonstrating their essential kinship, the anthropologist's account of colonial subjects, which since the turn of the century had stressed their "primitive" way of thinking, and the philosopher's account of the urban proletariat which, dating from the same period, had warned against the dangers of "mass society." Thus, on the one side, it was suggested that "the rootless masses" bore the main responsibility for the eclipse of "Western Reason"—in other words, that Nazism was a child of the "mob" (Arendt, 1951). On the other side, categories such as "the Mythical," by which nineteenth-century anthropologists had characterized the mentality of the peoples Europe had colonized, were extended to explain "Western" behavior.

The "Mythical," which, like the "prelogical," is part of a long colonial trajectory, was used by Ernst Cassirer in *The Myth of the State* (1946) to argue that Nazism was the surfacing of irrational powers, so far kept at bay in "the West." Nazism—Cassirer claimed—was the proof that the "Western" masses were vulnerable to the same "subterreanean instincts and drives" that had previously been mistakenly attributed only to the "uncivilized" (Cassirer, 1946: 2); among them being their preference for communal bonding, which Cassirer described as a typical trait of "savage" peoples, who lack any sense of individuality and moral responsibility (38–39, 284–85).

Like the appeal to "mass society" and the "evil in the heart of man," the assumption of a "Mythical" way of thinking served to foreclose a therapeutic reassessment of "Western Civilization" and to replace it with age-old devaluations of race and class that assimilated the "lower classes" to the "lower breeds," in a continuum of irrationality, emotionalism, and fanaticism.

Fear of the "irrational mob" further confirmed that faithfulness to "the West" could only be preserved by an intellectual retreat to purely ethical concerns. Coupled with the rise of McCarthyism, it served to create a climate where even ideas could appear suspicious. However, humility in front of our ability to affect historical change often stopped at the doorsteps of power. The same intellectuals who warned against political activism did not demonstrate a "plausible scepticism" in front of U.S. intervention throughout the world, nor did they object to being financed by that most *engagé* of all institutions: the United States government. William Barrett, who in his recollections about the origins of *Partisan Review* was to praise Dostoyevsky for having "understood that we are now in the Age of Ideology when ideas beget crimes and terror" (Barrett, 1982: 173), did not hesitate to join Henry Kissinger at Harvard in 1952 when, at the height of the cold war, Kissinger invited him to run an International Seminar for "chosen foreign intellectuals," "to teach them that American attitudes were not summed up in McCarthyism" and that there were left-wing American intellectuals who were anticommunists (Barrett, 1982: 189). Nor did his colleagues in the Congress for Cultural Freedom and *Encounter* feel compromised by receiving secret funds from the CIA (Lasch, 1969; Steinfels, 1979), or again display that "plausible scepticism" which, according to Stern, is the essence of the American intellectual tradition (Stern, 1965: 10).

Both intellectually and politically, the rescue of "Western Civilization" was paid at a high cost. The inexplicability theory trained a generation of intellectuals, who previously had felt confident concerning their ability to explain social phenomena, to assume that social reality could supersede their conceptual powers. So influential was the inexplicability theory that, through the 1950s and early 1960s, the appeal to the existence of inexplicable, irrational forces became a standard maneuver to deal with a wide range of recalcitrant phenomena, from the witch-hunt to nuclear war. In the same vein, the interpretation of Nazism as a manifestation of destructive psychosocial forces lurking within "the West" gave credence to the idea of the "enemy within," serving both to cast suspicion on any altruistic impulse and to annul sensibility in front of the escalating political repression.

By such strategies the normative status of "Western Civilization" was preserved. However, the explanatory power of the concept was gradually subverted, just as the Ptolemaic astronomer's attempts to deal with comets as sublunar phenomena and the unevenness of the solar year with equants had reduced the theory's legitimacy. As with the Ptolemaic equants, the extraordinary devices used to save the "Western Civilization" paradigm slowly undermined its *raison d'être*. For if "the West" was a "civilization" based on Reason, Equality, and respect for Law, then how could so much of its history be determined by irrational forces or remain enigmatic? And if "the West" was based on an unquenching belief in democracy, why were all the voices raised in its defense so concerned with the power of "the masses" and so thoroughly convinced that they were the primary cause of its debacle?

NOTES

1. The rationale and basic guidelines for "integrative" multiculturalism have been developed in the Report of the New York State Social Studies Review and Development Committee: *One Nation, Many Peoples: A Declaration of Cultural Interdependence* (New York, June 1991). Its recommendation for a "Curriculum of Inclusion" has provided the model for similar attempts to reform curriculum at the college level.

2. H. D. Schmidt describes some of the reasons behind the expulsion of "Christendom" from English. He points out that the choice of a more neutral "Europe" came from the opponents, in the late seventeenth century in England, of the foreign policies of Louis XIV, who liked to describe himself, hermetically, not only as the "Sun King" but also as "the most Christian King." In the 1670s and 1680s, the fortunes of "Christendom" and "Europe" fluctuated with the "Popish Plot," the succession crisis, and the defeat of the Turks at Vienna. But William of Orange's successful invasion of England in 1688 and the establishment of an almost century-long Whig hegemony over British politics condemned "Christendom" to oblivion. Schmidt concludes: "The term Europe established itself as an expression of supreme loyalty in the fight against Louis XIV. It was associated with the concept of a balanced system of sovereign states, religious tolerance, and expanding commerce" (Schmidt, 1966: 178).

3. "Civilization" and its cognates originated in eighteenth-century England, France, and Scotland to characterize the institutional, juridical, and economic reforms implemented by the bourgeoisie in its rise to power. In France the term, which originally referred to courtly manners, was popularized by the Physiocrats in the second half of the eighteenth century to define a specific stage of social development that the bourgeoisie considered as its achievement and ideal. "Civilized" indicated a stage in the social process characterized by the consolidation of private property (Elias, 1978), the introduction of monetary relations, and the reorganization of economic life on a commercial and industrial basis (Caffentzis, in this volume). Anthropologists of the last generation have elaborated an important self-critique of their use of "civilization" and "culture." Three good examples of this process are Diamond (1974), Clifford (1988), and Stocking (1987).

4. "Western" could now be used to indicate a racial entity that was no longer enclosed within Europe's boundaries, but had begun to settle in many other regions of the planet. This racialization of "Western" went a long way to solve the identity crisis of the Europeans, following their nomadic imperialist dispersal through lands inhabited in their view by semi-savages at best. For one remained a "Westerner" in Tasmania as much as he or she was in London (Stocking, 1987; GoGwilt, in this volume).

5. This passion for Oriental philosophies is evident in much of the literature of the period from Eliot's *Wasteland* to H. Hesse's *Siddhartha*. In the interwar period as well, "Orientalism" continued to be a European intellectual and political fad; as Caffentzis has shown, even John Maynard Keynes was not immune from it (Caffentzis, 1989: 225–26).

6. Among the defenders of "Western Civilization" were Henry Massis, the patron of the protofascist "Action Française"; Rene Johannet, author of *Eloge du Bourgeois* (1927), who included among civilization's enemies Germans, Jews, and revolutionaries, describing Bolshevism as a Judeo-Germano-Asiatic putsch (Cadwallader, 1981: 11); Paul Morand, who, in *Buddha Vivant*, warned against the inability of a westernized East to save "the West," and the danger posed by the "all consuming hatred" for Western Civilization that had seized the "racially inferior" (Cadwallader: 36–37). Among the journals that distinghuished themselves in the defense of "Western man" was *La Revue Universelle*, which "was always ready to publicize the horrors of Judeo-Soviet rule, to expose the proletarian enthusiasts and denounce Asian neophytes, but no less ready to identify and applaud those institutions and associations whose activities and ideas it held compatible with its own: capitalism and fascism" (Cadwallader: 66).

7. As is now well known, the ancestor of the present Western Civilization course was the "War Issues" course which, in 1917, the State Department, on behalf of the Student Army Training Corps (SATC) that was being established at the time in colleges throughout the country, asked Columbia University to set up (Bell, 1966: 14; Hall, 1986: 5; Levine, 1986: 96). "Aimed at building students' morale, by giving them an appreciation of the history and culture of the various warring nations, the War Issues course—also known as *War Aims*, a title that more accurately reflected an important part of its agenda—laid the groundwork for the Western Civilization survey courses" (Levine, 1986: 96). In 1919, under the name of "Contemporary Civilization," the War Issues course became the basis of Columbia's general education curriculum, serving as a model for many other universities in the interwar period. Later, during World War II, a committee of Harvard academics was appointed by the Faculty of Arts and Sciences and the Faculty of Education to plan a university curriculum that could respond to the ideological challenge of Marxism. The result was a policy paper, *The Objectives of General Education in a Free Society* (Harvard University Committee, 1945), which is often described as the Red Book. The Red Book was concerned with "[s]uch Problems as 'why we fight,' the principles of a free society, the need to provide a consistent image of the American experience, the definition of democracy in a world of totalitarianism, the effort to fortify the heritage of Western Civilization, and the need to provide a 'common learning' for all Americans as a foundation of national unity" (Bell, 1968: 39). The Western Civilization course reached its zenith, as an instrument of the cold war, in the immediate postwar period when, concomitantly with the McCarthy purges of academe, students were taught the inevitablity of the path "from Plato to NATO," with Sophocles' *Antigone* and Locke's *Second Treatise* being used as cultural weapons in the ideological war against "the communist threat."

8. Exemplary of the conceptual somersaults that became necessary in order to transplant "Western Civilization" on English and American soil and to bind it to the history of capitalism is the following account offered by Hans Kohn: "Modern Western Civilization has its roots in the Greco-Roman Civilization of antiquity and in the Western Christendom of the Middle Ages. Yet its spirit was unknown before the seventeenth century, being based upon the new realities of liberty, science, tolerance. The roots of the modern West go back to Athens, Jerusalem, and Rome; yet it was a new growth that sprang up in London, Amsterdam, Philadelphia, and Paris" (Kohn, 1957: 18–19).

9. At the beginning of the nineteenth century, in a climate of mounting nationalism, German intellectuals (e.g., Fichte in *Discourse to the German Nation*) challenged the

universalistic pretension of "Civilization," which they identified with Napoleonic France's imperial aspirations. To "civilization" (which they interpreted as a concept having purely materialist connotations) they opposed the notion of *Kultur*, intended as a spiritual entity presumably stemming from the unique fusion between the spirit of the *Volk* and the national "soil." Although the culture/civilization contrast was to remain a peculiar German problem, the introduction of the new term created a methodological crisis in the definition of civilization which is still to be resolved.

REFERENCES

Arendt, Hannah. (1945, Winter). "Approaches to the German Problem." *Partisan Review*, 12(1): 93–106.
———. (1946, Winter). "What Is Existenz Philosophy?" *Partisan Review*, 13(1): 34-56.
———. (1951). *The Origins of Totalitarianism*. New York: Harcourt Brace.
Bagby, Philip. (1963). *Culture and History*. Berkeley and Los Angeles: University of California Press.
Barraclough, G. (1955). *History in a Changing World*. Oxford: Basil Blackwell.
Barrett, Richard. (1984). *Culture and Conduct*. Belmont, Calif.: Wadsworth Publishing.
Barrett, William. (1958). *Irrational Man: A Study in Existential Philosophy*. Garden City, N.Y.: Doubleday.
———. (1964). *What Is Existentialism?* New York: Grove Press. (Part I was published in *Partisan Review* in 1947.)
———. (1982). *The Truants: Adventures Among Intellectuals*. New York: Doubleday.
Barthes, Roland. (1968). *Writing Degree Zero*. Translated from the French. New York: Hill and Wang. Published in French in 1953.
Beckett, Samuel. (1965). *Three Novels*. New York: Grove Press. (First edition 1955.)
Bell, Daniel. (1966). *The Reforming of General Education: The Columbia College Experience in its National Setting*. New York: Columbia University Press.
Brandon, William. (1986). *New Worlds for Old: Reports from the New World and Their Effect on the Development of Social Thought in Europe, 1500–1800*. Athens: Ohio University Press.
Bruhl, Lucien Levy. (1966). *The "Soul" of the Primitive*. Chicago: Henry Regnery.
Cadwallader, Barrie. (1981). *Crisis of the European Mind: A Study of Andre Malraux and Drieu La Rochelle*. Cardiff: University of Wales Press.
Caffentzis, C. G. (1989). *Abused Words, Clipped Coins, and Civil Government: John Locke's Philosophy of Money*. New York: Autonomedia.
Camus, Albert. (1948). *The Plague*. New York: Random House.
Cassirer, Ernst. (1946). *The Myth of the State*. New Haven, Conn.: Yale University Press.
Cesaire, Aimé. (1955, 1972). *Discourse on Colonialism*. Joan Pinkham, trans. New York: Monthly Review Press.
Chambers, Mortimer et al. (1987). *The Western Experience*. Vols. I and II, 4th ed. New York: Alfred A. Knopf.
Clair, Louis. (1947). "Ernst Junger: From Nihilism to Tradition." *Partisan Review*: 452–65.
Clifford, James. (1988). *The Predicament of Culture: Twentieth-Century Ethnography*,

Literature, and Art. Cambridge, Mass.: Harvard University Press.
Cooney, Terry. (1986). *The Rise of the New York Intellectual: Partisan Review and Its Circle*. Madison: University of Wisconsin Press.
Derrida, Jacques. (1982). "Differance." In *Margins of Philosophy*. Alan Bass, trans. Chicago: University of Chicago Press. (Originally published in French, 1972.)
Dostoyevsky, Fyodor. (1947). *The Grand Inquisitor*. Constance Garnett, trans., with reflections by William Hubben. New York: Association Press.
Duras, Marguerite. (1985). *The War: A Memoir*. Barbara Bray, trans. New York: Pantheon Books.
Elias, N. (1978). *The Civilizing Process*. Edmund Jephcott, trans. New York: Urizen Books. (Originally published in German, 1938.)
Eliot, T. S. (1952). *The Complete Poems and Plays, 1909–1950*. New York: Harcourt Brace.
Encyclopedia Britannica. (1910). Vol VI. New York.
Farias, Victor. (1987). *Heidegger and Nazism*. Paul Burrel and Gabriel R. Ricci, trans. Philadelphia: Temple University Press.
Fichte, Johann Gottlieb. (1922). *Addresses to the German Nation*. R. F. Jones and G. H. Turnbull, trans. Chicago and London: Open Court Publishing.
Fleischer, M. P., ed. (1970). *The Decline of the West?* New York: Holt, Rinehart and Winston.
Fritze, R. H., et al. (1991). *Reflections on Western Civilization: A Reader*. Vol. I: *Prehistory to 1600*. New York: HarperCollins Publishers.
Glaser, Hermann. (1978). *The Cultural Roots of National Socialism*. E. A. Menze, trans. Austin: Texas University Press.
Gless, Darryl J., and Barbara Herrnstein Smith. *The Politics of Liberal Education*. Durham, N.C., and London: Duke University Press.
Goldberg, D. T., ed. (1990). *Anatomy of Racism*. Minneapolis: University of Minnesota Press.
Greaves, R. L., R. Zaller, and J. T. Roberts. (1992). *Civilizations of the West: The Human Adventure*. Vols. I and II. New York: HarperCollins Publishers.
Hagtvet, Bernt. (1980). "The Theory of Mass Society and the Collapse of the Weimar Republic: A Re-Examination." In Larsen et al., *Who Were the Fascists: Social Roots of European Fascism*. Bergen, Oslo: Universitetsforlaget.
Hall, James W., and Barbara L. Kevles, eds. (1982). *In Opposition to Core Curriculum: Alternative Models for Undergraduate Education*. Westport, Conn.: Greenwood Press.
Hall, John. (1986). *Power and Liberties: The Causes and Consequences of the Rise of the West*. Berkeley: University of California Press.
Harvard University Committee. (1945). *General Education in a Free Society*. Cambridge, Mass.: Harvard University Press.
Hay, Denys. (1957). *Europe: The Emergence of an Idea*. Edinburgh: Edinburgh University Press.
Hegel, G.W.F. (1956). *The Philosophy of History*. New York: Dover Publications.
Hesse, Herman. (1919). "The Brother Karamazov, or the Decline of Europe." In *My Belief*.
———. (1974). *My Belief: Essays on Life and Art*. Denver Lindley, trans. New York: Farrar, Straus, and Giroux.

Hughes, S. (1952). *Oswald Spengler: A Critical Estimate*. New York: Scribner.
Hughes, W., ed. (1991). *Annual Editions: Western Civilization*. Vol. II. Guilford, Conn.: Dushkin Publishing Group.
Husserl, E. (1970). *The Crisis of European Sciences and Transcendental Phenomenology: An Introduction to Phenomenological Philosophy*. David Carr, trans. Evanston, Ill.: Northwestern University Press. (Originally written in German between 1934 and 1937.)
Jaspers, Carl. (1957). *Man in the Modern Age*. New York: Doubleday. (First edition in German, 1931.)
Kaplan, Martin. (1982). "The Wrong Solution to the Right Problem." In James Hall, ed. *In Opposition to Core Curriculum*. Westport, Conn.: Greenword Press.
Kateb, George. (1984). *Hannah Arendt: Politics, Conscience, Evil*. Totowa, N.J.: Rowman and Allanheld.
Keller, Evelyn Fox. (1985). *Reflections on Gender and Science*. New Haven, Conn.: Yale University Press.
Koestler, Arthur. (1945). *The Yogi and the Commissar and Other Essays*. New York: Macmillan.
Kohn, Hans. (1957). *Is the Liberal West in Decline?* London: Pall Mall Press.
Kohnke, K. C. (1991). *The Rise of Neo-Kantianism*. Cambridge: Cambridge University Press.
Kroeber, A. L. (1953). *Anthropology Today*. Chicago: Chicago University Press.
———. (1957). *Style and Civilizations*. Ithaca, N.Y.: Cornell University Press.
Kroeber, A. L., and Clyde Kluckhohn. (1952). *Culture: A Critical Review of Concepts and Definitions*. Cambridge, Mass.: Peabody Museum.
Krois, J. M. (1987). *Cassirer: Symbolic Forms and History*. New Haven, Conn.: Yale University Press.
Kuhn, Thomas S. (1957). *The Copernican Revolution: Planetary Astronomy in the Development of Western Thought*. Cambridge, Mass.: Harvard University Press.
———. (1962). *The Structure of Scientific Revolutions*. Chicago: University of Chicago Press.
Lakatos, I., and E. Zahar. (1978). "Why Did Copernicus' Research Programme Supersede Ptolemy's?" In Imre Lakatos, *Philosophical Papers*. Vol. I: *The Methodology of Scientific Research Programs*. Cambridge: Cambridge University Press.
Larsen, S. U., B. Hagtvet, and J. P. Myklebust. (1980). *Who Were the Fascists: Social Roots of European Fascism*. Bergen, Oslo: Universitetsforlaget.
Lasch, Christopher. (1969). *The Agony of the American Left*. New York: Alfred A. Knopf.
Levine, David O. (1986). *The American College and the Culture of Aspiration, 1915–1940*. Ithaca, N.Y.: Cornell University Press.
Linebaugh, Peter. (1991, Spring). "Jubilating, Or, How the Atlantic Working Class Used Biblical Jubilee against Capitalism, with Some Success." *Radical History Review*, 50: 143–80.
———. (1992). *The London Hanged*. London: Penguin.
Marvin, F. S. (1970). *The Unity of Western Civilization*. New York: Books for Libraries. (First edition, 1929).
McNeill, W. (1963). *The Rise of the West*. Chicago: University of Chicago Press.
Mehlman, Jeffrey. (1983). *Legacies of Anti-Semitism in France*. Minneapolis:

Minnesota University Press.
Mendelssohn, K. (1976). *The Secret of Western Domination*. New York: Praeger.
Michaud, Guy. (1977). "La Crisi della Civiltà Europea." In *Nuove Questioni di Storia Contemporanea*. Vol. II: *1433–1466*. Milano: Marzorati.
Neske, G., and E. Kettering, eds. (1990). *Martin Heidegger and National Socialism: Questions and Answers*. Lisa Harries, trans. New York: Paragon House.
Ormsy-Gore, David. (1966). *Must the West Decline?* New York: Columbia University Press.
Ortega y Gasset, José. (1985). *The Revolt of the Masses*. Notre Dame, Ind.: University of Notre Dame Press.
Oxford English Dictionary. (1989). 2nd ed. Oxford: Clarendon Press.
Perry, Marvin, et al. (1992). *Western Civilization: Ideas, Politics and Society*. Vol. I: *To 1789*. 4th ed. Boston: Houghton Mifflin Co.
Pois, Robert A. (1986). *National Socialism and the Religion of Nature*. New York: St. Martin's Press.
Popper, Karl. (1945). *Open Society and Its Enemies*. Vol. I: *The Spell of Plato*. London: George Routledge and Sons.
Quine, W. O. (1962). *Word and Object*. Cambridge, Mass.: MIT Press.
Redfield, Robert. (1953). "Relation of Anthropology to the Social Sciences and the Humanities." In A. L. Kroeber, *Anthropology Today*. Chicago: Chicago University Press, 728–38.
Richardson, M., and M. C. Webb, eds. (1986). *The Burden of Being Civilized: An Anthropological Perspective on the Discontents of Civilization*. Athens and London: University of Georgia Press.
Rickman, H. P. (1976). *W. Dilthey: Selected Writings*. Cambridge: Cambridge University Press.
Rockmore, Tom. (1992). *On Heidegger's Nazism and Philosophy*. Berkeley: University of California Press.
Rougier, Louis. (1971). *The Genius of the West*. Introduction by F. A. Hayek. Los Angeles: Nash.
Rudolph, F. (1978). *Curriculum: A History of the American Undergraduate Course of Study Since 1963*. London: Jossey-Bass Publishers.
Said, Edward W. (1978). *Orientalism*. New York: Pantheon Books.
Schlesinger, A. M., Jr. (1947, May/June). "The Future of Socialism." *Partisan Review*, 14(3): 229–42.
Schmidt, H. D. (1966). "The Establishment of 'Europe' as a Political Expression." *Historical Journal* 9(2): 171–78.
Schoenbaum, D. (1967). *Hitler's Social Revolution: Class and Status in Nazi Germany, 1933–1939*. New York: Doubleday.
Spengler, Oswald. (1947). *The Decline of the West*. Vols. I and II. C. F. Atkinson, trans. New York: Alfred A. Knopf.
Stace, W. T. (1942). *The Destiny of Western Man*. New York: Reynal and Hitchco.
Steinfels, Peter. (1979). *The Neoconservatives*. New York: Simon and Schuster.
Stern, Fritz. (1965). *The Politics of Cultural Despair: A Study in the Rise of Nazi Ideology*. New York: Doubleday.
Stocking, G. W., Jr. (1987). *Victorian Anthropology*. New York and London: Macmillan.

Summerscales, W. (1970). *Affirmation and Dissent: Columbia's Response to the Crisis of World War I*. New York: Teachers College Press.
Tasso, Torquato. (1962). *Jerusalem Delivered*. Edward Fairfax, trans., newly introduced by Robert Weiss. Carbondale: Southern Illinois University Press.
Thagard, Paul. (1992). *Conceptual Revolutions*. Princeton, N.J.: Princeton University Press.
Toynbee, Arnold J. (1934). *Study of History*. Vols. I–III. London: Oxford University Press.
———. (1939). *Study of History*. Vols I–VI. London: Oxford University Press.
Ullmann, Walter. (1975). *The Church and the Law in the Earlier Middle Ages: Selected Essays*. London: Variorium Reprints Publishers.
Wagner, J. (1981). *The Invention of Culture*. Chicago: Chicago University Press.
Wallerstein, I. (1984). *The Politics of the World Economy: The States, the Movements, and the Civilizations*. Cambridge: Cambridge University Press.
Weber, Max. (1958). *The Protestant Ethic and the Spirit of Capitalism*. Talcott Parsons, trans. New York: Charles Scribner's Sons.
Wiener, Philip P., ed. (1973). *Dictionary of the History of Ideas*. New York: Charles Scribner's Sons.
Wiesner, M. E., J. R. Ruff, and W. B. Wheeler. (1989). *Discovering the Western Past: A Look at Evidence*. Vol. II: *Since 1650*. Boston: Houghton Mifflin.

Satirical Appendix: Oedipus and the Coup

Sol Yurick

PROLOGUE, SCENE I

The curtain rises on a single set. Two-thirds upstage we see pillars, a huge gate and a wall representing the palace of Oedipus. From time to time we see through the wall, when the action takes place inside the palace. Above the set is a screen upon which are projected various images. Some action—small and secret conversations—will take place in various illuminated areas while the rest of the set remains in darkness.

We begin in 1968. As the curtain rises, a Teacher stands downstage beside a large table, which serves him as a desk, facing the audience. The students from time to time will respond from loudspeakers in the direction of the audience, but we never see them. The Teacher is reading out loud from Oedipus. *As he reads he makes gestures, picking up masks on his desk, representing the characters he's quoting and acting out the parts.*

As he's coming to the end of the reading, murmuring sounds grow among the students. The voices grow louder as the reading continues, but the Teacher seems unaware of them. As the noise mounts, we see on the screen student demonstrations.

Teacher (as Oedipus): Knowest you on what conditions I will depart? *(As Creon)* Name them. *(As Oedipus)* Send me to dwell beyond this land. *(As Creon)* You ask me for what only higher powers can give.

First Student Voice (Male): Hey man, what's the politics of this play? And what's the story about this plague that hit Thebes? We need some class analysis here.

Teacher: This is a universal tale, a lesson for all mankind.

Second Student Voice (Male): Last night I had a nightmare . . . I saw a crowd of Thebans. Everybody was starving, the kids had swollen bellies and they were calling us for help . . .

Third Student Voice (Female): Isn't it awful what they did to Jocasta? Everything gets blamed on women. How was she supposed to know she was committing incest?

First Student Voice: Who cares about these people anyway? What's the relevance of this story?

Teacher: Did I hear someone say "relevance"? Can't you see we're dealing with eternal values, transcending time and place? *(As Creon, repeating)* Thou ask me for what the Gods alone can give.

Female Student Voice: The gods, the gods; I bet it was the boys from Delphi.

Teacher: I won't allow a minority to disrupt my class. If you can't appreciate what the best minds that ever existed have to say about the human condition, then leave this room. *(As Oedipus)* It is time to lead us hence. *(As Creon)* Come then, but your children must stay. *(As Jocasta)* Don't take our children from us! *(As Chorus)* Dwellers in our native Thebes, behold, this is Oedipus, who solved the famed Sphinx's deadly riddle. Behold in what a stormy sea of trouble he hath sunk!

As he speaks, the murmurs begin to grow into a nasty discordant roar of protest from all the students. On the screen appear pictures of demonstrations and students' revolts from the sixties. Books coming in the direction of the audience start flying through the air.

First Student Voice (sounding as if it were through a bullhorn): Lies, lies, and they call it knowledge. *(On the screen the images of students start rushing forward.)*

Teacher: It's the attack of the primal horde! *(Screaming)* Barbarians! *(He throws the book away and flees.)*

SCENE II

A committee comes in. They're carrying attaché cases and folders. They are a strategist, a think-tank scientist, a psychologist, an agricultural expert, a PR person, an economist, an anthropologist, an intelligence officer, and the Teacher. They sit around a conference table. We're at an emergency meeting of the Committee for the Defense of the Free World. The meeting is chaired by the geopolitical strategist.

Teacher: They cry for anarchism, nihilism, activism, democracy now! They say their demands are nonnegotiable. They say that nothing will stop them but the end of racism, sexism, classism, and they want control over the schools. They want open admission, a new curriculum, and no more Western Civ courses.

Think-Tank Scientist: The students are under the illusion they have heard a scream from the past and their juvenile interpretation of history has set up a wave that reverberates from past into the present, creating a crisis of confidence.

All (chanting): The rites of loyalty are wearing thin. It is the beginning of disorder. Things are falling apart.

Teacher: They made me rewrite the play to suit their whims. They resurrected Jocasta—that *organum Satanae*, as the Church Fathers would say. You can imagine the effect these disruptions are having on Thebes, our strategically placed client state. If this goes on, the geopolitical consequences will be incalculable. We'll have a domino effect throughout the Third World.

All (chanting): The center cannot hold. Things are falling apart.

Teacher: Now many versions of the events emanating from the students are invading our collective memory. History's being assaulted. The past we so carefully constructed is dissolving into indecipherable chaos. In one version Jocasta sends Oedipus to exile and happily goes on to rule alone; in another, more dangerous one, it is our client Creon who's exiled, while Oedipus rouses the masses against Delphi and foreign intervention.

Strategist: Oedipus has got to go. If things go on this way the Theban masses will wake up and that's the last thing we want. I can already see what's going to happen. To offset the internal unrest Thebes will ally with Corinth and Sparta and move against Athens. This triad will win the Peloponnesian War; then a fraction of the Athenians will ally with the totalitarian Persians, switch to their Asiatic mode of production, and establish a tyrannical Pan Mediterranean hegemony. Classic Greece, as we used to know it, our bulwark against totalitarianism, will collapse. The philosophers will not have a chance to arise; defeat will follow defeat and the decline of the West will have begun twenty-five centuries ago. We've already lost Cuba, China, we're losing Vietnam, Latin America, and now we're in danger of being deprived of the most important commodity of all. With Greece there goes Western science and technology, abstract reasoning, the deductive method, not to mention democracy and all those values of Western Civilization. If this happens, the despotic East will win the war of Darkness against Light and we'll all be dead. Gentlemen, we're in deep trouble. We must reverse this trend. What can be done?

Scientist: Let's not despair. There is a way to intervene, we have agents who can handle the situation on the spot. We know that any change, even of a single particle, is instantaneously felt all over the universe.

All (chanting): Time present is time past and both are present in time future. If all time is eternally present, then all time is redeemable and we can recover our investments.

Strategist: Oedipus' position is solidly entrenched.

Scientist: We have contingency, off the shelf, destabilization scenarios . . . germ warfare . . . Anthrax for the sheep. . . .

Economist: We need a crop failure. Agent Orange served us well; besides, the pesticide industry needs a boost. Suppose we add an epidemic . . . a life threat gets them all the time. Then we start circulating rumors . . . the usual thing. . . .

Psychologist: I have made profiles of all the main characters. We'll feed them into a computer and project what they will do in a variety of situations. Oedipus is always too quick to act. Basically he's a bull, he has a certain shrewdness, but just enough to be suspicious of everyone around him, including his wife. He's the ideal dupe. And we've got a lot on Creon. He's bitter because Jocasta first lured him into setting up Laius, then when Oedipus came along she married him and Creon was out. He never forgave her for this. We can handle him. The most dangerous is Jocasta. She is the power behind the throne and has support. She will sense immediately that something is wrong. We have to neutralize her; we should find a way to put her against her husband.

Strategist (turning to Tiresias, the Intelligence Officer in Delphi): I like it, I like it. . . .

Tiresias: I hear voices running down the channels of time, speaking wisdom into the porches of my ears . . . I have an idea. I'll hire a playwright, Sophocles, and place him as the advisor to the Theban king and queen. He'll be briefed about what we want. The committee in charge of the Dionysian festival will produce the play as it was to have been originally written. Aristotle will write the reviews. We'll forge old manuscripts and plant them in the Renaissance where they can be discovered at the proper time.

Strategist: The one who rules best is a shadow to his subjects. When his task is accomplished the people will say that "it happened naturally." But the fish must not be allowed to leave the deep.

ACT I

Characters

The Leader of the Chorus, who is a priest of Zeus and an agent of Delphi; Oedipus, King of Thebes; Jocasta, his wife; Creon, her brother; and Tiresias, who's chief of intelligence operations in Delphi. He is not blind, but he carries fake eyeballs that he wears when the occasion requires it.

SCENE I

In front of the royal palace of Oedipus at Thebes. The time is generally classical Greece.

The Leader comes on the stage. He's accosted by Tiresias who gives him a bag of money. The Leader kicks back a little to Tiresias. Now supplicants, petitioners, old men, and youth come on stage. As the curtain rises they're being arranged before the palace by the Leader. They will act as the Chorus. They're obviously well fed, but their masks indicate they're starving.

The Leader, a venerable man, approaches the gate. An advisor to Oedipus comes out. It is Sophocles. He holds a script which, throughout the play, he will consult from time to time.

The doors are now thrown open. Oedipus wearing kingly robes emerges. Sophocles takes his place by his side. He proceeds carefully to position Oedipus. He whispers in his ears, checking where the best light is coming from, to present the most noble aspect to the crowd. At a signal of the Leader, the crowd begins to wail and complain. Oedipus gazes silently, then he speaks.

Oedipus: My children, latest born to Cadmus, founder of this State, why have you come here in supplication? Why does this city reek with incense and rings with prayers and cries of woe?

Leader of the Chorus: Oedipus, ruler of our land, in front of you stand the chosen youth and the heads of the ruling families. The rest of our folk are in the marketplace before the shrines, bowing before the prophetic fire, waiting for an answer from the ever-shifting flames. Our state is in terrible straits. A mysterious plague is on us; it strikes the amber waves of grain, it decimates the herds; it makes women barren. And we, we come begging you, the first among the men, you, to intercede with the gods. In the past you came to Thebes to free us from the oppression of the Sphinx, mother of civil war. Now, once again, we raise our hands and pray you. Find some remedy for us. Cure us, make us happy again.

Oedipus (to his advisor Sophocles): This was supposed to be a purely ceremonial occasion. It was agreed that they would not discuss everything out here in public. Tiresias has forced our hand too soon. Send Creon immediately to Delphi. *(To all)* My wretched children, I've wept and kept awake many nights wondering what can be done. I've consulted wise men; I have appointed an investigative commission. I've sent Creon, my brother-in-law, to Delphi to consult the Python sacred to Apollo, to learn by what deeds this town can be delivered. I shall do everything the god demands.

SCENE II

We are in Delphi. Present are Creon and Tiresias, who appears for the time being as an ordinary man, seated behind a desk, wearing opaque sunglasses.

Creon: Oedipus told me to come.

Tiresias: I would have hoped you came of your own will. You neglect us, Creon, then when things get sticky you run to us.

Creon: Are the gods angry?

Tiresias: The gods, the gods . . . whenever there is a problem everyone blames the gods.

Creon: I mean, couldn't Delphi float Thebes a loan to buy food and medicine?

Tiresias: As it is, you're already falling behind your interest payments. Your credit is exhausted. Year after year we've warned you that unless you cut back your expenditures, things could go wrong. Why can't you learn from the Athenians? They always manage to balance their budget, and they've got the most stable currency in the whole Mediterranean. That's a free market economy! In any event a loan won't solve your political problems; moreover, your king has got lots of money stacked away. Tell him to buy some grain. The Egyptians have had a big harvest and are selling on the open market. . . .

Creon: Oedipus will never agree to that. He wants to beef up his bodyguards.

Tiresias: He should be careful. Soon he'll have a revolt on his hands. But if you play your cards right maybe your turn is coming.

Creon: Forget it. He and his sons have taken over. As for your promises, you've broken them too many times.

Tiresias: Those were policy decisions, you shouldn't take them personally.

Creon: You talked differently when you needed me to do that job on Laius.

Tiresias: I needed you? What job? Can you prove it? Do you have it in writing?

Enough, you're making the gods angry. The times are changing, Creon. Oedipus is in deep trouble.

Creon: What are you talking about?

Tiresias: I'm saying that if you're willing to take a few risks, you'll find you've good friends in high places. Listen to me. There is a way to handle this crisis. *(He leans forward, taking Creon by the lapel, and whispers in his ear. The lights go down.)*

SCENE III

We are back in Thebes. The lights come up on the palace courtyard.
Creon enters. Oedipus tries to pull him aside for a private conversation, but Creon resists. Oedipus is forced to speak before all.

Oedipus: Speak, my kinsman, what does the oracle say?

Creon: Apollo warns us: to heal our country we must put an end to its defilement. Blood must be shed in retribution for the blood shed in the past. An unrevenged corpse contaminates the soil.

Oedipus: Whose blood was shed?

Creon: Laius's blood.

Oedipus: What has Laius's death to do with our problems? He died fifteen years ago. Why bring it up now?

Creon: His blood cries for revenge like an unpaid debt.

Oedipus: Let the dead lie. Stirring up old corpses will rouse forgotten grudges and suspicions. Moreover, the track of this crime must be cold.

Creon: The god said the killer is alive, and he's still in this country.

Oedipus: Where did Laius meet his bloody end?

Creon: He went to visit Delphi, but he never returned.

Oedipus: Delphi, Delphi . . . the hands of those priestly spies are everywhere. Are there any witnesses to Laius's murder whom we can question?

Creon: All Laius's people perished except for one. He told us many robbers fell on them.

Oedipus: How would any robber dare to kill a king, unless there was trafficking in bribes from here?

Tiresias comes out of the crowd and pulls Sophocles to the side. Lights go down on the courtyard; up on the two, isolating them.

Tiresias: No, no, Sophocles, that was careless of you. We don't want to hear words like "bribes" in Oedipus' mouth. This is not the message we want to send to the audience. It's also a question of timing. At this point we want Oedipus to appear grand, fit to be tragic. His must be a mighty fall, not a stumble. From now on, clear everything with me before you write it.

The lights come up on the whole courtyard. Creon is still talking to Oedipus.

Creon: We considered such things. But remember Laius was killed during the Sphinx trouble, the peasants were restless, and the slaves were rising up. We had no time to avenge Laius.

Oedipus: Delphi wants us to take up Laius's case again. *(Aside)* I wonder why . . . but I don't see what I have to lose. It's in my interest that Laius's killer does not remain unpunished, it sets a bad precedent, which might give ideas to ambitious people here in the palace. *(To all)* Make haste, my children, with the gods' help, our city's health will be restored.

Lights go down on the courtyard. Lights come up behind the palace walls. A conference is taking place. There are Oedipus, Creon, Jocasta, and the ever-present Sophocles.

Oedipus: How can we find the killer? I'm sure he came from this palace.

Creon: Why do you keep assuming that he came from your household? Laius had many enemies at home and abroad. You must issue a statement saying you're going to take the strongest measures possible, that will give the populace confidence and engage them in the search.

Jocasta: I don't like it when Delphi meddles. I hear they believe our problems come from the fact that my husband's death was not avenged. But why couldn't they say something fifteen years ago? Think carefully, Oedipus. We cannot commit ourselves to anything until we understand what is going on.

Oedipus rolls his eyes in faked despair. Creon winks to him showing he understand he has to put up with his strong, domineering wife.

Oedipus: I've decided. I'm going to engage the Thebans in the hunt for the killer. I'll promise strong rewards and threaten severe penalties for whoever gives him shelter.

Jocasta: No, no . . . let's do what needs to be done, but let's keep it among ourselves. First, are you sure this is really the oracle's message?

Oedipus: You have a point! But I'll do things my own way.

Jocasta: All I say is "be careful." The situation might change and call for another course.

Lights go down. Lights come up in the courtyard. Tiresias and Sophocles come down stage.

Tiresias: Cut this scene. This is going to make all characters look bad. Where is the hero? Where is the moral redemption?

Sophocles: Morality makes for dull characters.

Tiresias: Stick to the lines I gave you.

Sophocles: I thought I had creative control.

Tiresias: Creative control is the province of the gods; don't forget, you're getting paid for this and a good bundle too. Audiences expect to hear what they've already heard. So don't complicate things. Cut that scene out.

Lights go down: lights come up in the whole courtyard. As Oedipus enters, he's intercepted by Tiresias who steps out of the throng.

Oedipus: What are you doing here?

Tiresias: I had a prophetic feeling you would send for me.

Oedipus: Did Creon arrange for you to come?

Tiresias: I don't know how to say this. Maybe you have been plotted against.

Oedipus: By whom?

Tiresias: Certain gods . . .

Oedipus: Come on! These superstitious Theban nobles? Is it Creon? Or Jocasta? Both of them?

Tiresias: I came here to help you. We have a vested interest in you.

Oedipus: What do you want?

Tiresias: First you must cut back on government. Your nobles have too much to say and too much to spend. We would like to put a management team in place, a few accountants. . . . We could issue some bonds.

Oedipus: I cannot share rule. Put a price to your help, and let it be counted in drachmas.

Tiresias: You're a hard man. Suppose we say another ten points added to your interest payments. Of course there will be service charges. . . .

Oedipus: I will go out now to address the Thebans.

Enters courtyard. Tiresias fades back into the throng. As Oedipus talks, he works himself up to a frenzy.

Oedipus: It is good to pray, but prayers must be supplemented by deeds. I have a plan. I will make an offer to the assassin of Laius. Let him confess his crime, and he shall be permitted to leave unhurt. But if any of you knows the assassin, speak up. I will order that no citizen of this land shall give the murderer shelter or food or speak to him, whoever he is. Everyone must ban this assassin from their homes because, as the oracle warned us, he's the defiler of the land. And I pray that the slayer fall under my curse, even if he should be a member of my house.

The lights go down in the courtyard: lights come up on Jocasta in the palace. She has been listening to what Oedipus has said. Creon is by her side.

Jocasta: He said too much. You're to blame for this.

Creon: It was his idea. Has it occurred to you that he's implicated us all in his hunt for the assassin? He wants suspicion to fall on us so that he can rule alone.

Jocasta: An ancient rule says Man alone can rule. But if Oedipus were to rule alone, it would be a disaster. He's not clever enough to maneuver.

The light illuminates the courtyard, while it goes down on the palace.

Oedipus: We cannot leave guilt unpurged. I have inherited the power once Laius held. I possess his bed and his wife. Had his hope of issue not been frustrated, my children, born from our wife, would be his own. These ties make me one with the dead king.

Light focuses on Jocasta in the palace.

Jocasta's advisor: What is he saying? Because you copulated with both of them, he and the dead man are bonded comrades? The insufferable arrogance of men! What does he think? That a woman's body is a chamber where men make compacts with each other?

Light comes up in the courtyard.

Oedipus: The unpunished murder of a king sets a terrible example. I will leave nothing untried to find whose hand shed that blood.

Leader: My King, none of us is the slayer, nor I can point to one. The rumors are faint and old.

Oedipus: What rumors?

Leader: Laius's surviving servant told us that wayfarers killed him.

Oedipus: I've heard this rumor. Where's the survivor?

Leader: It will not do us much good to ask him. But Prince Creon said that we might learn the truth from Tiresias the seer and has bid me to send for him.

Oedipus (aside): This proves Creon is plotting against me. I don't trust either man. It can't hurt to protect myself against all contingencies. *(To all)* Tiresias is all-seeing, but I must say that this great sage once gave me a devious answer. When I was in need, did he tell me what to do? No. I had to work it out for myself. You know what I say? Exterminate the sage, discard the wise, and the people will benefit a hundred fold.

Sophocles (pointing to the script): Wait, wait . . . it says nothing here about . . .

Oedipus (to Sophocles): Oh shut up!

Tiresias in the crowd puts on the fake eyeballs which render him blind. He walks to the wings and comes on again, led by a boy.

Leader: Here comes the only man in whom truth lives.

Oedipus: Great prophet, be our protector. Creon brought us puzzling answers from Delphi. Apollo says we can get rid of this pestilence only if we can learn who the slayers of Laius are. Tell us then what the voice of the birds, the discourse of the entrails, or any other seer craft at your disposal reveals. We're in your hands.

Tiresias: Although blind, I know the world and the way of the heavens. But alas I have forgotten how painful it is to have wisdom when no one listens to a prophet.

Oedipus: What's wrong? You seem troubled.

Tiresias: If you bear your terrible burden to the end it will be easier for all. I will go if you consent.

Oedipus: Your words bring no comfort. Why are you hoarding your knowledge?

Sophocles: Being beseeched is part of Delphi's routine.

Tiresias: I dare not speak lest your curse fall on me too.

Oedipus: If you have any knowledge, for the love of the gods don't turn away. *(Aside to Tiresias)* I thought we had made a deal. If you're not going to tell us anything, why did you come?

Tiresias: Don't ask. You will learn nothing from me.

Oedipus (aside to Tiresias): All right, all right. This has gone on long enough.

Tiresias: Whether I say something or nothing the future will happen.

Oedipus (to Sophocles): I am getting tired of this game. People are dying and he plays the reluctant bride. *(To Tiresias)* I bet you helped set up the murder of Laius; and if you had eyes to see I would say you killed him yourself.

Tiresias: I order you: abide by the conditions of your curse. From this day you shall not speak either to these before us nor to me. You are the defiler of this land.

Oedipus (to Sophocles): I knew he had an agenda. He's trying to pin it on me. *(To Tiresias)* You've tricked me, old dissembler.

Tiresias: Are you tempting me to talk?

Oedipus: Speak. I dare you.

Tiresias: You are the killer of the man whose killer you seek. And you've been living in shame with your nearest kin.

Oedipus: Beware, Tiresias! Blind you walk in endless night; but those who have eyes can see your accusations are politically motivated. Is it Creon who inspired these words?

Tiresias: Creon is no danger to you. You are your own danger. *(Aside to Sophocles)* You see, writer, what trouble you've caused? You see now why I say that every utterance must be carefully screened? Drop a few innocuous words and before you know it, you've planted suspicion everywhere. Soon everybody is going to blame Delphi.

Oedipus: I see, now . . . that cunning plotter has leased your oracular voice. Envious of the power the city has placed in my hands, Creon, my old friend, sought to supplant me and schemed against me. And you, Tiresias, tell me, when did you prove yourself a seer? Do you remember the half truths you told me when I came to Delphi all those years ago? And when the Sphinx wove her mystifying song, why didn't you say a word to free the Theban people? Our land needed a seer then; but not one in your tribe of charlatans could answer the riddles of the Sphinx. Then I came, and with my wit alone, without help of mind-bending vapors or entrails, silenced the Sphinx. This won me popular support, a thing you could never forgive me for and now you're trying to oust me, helping Creon to the throne.

Tiresias: Oedipus, you taunt me with my blindness; but you're blind to the misery you're in. When the truth about your birth will be revealed, and when you learn what nuptials, within that house, gave you a fatal haven, your shrieks of agony will fill Kithairon and echo down the centuries as if they were immortal.

Oedipus: What about my birth? Stop speaking in riddles.

Tiresias: I have performed my errand. I can only say again: the man you're looking for, the assassin of Laius—that man is here. He shall be found to be father and brother at once of the children with whom he consorts, son and husband of the woman who bore him, heir to his father's bed, shedder of his father's blood. When he shall be discovered, he who sees shall be blind, he who is rich shall be a beggar, and he who dwells in a palace shall make his way to an alien land. *(Tiresias exits.)*

ACT II

Lights up in front of the palace. It is later the same day.

Leader: Has the unknown murderer heard the message? Where is he? Does he run among caves and rocks, fierce as a bull, forlorn on his wretched path? Or does he hide in the tangled woods of his mind? Wherever he conceals himself, he cannot flee the Fate that stalks him.

Creon enters.

Creon: Fellow citizens, Oedipus our King has charged me with foul crimes . . .

Enter Oedipus.

Oedipus: How dare you come here, you traitor of your master's reputation! Tell me. What did you offer Delphi for their support? Did you promise them that with you enthroned they could have a hand in our country's policy-making? And Tiresias? Since when have you been plotting with him?

Creon: I sent for him because I thought he would offer the best advice.

Oedipus: How long ago was Laius assassinated?

Creon: Fifteen years ago.

Oedipus: Did Tiresias say anything about me at the time of the crime?

Creon: No, I told you. We searched and searched but found nothing.

Oedipus (aside): Funny. Earlier he told me they did not have time to search. *(To Creon)* And how is it that this sage didn't peer into the god's smoking mouth and see the assassin's face through the vapors?

Tiresias (to the Chorus): Oh, oh. Creon is running into trouble. We've got to do something. It's time to get Jocasta on stage before Oedipus works himself up and kills Creon.

Creon: I can't speculate about what I don't know and not in front of all these people. Let's talk it over in private.

Oedipus: You know more than you're telling me. You know why Tiresias has named *me*, after all these years, as Laius's murderer.

Creon: Oedipus, everyone reveres me. Those who need something from you come to me with presents and I've paid you your share. I'm almost like a king without the responsibilities. Why should I give up these things for the uncertainties of kingship and a possible short life? Who wants to be the target of envious eyes? And how, with your insight, could you have failed to spot a snake in your bosom? So don't accuse me of an unproved surmise. Investigate before jumping to conclusions. If you find I have plotted against you, take my life. But remember, time alone reveals the innocent and the just.

Leader: Well has he spoken, oh King. He talks like one who does not care if he fails . . .

Oedipus: Spare me your folk wisdom. *(Aside)* Distrust those closest to you: that's the fundamental rule of statecraft. *(To Creon)* Creon, the whole world will learn how the King of Thebes treats a traitor.

   Enters Jocasta from the palace.

Jocasta: You mindless men . . . aren't you ashamed of arguing in front of everyone when our land is sick? *(To her advisor)* These fools . . . can they ever forget their egotistical selves? Don't they realize they're putting us all in danger? *(To Oedipus)* Let us go into the palace and you too, Creon, go home.

Oedipus: Jocasta, stop meddling. I can't stand these feminine guiles. Don't you see all Thebes will suspect I'm trying to protect Laius's murderer?

Jocasta: How did the quarrel begin?

Oedipus: Creon says I'm guilty of the blood of Laius.

Jocasta: Did he really say that?

Oedipus: He had the soothsayer as his mouthpiece.

Jocasta: There are times, Oedipus, when I despair of you . . .

Oedipus: Just what I need . . . a motherly lecture.

Jocasta: I'm not your mother . . . I'm your wife, and as usual I have to repair the damage you've done.

   Tiresias pulls Sophocles aside for a whispered conference. Lights down on courtyard. Lights up on the two of them.

Sophocles: The lines you make me write create psychological difficulties.

Tiresias: Take my word. These are the traditional sacred lines.

Sophocles: Yeah . . . but we're running into serious trouble. Jocasta is going to make a dangerous speech which will raise more questions than we can answer. Then the whole drama will look ridiculous.

Tiresias: People have believed these words for two and a half millennia.

Sophocles: Listen to this. Jocasta says . . .

Lights down on the two and lights up on the whole courtyard.

Jocasta: You worry too much. It is impossible for human beings to see the future. I'll prove it to you. The oracle prophesied a long time ago that Laius was doomed to die at the hand of our child. So Laius pinned the child's ankles together and when he was just three days old had him thrown on a trackless mountain in Kithairon. Then one day it was reported to us that Laius had been murdered by foreign robbers at a plaza where three highways meet. How, then, could the son have killed the father, seeing that he was dead? Pay no attention to these oracles. What the god wants to have happen he'll make it happen.

Lights down. Lights up on Tiresias and Sophocles.

Tiresias: What's wrong with that speech?

Sophocles: In the first place, the survivor from the attack on Laius should have showed up already. The audience must be wondering what's happened to him.

Tiresias: He'll come. Don't worry. It's a matter of timing.

Sophocles: Moreover, when Jocasta tells Oedipus about the prophecy that Laius would be killed by his own child, and when she mentions the crippled ankles, Oedipus should get upset, because he has heard the same prophecy about himself when he was in Corinth, and later we find out that his ankles always hurt him. But does he act surprised or alarmed? Not at all. Then . . . can you believe it that in the fifteen years that Oedipus and Jocasta were married they never had a good discussion about Laius's murder? And how come Jocasta did not notice that her husband's ankles had marks? You see how difficult it is for me to make this story believable? I hate to make the whole thing so predictable, pulling the strings just at the right time.

Lights down on the two. Lights up in the courtyard. Oedipus acts startled and obviously troubled by what he's heard from Jocasta.

Jocasta: Oedipus, what's wrong? Why are you so upset?

Oedipus: You said that Laius was killed in a plaza where three highways meet?

Jocasta: That is the story we were told.

Oedipus: Where is this plaza?

Lights down on courtyard. Lights up on Sophocles and Tiresias.

Sophocles: You see what I mean? Can you believe it that after fifteen years this is the first time they talk about this? And why is he so slow in piecing things together?

Tiresias: You wonder? He's placed a terrible curse on the killer.

Sophocles: I see. . . . You've really set him up!

Tiresias: Be careful, writer, sometimes it's not wise to know too much.

Sophocles: And another thing . . . all these coincidences. I hate them. They're such a cheap trick. The audience will see right through them. They know that in real life such things never happen.

Tiresias: Leave the audience response to us. Our Warfare Section has taken surveys on audience response and expectations. Audiences love coincidences, particularly when they think they see something the characters don't see. It makes them feel smart. They don't care if there are some loose ends.

Sophocles: Say what you want, but my reputation is on the line. I'm also afraid the actors will object.

Tiresias: Your words will weave a magic spell that actors and audiences and even yourself as a writer can't escape from. Texts are a web of cosmic wires etching invisible but inexorable pathways in psychological space.

Lights go down on the two. Lights go up in the courtyard.

Jocasta: The name of the plaza is Phocis. From it roads branch to Delphi, Dealy, and Athens.

Oedipus: How long ago was this?

Jocasta: It happened shortly before you arrived at our country.

Oedipus: Oh Zeus, what are you doing to me? *(Aside)* Let's get out of here.

Oedipus and Jocasta try to leave but find it impossible. It is as if they were held in place by a mysterious magnetism.

Oedipus: How was Laius built, and what did he look like?

Jocasta: He was tall. The silver just lightly strewn among his hair. His body was similar to yours.

Oedipus: Oh gods of Olympus, I've put myself under my own curse. . . .

Jocasta: You scare me. Let's go inside . . . *(Again they try to leave, again they cannot.)*

Lights down on them. Lights up on Tiresias and Sophocles.

Tiresias: Beautiful . . . beautiful . . . this is worth a Nobel Prize.

Lights down on the two. Lights up on Oedipus and Jocasta.

Oedipus: Where was Laius going? Was he alone?

Jocasta (to herself): He was sneaking off to his lover Chrysippus. *(To Oedipus)* There were five of them. One was a herald. They ran before and beside him. Laius was in the carriage with a charioteer.

Oedipus: I see . . . I see . . . Who brought the news?

Jocasta: Only one servant survived.

Oedipus: Didn't we send for him? What is taking him so long to come? Does he live in the palace?

Jocasta: No. As soon as he came back and found you reigning, he begged me to send him to the pastures where he had tended the flock in his youth. He had served us long and well. I let him go.

Oedipus: Send for him again . . . I fear my lips have been unguarded.

Jocasta: What is there to fear?

Oedipus: I have a premonition of doom. My father was Polybus of Corinth, my mother the Dorian Merope; and I was heir to the throne. But one day at a banquet a drunken man said I was not my father's son. I questioned my mother and father. They were angry and wanted to punish the drunk, but he disappeared. That smacked of a put-up-job. Yet this thing kept rankling in my mind. Unknown to my mother or father, I went to Delphi. Apollo sent me away after telling me things full of sorrow and woe. I was fated to defile my mother's bed and I would have children no one could bear to look at, and to pile Pelion on Ossa, he told me that I should be the slayer of my sire.

Jocasta: Didn't you ask what you could do to avoid your fate?

Oedipus: I did, but Delphi would reveal nothing to me. I fled from the land of Corinth as far as I could get. Anywhere so long as those infamous prophecies could not be fulfilled. In time I came to Athens and lived there for half a year. One day I was approached by a writer. He was the same person who at the banquet, masked as a drunk, had told me that Polybus was not my real father. He was a glib talker and I fell under his spell. He said I could find favor with the gods and maybe escape my fate if I did something for some people he worked for. I had to kill a man. I was not told who he was, but I was sent to the same region where your husband is said to have been killed. Now Jocasta, I will tell you the truth. When I came to the plaza where three roads cross, I met a herald, behind him was a man seated in a chariot as you described. To my surprise the old man ordered me to have sex with him.

Jocasta (aside): That sounds like him.

Oedipus: In anger I struck the men who tried to pin me down. The old man, seeing this, brought his goad down my head, but I paid him back; by one swift blow from my staff he was rolled right out of the carriage and I slew every one of them.

Jocasta: Everyone? You're sure?

Oedipus: Yes, but if this stranger was Laius, who's more wretched than me? Am I that one I cursed, the one no citizen is allowed to receive in his house? And do I pollute the bed of the slain man with the same hands by which he perished?

Jocasta (to her female advisor): I knew there was something thrilling about those strong hands I guided to caress my body. . . .

Oedipus: Am I utterly unclean? Must I be banished, never to see my people or set foot on my land again? Will the old prophecy come through after all? If so, forbid, you gods, that I should see the light of day. May I be swept from the company of men before I behold myself visited by such doom.

Lights down on the two. Lights up on the whole courtyard.

Leader of the Chorus: Now we've got him.

Sophocles: No, not yet. The timing is wrong. The play would end too soon. Rally to his support.

Leader: To us, oh King, these things are fraught with fear. Yet have hope until thou gain full knowledge from him who saw the deed.

Oedipus (turning to Jocasta): You said Laius's servant reported Laius was killed by robbers, that means more than one. If his story is still the same, how could I have been the assassin? But if he says there was only one man, then no doubt I'm the guilty one.

Jocasta: Don't worry. Why should he change his story? Unless he was in league with the assassins. In any event the prophecy was false. Delphi said Laius was to be murdered by my child, but the poor child did not grow to slay him. He was killed. That's how we dealt with the divination.

Oedipus and Jocasta enter the palace.

Sophocles (to the Chorus Leader): Now we begin to change the tune; slowly we start blaming Oedipus and we increase our support for Creon.

Chorus: When a man walks haughtily, with no fear of justice or reverence for the gods, the State becomes corrupt and no citizen is mindful of its power.

When a man performs unholy deeds and such deeds are held in esteem, why should we bow in the sacred dance of obeisance?

Leader: If the world is unbalanced, no longer will I consult the inviolable shrine of Delphi. No more shall I go to the Acropolis's temples, for men shall point the fingers of shame at them. Nay, King, if thou are rightly called, observe Fate's all-ruling dictates.

Lights go down on the courtyard. Lights go up on Tiresias, Sophocles, and an unidentified man.

Tiresias (to the man): You're to leave and come back in the guise of a man from Corinth. Here is what you have to say. . . . *(He whispers in the man's ear.)*

Jocasta comes forth into the courtyard bearing a branch wreathed with festoons of wool which, as a supplicant, she is about to lay on the altar of her secret household god Dionysius.

Jocasta: I have come as a supplicant with these symbols of prayer to thee, Dionysius, for thou are nearest to women's desires.

While Jocasta is offering prayers to the gods, a messenger, evidently a stranger, enters and addresses the elders of the Chorus. He resembles the man Tiresias was briefing.

Messenger: Might I learn from you where the house of King Oedipus is . . . or better still, can you tell me where he himself is?

Leader: This is his dwelling and he's inside. The lady is his consort and mother of his children.

Messenger: Good tidings, lady, your lord, Oedipus, will now reign over Corinth and Thebes.

Jocasta: How then? Is Polybus no longer in power?

Messenger: Polybus is dead and gone.

Jocasta: These are sweet and bitter words to my ears. Handmaid, go tell the news to your master. Oracles of male gods, where is the truth in your prophecies? The father Oedipus was afraid he would kill has died in the course of destiny.

Enter Oedipus.

Oedipus: Messenger, what news you have brought for me?

Messenger: Polybus is gone. Sickness and long years have killed him.

Oedipus: Dead! Polybus is dead, and from old age! Messenger, you have freed me from a dreadful fear. You'll be well rewarded. They said I was doomed to slay my father; but he's dead, buried beneath the earth, and here's me who has not even put hand to the spear, unless making my father long for me counts as parricide.

Messenger: Oedipus, set your mind at rest; I'm here to free you twice.

Oedipus: How so, old man?

Messenger: Polybus was nothing to thee in blood.

Oedipus: He was not my father?

Messenger: Nay, he received you as a gift from my own hands. I found you in Kithairon's wild glens near our lands' borders. Then too I freed you; your ankles were pinned together.

Oedipus: Yes, those wounds still trouble me in damp weather.

Lights down on courtyard. Lights on Tiresias and Sophocles.

Sophocles: This is very lame. You've arranged it all, didn't you?

Tiresias: Enough! Maybe we should assign you to a different project.

Sophocles is grabbed by two men, dragged off stage, and shortly after returned, evidently crippled. He appears frightened and shows signs of beatings. Lights up on the courtyard.

Messenger: Because of that stroke of luck, you were called Oedipus, which means, I think, swollen feet or swollen head.

Oedipus: How did you find me?

Messenger: Another shepherd, a herder in Laius's service, gave you to me.

Oedipus: Where is this man? The hour has come for these mysteries to be resolved.

Tiresias (to the Chorus Leader): Now. Now, drive him here.

Leader: He's the peasant thou has sent for. But our lady Jocasta might best tell.

Oedipus: You mean to say that the man who survived Laius's murder is the same man who gave the infant to this shepherd?

Jocasta: Oedipus, I implore you. Don't you see what's happening?

Oedipus: Let what will happen, happen. No matter how low my origin might be, I must learn where I come from. The queen has used me as an instrument of rule, turning my phallus into her scepter; now she fears I am of common birth. . . . Here come my servants with the old man. . . . Is he the herdsman?

Messenger: Yes, he's the man who was in Laius's service.

Oedipus: Old man, I want you to answer everything I ask you. Were you once in the service of Laius? And if so, what were your tasks?

Herdsman: I was a slave reared in Laius's house. For the better part of my life I tended the flock; sometimes it was in Kithairon, sometimes in Corinth's neighboring ground.

Oedipus: Do you know this man?

Messenger: Come now. Don't you remember giving me an infant boy in those days, for me to rear as a foster son?

Herdsman: Why do you ask?

Oedipus: Do you remember giving this man an infant? Speak or you'll die.

Herdsman: For the gods' sake, master, don't ask any more.

Oedipus: Whose child was it?

Herdsman: Heavens forgive me. It was a child from the house of Laius.

Oedipus: A slave's or Laius's?

Herdsman: It was said to be his own child . . . but your wife can tell you best.

Oedipus: It's she who gave you the child?

Herdsman: She did, bidding me to do away with it. A prophecy warned that the child would grow to kill his father.

Oedipus: But why did you give the child to this old man? Why did you not kill him?

Herdsman: I pitied him, master. I thought this man would take the child away. But when I turned him over to him, he gave him to the King. Some say Polybus had made a deal with your mother . . . she wanted an alliance between Thebes and Corinth so that she could rule alone.

Creon (aside): Never trust women. . . . They are always plotting your demise!

Tiresias: Everyone now suspects Jocasta is the culprit. She arranged to have her son saved; she followed his career carefully. When he became sixteen, she schemed to have him driven from Corinth by planting disturbing rumors about his parents. Carefully guiding his steps, she plotted to have him arrive at a certain place, the plaza at the crossroad. She conspired to have Laius arrive at the same place, setting up his assassination. She then provided Oedipus with the answers to the riddle of the Sphinx, with whom she had made a deal. She thus betrayed the fierce creature by having Oedipus unmask the Egyptian agents hiding behind Operation Sphinx.

Jocasta: None of this is true.

Tiresias: Not to anyone in this room. But for those simpletons out there it is a different story. Don't forget, Thebes is in trouble: there is a plague; there is a harvest failure; women's milk has dried and they're issuing dead offspring. The Theban nobles are looking for a scapegoat.

Jocasta: What is going to happen?

Tiresias: Abdicate. You'll be permitted to leave. We'll stage it in such a way that not only people will take pity of you, but everyone will remember your story for generations and generations to come.

Oedipus: Alas . . . I'm accursed in birth, accursed in wedlock, accursed in the shedding of blood. *(He rushes back to the palace. Jocasta runs after him.)*

Chorus: A fluttering shadow do I count your life. Oh, renowned Oedipus, how can the soil where your father sowed have suffered you in silence so long?

   Second messenger enters from palace.

Second Messenger: You who are the most honored nobles in this land, of what deeds shall you hear. The Danube or the Phasi River could not wash this house clean, so many are the ills that it shrouds.

Leader: What else have you got to say?

Second Messenger: Jocasta is dead. Frantic she had rushed to the nuptial couch, clutching her hair with both hands. Once in the chamber she slammed the door behind her, then called the name of Laius, bewailing the wedlock wherein she had borne a twofold brood, husband by husband, children by her own child. Oedipus tried to follow her; to and fro he paced, asking us to give him a sword, asking us where was the wife who was not a wife, but a mother whose womb had borne both him and his children. None of us could calm him. With a dreadful shriek, he sprang the double door and rushed into the room. There we beheld the woman hanging by the neck in a twisted noose. Oedipus, upon seeing her, with a deep cry of misery loosed the halter whereby she hung. . . .

   Lights down in courtyard. Lights up in the palace. Oedipus pretends to see his wife swinging there and begins to loosen her.

Jocasta: Be careful, you're hurting me. Slow, slow . . .

   Lights go down in the palace. Lights go up in the courtyard.

Second Messenger: And when the hapless woman was stretched to the ground, then was the sequel horrible to see. For he tore from her raiment the golden brooches wherewith she was decked and stabbed them full on his own eyeballs. . . .

Satirical Appendix

Lights down in the courtyard. Lights go up in the palace. Oedipus is splattering blood on his eyes.

Oedipus: Eyes, my eyes, no more shall you behold such horrors. Long enough have you looked on what you never ought to have seen. Henceforth all shall be darkness! *(He screams.)*

Second Messenger: To such dire refrain not once alone, but oft he struck his eyes, and at each blow the ensanguined eyeball bedewed his beard. Such ills have issued from the deeds of these two. The ancestral fortune is gone. Today lamentation, ruin, death, shame, all earthly ills are theirs. He cries for someone to unbar the gates and show the Cadmeans his father's slayers. He proposes to cast himself out of the land. His anguish is more than anyone can bear. Soon, thou too shall behold a sight which even he who abhors him must pity.

The central door of the palace is opened. Oedipus comes forth, leaning on attendants; the bloody stains still upon his face.

Oedipus: Woe is me! Alas, whither am I borne in my misery?

Creon (aside): He acts well.

Tiresias: Every politician has to be a good actor. His voice will carry through a thousand aeons and a thousand lands. Remember this when your time comes.

Oedipus: Oh horror! Oh darkness! Thou enfolds me unspeakable, sped by a wind of inevitability. Ah, my friends . . . are thou still steadfast in your defense of me?

Chorus: Man of dreadful deeds, how could thou quench thy vision?

Oedipus (aside): What hypocrites! They know I had no choice. *(To all)* It was Apollo's voice sounding through Delphi's mouth that brought these woes to pass.

Lights down on courtyard. Lights up on Tiresias and Sophocles.

Tiresias: Watch him. I don't want him to drop any hint of our arrangement.

Sophocles: But I have to make his lamentations sound realistic. I have to arouse their pity.

Lights up in the courtyard.

Oedipus: Friends, what more should I behold? Why should I see when sight will show me nothing good? Lead me from the land friends . . . the utterly lost, the thrice accursed.

Chorus: Thou were better dead than living.

Oedipus: If I had died after my birth I could not have shed my father's blood, nor mated with the spouse of him from whom I sprang. But consider . . . was it my fault? Did I plan it? It was done to me. They've tried . . .

Tiresias (to Sophocles): Stop him. Stop him. Don't let him write his lines.

Leader: No, no. Man makes his destiny.

Oedipus: Nothing will ever be lovely to my eyes again. Not this town with its towered walls, nor the sacred statues of the gods, since I, the noblest of the sons of Thebes, have doomed myself to see these no more. And if there was but a way to choke the fountain of my hearing, I would not hesitate to make a senseless prison inside my wretched frame, so that I should know no sight nor sound, for 'tis sweet for our thought to dwell beyond the sensory sphere of grief. Alas, Kithairon, why did you save me? Ah Polybus! Ah Corinth! And you that was called the ancient house of my fathers. What ills were festering beneath? O ye three roads and you secret glen, do you remember what deeds I wrought for you to see? You drank my father's blood shed by my hands and yet, when I came here to Thebes, what fresh deeds I was made to do . . .

Tiresias (to Creon): He's going on too long. I don't like it. There are still people who support him. He's going to turn them around. They are going to pity him and say it wasn't his fault. Cut him off.

Oedipus: Oh marriage rites, creating an incestuous kinship of fathers, brothers, sons, brides, and mothers . . . yes, all the foulest shame that is wrought among men. *(Aside)* But all the gods commit incest; aren't we supposed to follow in their footsteps?

   The lights go up behind the palace walls and down on the courtyard.

Tiresias: Stop him! *(He makes various signs: "T" for "time," a hand across his throat for "cut off.")*

   Enter Creon from palace.

Creon: I have not come in mockery, Oedipus. I will not say "I told you." *(To the attendants)* Spare the world the sight of a pollution such as this, one which neither earth can welcome, nor the holy rain, nor the light. Take him into the house as quickly as you can. Pity demands that kinsfolk alone should see and hear a kinsman's woes.

Oedipus: It's time to lead me hence. Send me into exile.

Creon: You may go but without your children.

Oedipus: No! Don't take them from me!

Teacher steps to the front as if lecturing a class of students or acting as a Chorus.

Teacher: Behold this is Oedipus, who was once a most mighty man, the man who answered the famous riddle. On his fortune who did not gaze with envy? Behold into what stormy sea he has been plunged! Ponder deeply on this lesson. Until destiny unfolds, we must call no one happy who is a mortal. Any questions?

Lights isolate Tiresias and Sophocles.

Sophocles: You've turned my tragedy into a soap opera. It is worse than . . .

Tiresias: Writer, you are hopeless. Aren't you proud of what you've done? Has it occurred to you that we've just saved Western Civilization? Now things are back in order, and for centuries to come men and women will turn to these words of yours in awe and fear—fear of the gods, fear of the state. . . .

Sophocles: No! These are nothing but lies. I'll write another play to tell the truth!

Tiresias shakes his head, signalling. Sophocles is forcibly taken away. Soon the real screams begin.

Part II

One or Many Civilizations?

5

Mathematics and Eurocentrism

George Gheverghese Joseph

In recent years, especially since the publication of the Swann Report, *Education for All* (Department of Education and Science, 1985), there has been a recognition that the British school curriculum suffers from an ethnocentric bias, which an increasing number of teachers find unacceptable in a multicultural Britain. However, despite some institutional and professional backing even in mathematics (In London Education Authority [ILEA], 1985a, 1985b; The Mathematical Association, 1988), the attempt to counter ethnocentrism in the classroom is meeting a growing resistance by politicians and academics, who believe that an important goal of educational policy is to instill a greater awareness of British culture and history. The rationale for this position was well expressed by the secretary of state for education, Keith Joseph, on his last day in office (May 20, 1985), when he addressed the question of the role of education in an ethnically diverse society: "British history and cultural traditions are, or will become, at least, part of the cultural heritage of all who live in this country. . . . Schools should be responsible for trying to transmit British culture—enriched as it has been by so many traditions."

These sentiments have been echoed in an even more strident way by Keith Joseph's successors. They have also inspired the National Curriculum recently introduced into British schools, which aims at "removing" (some would say "suppressing") the social, linguistic, and cultural diversity present in British society.

The argument in favor of bolstering the British cultural tradition is that it fulfills an integrating and equalizing function. But it is only a short step from promoting British traditions to fostering cultural chauvinism, particularly in view of the resilience of the imperial legacy, which sees in the preservation of "our culture" the fulfillment of Britain's "civilizing mission" with respect to the "lesser breeds." There is, in fact, a historical continuity between the educational policy that imperial Britain applied in the colonies and the treatment it has meted out in the late twentieth century to its "internal colony" of "New Commonwealth immigrants," as nonwhite immigrants to Britain were euphemistically referred to until recently.

In both cases, the key to successful integration has been not just the knowledge of English and of the "British way of life," but the demotion of "native" cultural traditions. The labels have changed. We have had "immigrant education" in the fifties, then, in succession, "multiracial education," "multiethnic education," and, by the mid-seventies, "multicultural education." Yet, the hidden message has remained the same. In the same way as some native children were discouraged in Britain's colonial boarding schools from speaking their own "local" language, so are the immigrants to Britain made to understand that the faster they leave their cultural world behind, the better their prospects for adaptation. In other words, the key to good race relations is still following the dictum: "When in Rome do as the Romans do."

In this context, it is feared that the recent change in British educational policy, by its emphasis on *one* cultural tradition, would reinforce the ethnocentrism that has characterized the British curriculum in the past and at the same time "disempower" students from different ethnic backgrounds, who are taught that their cultural experience is of little value. In this process, all students would be deprived of the richness that other cultural traditions bring to Britain.

Are these fears justified? This question can be answered by examining how the mathematics curriculum has traditionally been shaped, and the recent attempts that have been made to develop multicultural and antiracist approaches to the teaching of mathematics. To appeal to British, or for that matter Western, "traditional" values as a factor of social cohesion is at best to foster an illusion, given the racist content of this tradition, forged as it was in the heyday of imperialism. In addition, mathematical education in Britain, as presently carried on, shows what Britain stands to lose by remaining ignorant of other traditions. This essay outlines an alternative approach to mathematics, which in its guidelines may serve to inspire similar efforts in other disciplines.

THE IMPERIAL LEGACY

To connect mathematics education to imperialism may seem anathema to those who believe that mathematics is the most universal of all disciplines and as such is value-free. In reality, not only has mathematics in the Western tradition been a vehicle for hierarchical values but also, in the case of British education, mathematics has compounded the Eurocentric biases of the "Western" approach with those congenial to the imperial experience.

The British mathematics curriculum, like that of other school subjects, was forged in the closing decades of the nineteenth century; thus, it was steeped in imperial ideology and deeply affected by the needs posed by imperial expansion. It could certainly be objected that the imperial enterprise produced a greater "multicultural awareness" both in the schools and in society than the nation has at present. It is not unusual, for example, to find in mathematics texts of the turn of the century questions such as the following (Colenso, 1892: 188): "A rupee contains 16 annas and one anna contains 12 pice. Find in French money the annual interest at 3.5 percent on 5,217 rupees, 3 annas, and 6 pice if the exchange rate is 2.63 francs per rupee." (The answer is: 480 francs and 24.5 cents.)

But in no way can the presence of this type of question be construed as a step toward an authentic cross-cultural perspective. The provision of a culturally diversified menu of mathematical examples stemmed from the need to equip the future imperial officers with the skills and information that their service in the colonies required. Thus, it legitimized a strictly utilitarian view of other populations, which well illustrates the pitfalls of a simplistic approach to multicultural education, oblivious to the political realities underlying the production and communication of culture. Indeed, the textbooks of the imperial era show how justified are those who insist that incorporating multicultural ideas in the curriculum is counterproductive, if we fail to address the question of power relations and racism. For preoccupation with cultural differences can be as divisive as preoccupation with racial differences.

It was mainly through the history and geography texts, as well as through juvenile fiction, that imperialist ideology was transmitted to the classroom (MacKenzie, 1984). Its main theme was the beneficial function of the colonial enterprise for the colonizers and colonized alike. The Europeans were seen as spreading a hard-won, dynamic civilization among inferior races that were inherently indolent (partly because of climatic reasons and partly because of their nature), not fit to rule themselves, and unable to engage in the type of higher thinking that technological and scientific progress allegedly require. Typical of this imperial belief, as transmitted to the classroom, is the following passage taken from a geography text that was still in use in Britain during the 1950s: "Under the guidance of Europeans, Africa is steadily being opened up. Doctors and scientists are working to improve the health of the Africans—missionaries and teachers are educating the people. . . . The single fact remains that the Europeans have brought civilization to the people of Africa, whose standard of living has, in most cases, been raised by their contact with white people" (Stembridge, 1956: 347).

The imperial experience prepared the students to consider it unthinkable that non-Europeans could produce mathematical knowledge. It fostered the myth that mathematics was a civilizing gift that Europe brought to the colonies, a Promethean spark that in time would enable the backward natives to penetrate the secrets of science and technology and enter the modern world. The prevalence of a Eurocentric bias among scholars is well illustrated in a review of Indian astronomy by John Playfair, first published in 1789, but included in an interesting anthology on the history of Indian science and technology edited by Dharampal (1971: 69–124). Playfair, a mathematician of note, carefully examined the evidence regarding early Indian astronomy. He was struck by the accuracy of the astronomical observations pertaining to the year 3102 B.C., which is the start of the Indian *Kali Yuga* era. Such accuracy could be explained either by assuming meticulous direct observations in that year or by using advanced analytical methods, including integral calculus, to extrapolate back in time. Playfair chose the first option. His reason for doing so is revealing:

Of such high antiquity, therefore, must we suppose the origin of this astronomy; we can believe that all the coincidences which have been enumerated are but the effects of chance; or what indeed were still more wonderful that, some ages ago, there had arisen a Newton among the Brahmins, to discover the universal principle which connects not only the most distant of space, but the most remote periods of duration; and a De LaGrange, to trace through the immensity of both, most subtle and complicated operations. (Playfair, 1789, quoted in Dharampal, 1971: 118)

It was easier for Playfair to concede the antiquity of the observations than to grant the sophistication of the mathematical calculations and astronomical theories, for it would have meant accepting the idea that India could have mathematicians of the stature of Newton and LaGrange.

More often the dismissal of the "native" was forthright. In a well-known geography textbook of the Edwardian period, still in print in the 1930s, we read, for instance: "The natives of Australia . . . were among the most miserable men. They roamed nearly naked, and were ignorant of everything except the chase. The explanation of their degraded condition lies in the arid climate of Australia. Their great poverty led them to practice vices like cannibalism and the murder of the sick and the helpless" (Hebertson, 1902: 1–2).

As for the African, he or she was typically described as "an overgrown child, vain, self-indulgent and fond of idleness," not indeed, an individual likely to contribute to any art, far less to mathematical creation.

By creating a "savage" counterpart to the "Western Mind," the imperial ideology legitimized the "traditional" account of mathematical development as a purely European product. As in the case of other equally pernicious social and intellectual biases, the tendency to trace mathematical development to an almost exclusively European origin predates and postdates the colonial venture. But the impact of colonialism was particularly pernicious in this regard, for imperial education propagated a Eurocentric bias not only in the British classroom, but also in every classroom of the Empire. Even after the demise of the Empire, the prejudices concerning the origins of mathematics and science have been especially difficult to combat, as they are still very functional to the legitimation of the economic and political supremacy of Western powers in the contemporary world. Thus, to this day, minority students in the British classroom are offered similar fare to that which was brought to yesterday's students in the colonies—an education whose pitfalls the proposed new policy can only reinforce.

ORIGINS AND NATURE OF MATHEMATICS

A crucial step toward building a multicultural mathematics curriculum is to dispel the assumption that mathematics is a purely European creation. Two tactics have been used to propagate this myth: simple omission—a tactic that is particularly evident at the lower echelons of the educational process—and the denial that the mathematics that was produced outside of Europe fits the criterion of genuine mathematical activity. The shaping of a Eurocentric account has in fact gone hand in hand with a definition of mathematics which ensures that certain strains of mathematics cannot be included in the mathematical tradition.

Omission and Appropriation

Prior to the "Renaissance," Europe's acknowledgment of the debt it owed to Arab mathematics was fulsome both in words and in deeds. Scholars from different parts of Europe congregated in Cordoba and Toledo in search of both ancient and contemporary knowledge. It is reported, for example, that Gherardo of Cremona (ca. 1114–87) went to Toledo, after its recapture by the Christians, in search of Ptolemy's *Almagest*, an astronomical text of great importance, produced in Alexandria in the second century A.D. He was so taken by the intellectual activity in the city that he remained there for twenty years, during which period he presumably translated (from Arabic into Latin) eighty manuscripts of Arab science or Greek classics, which he then took back to his homeland. Gherardo was one of a number of European scholars, including Plato of Tivoli, Adelard of Bath, and Robert of Chester, who flocked to Spain in search of knowledge. Up to the end of the sixteenth century, there was virtually a one-way traffic in mathematical knowledge into Europe. By the seventeenth century, however, the perception concerning the origins of mathematical knowledge had begun to change, owing to the operation of a number of forces. With the European expansion into the American continents, the development of the slave trade, and later the imposition of colonial rule in many parts of the world, the assumption of white superiority became dominant over a wide range of activities, including the writing of the history of mathematics. The rise of nationalism in nineteenth-century Europe and the consequent search for the roots of European civilization led to an obsession with Greece and the myth of Greek culture as the cradle of all knowledge and values. As Martin Bernal (1987) has shown, in the "Greek miracle" the Afro-asiatic roots of Greece were virtually buried. An account of the production of mathematical knowledge emerged that followed a purely Eurocentric trajectory (Figure 1) and ignored or devalued the contribution of the colonized, despite ample evidence of significant mathematical developments in Mesopotamia, Egypt, China, pre-Columbian America, India, and the Arab world, showing that Greek mathematics owed a great debt to some of these cultures (Ascher and Ascher, 1981; Gillings, 1972; Joseph, 1991; Neugebauer, 1962). This had been recognized by the Greeks themselves, beginning with Plato who reputedly declared that "compared with the Egyptians we are childish mathematicians."

According to the classical Eurocentric account, mathematical development took place in two distinct areas and two phases, separated by a period of inactivity that lasted 2,000 years: Greece from about 600 B.C. to A.D. 300, and post–Renaissance Europe from the fifteenth century to the present. The intervening period of inactivity is still referred to as the "Dark Ages"—a label forged during the Enlightenment that serves to devalue any cultural accomplishment predating the "rediscovery of Greek culture" in fifteenth-century Europe. That this "rediscovery" was made possible by the work of Arab intellectuals, and the culture thus appropriated was grounded on Egyptian and Arab knowledge, was not recognized. The very concept of "Renaissance" postulates, in mathematics as in other disciplines, a direct continuity between Greece and "modern Europe."

In recent years, a grudging recognition of the debt Greece owed to earlier civilizations and of the crucial contribution of Arab mathematicians has led to a revised Eurocentric trajectory (Figure 2). However, this figure also ignores the routes through which Hellenistic and Arab mathematics entered Europe, and it takes no account of the mathematical knowledge produced by India, China, and other cultures. Even the texts that do introduce Indian and Chinese mathematics often confine their discussion to a single chapter that may go under the misleading title of "Oriental" or "Eastern" mathematics. There is little indication, instead, of how these cultures contributed to the mainstream development of mathematics, and no consideration is given to the historical research on mathematics that is currently taking place in these and other "non-Western" regions. In the history of mathematics, non-European traditions appear as "residual dumps" that presumably can be ignored without prejudice for the main story. And the histories of mathematics still indulge in the misleading practice of naming mathematical results after Greek and European authors, even when it is known that these results had already been achieved by non-European mathematicians. For instance, the earliest known proof of Pythagoras's theorem is found in an ancient Chinese text, *Chou Pei Suan Ching*, conservatively dated around the middle of the first millennium B.C. Earlier antecedents of the "Pascal Triangle," or the "Gregory Series," or "Horner's method," are found outside Europe.

Figure 3 provides an "alternative trajectory" of mathematical transmission from the eighth to the fifteenth centuries. The cross-transmission that occurred between different cultural areas, and the critical role of the Arabs in taking mathematics westward, are illustrated in this figure. They are not discussed here; the interested reader may consult Joseph (1987, 1991).

Challenging the Eurocentric bias that so far has permeated mathematics teaching has more than one positive consequence. First it allows the teacher to tailor mathematics education to the students' experience of their social environment which, in contemporary Britain, includes different ethnic groups with their own mathematical heritage. It also provides cultural validation for minority students who are always being reminded, even if indirectly by the absence of any reference to it, that they have no mathematical tradition. Thus, it can help to counter the entrenched historical devaluation to which nonwhite minorities have been traditionally exposed. Finally, challenging Eurocentrism in mathematics allows us to achieve a more holistic approach to mathematics—one that acknowledges its relation to a wide range of disciplines that it conventionally ignores (including art, music, architecture, linguistics, and history)—and in the process construct a much needed redefinition of what we understand as "mathematical thinking."

One of the most unfortunate aspects of mathematics' development over time is its remoteness from other areas of knowledge, even those that are interested in ordering, sequencing, pattern, and color. Much can be learned, for example, from the close association that existed between the development of mathematics and that of linguistics in ancient India, and from the role of spatial intuition in the creation of African geometric designs. Woven into traditional African material culture—in the baskets, mats, pots, houses, fishtraps—are many "hidden" examples of geometrical thinking (Gerdes, 1986, 1988a, 1988b; Zaslavsky, 1973). The manufacture of these objects reveals a practical knowledge of the properties of circles, rectangles, cones, pyramids, or cylinders, as well as "deeper theoretical" principles, such as the one relating to the sides of a right-angled triangle, commonly attributed to the Greek mathematician Pythagoras. Unfolding this "hidden" mathematics poses an intellectual challenge to any mathematician and would encourage a study of the relation between geometry and material production. This is the message that Gerdes (1986) conveyed to a seminar for mathematics educators, when he presented the following nonstandard problems that (illiterate) Mozambiquan artisans solve as a matter of course:

- Construct a circle, given only its circumference: a problem encountered in laying out a circular floor for a traditional Mozambiquan house.

Figure 1
The "classical" Eurocentric approach

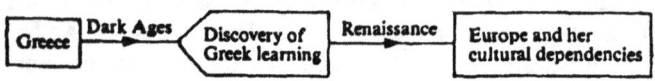

Figure 2
The "modified" Eurocentric trajectory

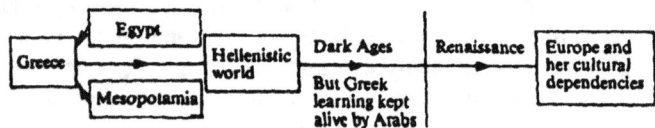

Figure 3
An alternative trajectory (from 8th to 15th centuries)

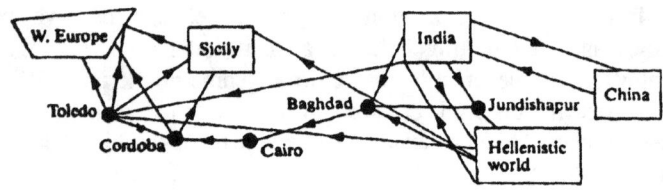

- Construct angles that measure 90, 60, or 40 degrees with strips of straw: a problem in basket weaving.
- Fold an equilateral triangle out of a square: a problem in making a straw hat.

None of these problems is trivial in a mathematical sense.

The discovery of this hidden but plastic mathematics would provide practical and creative examples for the mathematics class, and stimulate a child's imagination and spatial sense. This, however, is impossible if we keep considering mathematics as a purely theoretical activity, as has been the case in the European mathematical and philosophical approach.

Exclusion by Definition

It is not sufficiently recognized that a Eurocentric approach to the history of mathematics is intimately connected with what is still the dominant view of mathematics as a social/historical practice and intellectual activity. Despite the development of contrary trends in the nineteenth and twentieth centuries—Empiricism, Conventionalism, Behaviorism—the standard textbook approach generally conceives mathematics as a deductive, a-prioristic system, ideally proceeding from (and providing) axiomatic foundations and revealing, by the necessary unfolding of its pure abstract forms, the eternal and universal laws of "the Mind."

The Indian or Chinese concept of mathematics is very different. Its aim is not to build an imposing edifice on a few self-evident axioms, but to validate a result by any method, including visual demonstrations. Some of the most impressive works in Indian and Chinese mathematics (the summations of complex mathematical series, the use of the "Pascal Triangle" in solutions of higher order numerical equations, and the derivations of infinite series and "proofs" of the so-called Pythagorean theorem) involve the use of visual demonstrations that are not formulated with reference to any formal deductive system. Furthermore, the Indian view concerning the nature of mathematical objects, like numbers, is based on a framework developed by Indian logicians (and linguists), and differs significantly at the foundational level from the set-theory universe of modern mathematics.

The view that mathematics is a system of axiomatic/deductive truths inherited from the Greeks and enthroned by Descartes and Kant has been traditionally associated with a cluster of values that reflect the social context in which it originated. Prime among them are an idealist rejection of any practical, material(ist) basis for mathematics, from which stems the tendency to view mathematics as a value-free pursuit, detached from any social and political concerns; and an elitist perspective that sees mathematical work as the exclusive province of a pure, high-minded, nearly priestly caste, removed from mundane preoccupations and operating in a superior intellectual sphere.

Non-European mathematical traditions (from Egypt to Mesopotamia, India, and China) have therefore often been dismissed on the ground that they are purely empirical and dictated by purely utilitarian aims. To this day, great care is exercised to project an image of mathematics as a purely speculative activity, free from material preoccupations, and to ensure that it remains the property of an elite. At a conference that I recently attended, it was emphatically stated that "Mathematics is not learned in the streets." This brought to my mind the great eleventh-century Islamic scientist, Ibn Sina (or Avicenna, as he was known in Europe), who declared that he had learned the new (Indian) arithmetic from a street vegetable vendor. I was also reminded of my own experience as a young boy in India, when I used to observe street astrologers performing an incredible mental arithmetic, through methods akin to the so-called Vedic multiplication procedures (Nelson, Joseph, and Williams, 1993: 106–16). In the "West," however, the idea of "pure" mathematics still prevails, even though the history of the subject in this century indicates that, despite its seeming abstraction from social reality, it has found very "practical" applications indeed. An outstanding example is its usage in nuclear physics and the development of atomic weaponry. Equally important, even a cursory look at today's mathematics curriculum would show that what is being taught in the classroom is dictated by very practical social and political goals.

THE HIDDEN IDEOLOGY OF MATHEMATICAL EDUCATION

Consider the range of topics covered by school mathematics today in Britain. There might be legitimate reasons for teaching social arithmetic, numeracy skills, measures, ratios and proportion, variation, and percentages. There are, however, no strong mathematical justifications for including percentages in the curriculum. Percentages are taught for practical purposes, for example, in order to inculcate in the students the skills required for servicing the commercial and financial sectors.

That the mathematics curriculum is not above social and political concerns is evident at more than one level. Questions referring to stocks and shares, which were common in school mathematics of the 1950s and 1960s, served to habituate children to view "matter-of-factly" the language of financial capital, long before the majority of the students could have any experience of it. Similarly, the questions on bath-filling in earlier decades presented as the norm the physical environment of the upper classes, and dismissed the reality of the many children who did not have this facility in their homes. Practical concerns are also evident in the debate about the uses of classroom mathematics found in the early discussions of the National Curriculum. This debate is reminiscent of the one that took place in England a hundred years ago among industrialists and educators on the goals of mass education. At that time, the "industrial" lobby emphatically stressed that education should serve the needs of industry and commerce; the "public education" lobby wanted education to contribute to the development of the "whole" individual and to bolster democratic citizenship; and finally, the academic ("old humanist") lobby argued that school subjects should be studied for their own sake and that knowledge should be an end in itself. Later, when science was introduced into English education around the middle of the nineteenth century, there was a move, led by educationists such as Richard Dawes and Michael Moseley, to devise a curriculum based on the experience and knowledge that students derive from everyday life (Layton, 1973). This approach, described as the "science of common things," involved teaching science through common everyday problems: cottage ventilation, personal hygiene, family nutrition, and gardening. This approach was consistent with the "public education" perspective, although it made concessions to other lobbies, emphasizing (for the benefit of the humanist) the objective of raising "them [students] into the scale of thinking beings" (Layton, 1973: 189), and (for the benefit of the industrialist) the vocational usefulness of scientific knowledge.

The "science of common things" lost, and the reasons why are interesting from our viewpoint. One reason implied, though not necessarily stated, was that by giving to the masses a practical scientific knowledge that the upper classes might not possess, education would subvert the existing social order. Liberal educators also argued that a curriculum selected because of its utility to a particular social group (in this case the working class) would ghettoize the students and discourage them from moving beyond their immediate environment. Third, modern science and its industrial applications were thought to be better served by the application of mathematics to scientific problems, especially physics. The mathematics of science was presented as the antithesis of the "science of common things" because of its supposedly universal abstractions.

There are close parallels between the nineteenth-century debate on the science curriculum and today's deliberations on mathematics teaching. When a teacher is asked today why mathematics should be a core subject, the answers ring a familiar note. We hear the humanist argument that mathematics offers rigorous training in the process of "reasoning," that it cultivates logical and critical thinking and problem-solving abilities, despite justifiable skepticism on the part of many who are directly involved in the teaching of mathematics. We then have the analogue of the "industrial" lobby argument: the primary purpose of mathematical education is to deliver skilled manpower to the workplace. This is something the math class is apparently failing to accomplish, if we credit the frequent complaints on the part of British politicians and industrialists. Finally, we are again told that mathematical education contributes to the formation of the "whole" individual and that it is indispensable for citizens who are expected to make informed judgments on various aspects of their society on the basis, among other things, of statistics and other quantitative indicators. This approach is consistent with the idea of science education promoted by Dawes and Moseley and might be described as the "mathematics of common things" (Layton, 1973).

An important question arises when we examine these three perspectives: What does each imply about the relationship between mathematics and society? The academic/humanist approach does not acknowledge any social dimension in the study of mathematics. The utilitarian/"industrial" approach recognizes a one-way relationship between mathematics and the outside world—mathematics as an input into training for specific skills and expertise. Both approaches, which have deeply influenced the mathematics curriculum of Britain, see mathematics as free of social considerations and values. The third approach permits a more dynamic relationship between mathematics and society; it takes into account different constituencies and the specific cultural interests of the learner. However, if we define too narrowly the constituency to whom mathematics is addressed, then we may have a curriculum that marginalizes the students and devalues both the content and context of the mathematics taught. One way of safeguarding against this danger is to emphasize both the practical use of mathematics and its relevance to the development of a universal language and discipline. It is here that a historical approach could be helpful, and this is precisely what a non-Eurocentric, multicultural, antiracist approach to mathematics contributes.

THE OBJECTIVES OF MULTICULTURAL/ANTIRACIST MATHEMATICS

In 1987, at the Annual Conservative Party Conference, Prime Minister Margaret Thatcher stated: "Children who need to count and multiply are being taught anti-racist mathematics, whatever that may be."

Thatcher's puzzlement is shared by many, including a number of teachers. Multicultural/Antiracist (MC/AR) mathematics is perceived as a strange and incongruous subject to be added to an already overladen math syllabus, rather than as an approach that permeates all topics in the syllabus. This confusion is present in the section entitled "Ethnic and Cultural Diversity" (paragraph 10.18–10.23) of the National Curriculum Report (Department of Education and Society, 1988) entitled *Mathematics for Ages 5 to 16*:

It is sometimes suggested that the multi-cultural complexion of society demands a "multi-cultural" approach to mathematics, with children being introduced to different number systems, foreign currencies and non-European measuring and counting devices. We are concerned that undue emphasis on multi-cultural mathematics, in these terms, could confuse young children. Whilst it is right to make clear to children that mathematics is the product of a diversity of cultures, priority must be given to ensuring that they have knowledge, understanding, and skills which they will need for adult life and employment in Britain in the twenty-first century. We believe that most parents would share this view.

And again: "Many of those who argue for a multi-cultural approach to the mathematics curriculum do so on the basis that such an approach is necessary to raise the self-esteem of ethnic minority cultures and to improve the understanding and respect between races. We believe that this attitude is misconceived and patronizing."

These quotations from the National Curriculum Document summarize well the attitudes and misconceptions that exist about MC/AR mathematics. What is missing in this view of MC/AR mathematics as irrelevant, peripheral, patronizing to "minorities," and pedagogically ineffectual is an understanding of the general objectives of and conditions for learning mathematics.

An important purpose of learning mathematics is to acquire a new language with its rules of operation, opening a whole range of possibilities for the articulation of our experiences and apprehension of the surrounding world—an acquisition that necessarily depends on the students' ability to connect mathematics with other aspects of their reality, and their conviction that this is a knowledge in whose production they too are daily involved.

MC/AR mathematics provides a strategy for making mathematics more accessible and less anxiety arousing among a wider public. As it is all too well known, as presently taught, mathematics fails to reach the vast majority of students; even for those who expect to make it part of their higher education, it causes more anxiety than any other subject. This is because it is often taught as a sequence of disconnected skills, in isolation from real-world applications and abstracted from its historical roots.

By contrast, MC/AR mathematics has five overlapping objectives (The Mathematical Association, 1988: 4–9):

1. *Drawing on the student's experience as a resource.* Abstract concepts can be presented in a concrete form through examples that are familiar to the class. In a class with children from Hindu and Sikh households, the *rangoli* patterns used to decorate their homes on festive days can serve as a useful introduction to different geometrical notions of patterns, symmetry, transformations, and equivalence. For children from an Islamic or Jewish background, time measurements involving the principle of constructing calendars and demarcation of eras, including the role of lunar calendars, could be developed from a few questions regarding the religious practices of these groups. An ability to convert from one system to another would not only be a useful arithmetic exercise, but would also help students to appreciate the diversity of the local environment. Students would understand, for example, why their Chinese and Jewish neighbors do not celebrate their New Year's Day on January 1.
2. *Recognizing different cultural heritages.* It is important that students understand

the development of mathematics as a truly global endeavor that evolved through centuries of cross-fertilization between different cultures. Students should learn, for instance, that our number system grew out of the work of mathematicians from the Indian subcontinent about 2,000 years ago and was transmitted by the Arabs to Europe in the twelfth century. Manipulations and representations of plus and minus quantities, the distinction between real and imaginary numbers, and the concepts of zero and infinity excited the imagination of Indian, Mayan, Chinese, and Italian mathematicians. We owe the foundations of algebra (an Arabic word) and the development of trigonometry to non-European civilizations. This international dimension must be stressed in the teaching of mathematics. We are not suggesting that learning mathematics must involve a detailed historical investigation, even though the "History of Arab Mathematics," or "Egyptian Arithmetic," or "Calculus Before Newton" would make interesting projects. Instead, a cultural and historical perspective on mathematics could take two forms:

- Math teachers should have a fund of interesting stories on the origin and development of various topics in mathematics, emphasizing its practical origins and reinforcing the view that mathematics is a universal activity which, however, always takes a specific cultural form. The sources for such materials are not only the standard histories of mathematics, which tend on the whole to be Eurocentric, but the growing literature on non-European traditions examined, for example, in Ascher (1991) and Joseph (1991).
- New approaches to curriculum development recently adopted in France can be usefully introduced into the mathematics classroom. These involve using the original texts in which a problem and its solution first appeared. For instance, a student who is introduced for the first time to non-Euclidean geometry will profit by a study of selections from the original texts of, say, the thirteenth-century Arab mathematician, Nasir al-Din al-Tusi, and the seventeenth century Italian mathematician, Sacheri, whose unsuccessful attempts to prove Euclid's "Parallel Postulate" were important signposts in the discovery of non-Euclidean geometry. It would also help the students to understand, at least in broad outlines, the social context in which these mathematical works were produced and the practical implications of the specific problems tackled.

3. *Developing knowledge and empathy with cultures other than one's own.* A math teacher has a role to play in fostering mutual understanding and respect in societies where different cultures live side by side. Not only should teachers draw on the experiences and highlight the historical heritage of different students, but they should also create opportunities for them to learn about customs and cultures other than their own. Making judicious use of the names of members of different ethnic groups and encouraging the publication of texts that acknowledge the existence of other measuring systems, different calendars and monetary systems are obviously important ways of giving a non-Eurocentric dimension to classroom work. It might also be advisable to stress the cultural contributions of nations that have received negative comments from the media. For instance, mentioning the historical contribution of Persian mathematicians such as Omar Khayyam and Jamshid al-Kashi could counter the stigmatization of Iran in the public eye in recent years.

4. *Combating racism.* A number of reports, including the Swann Report, have high-

lighted the considerable level of racism that exists in both British society and British schools. Here too the math teacher must be sensitive to the ways in which racism enters the classroom and can be countered. A publication entitled *Everyone Counts* (ILEA, 1985a) provides the following checkpoints for detecting how mathematics materials can be biased or insensitive to racial minorities:

- Using examples that make reference to selectively chosen "lifestyles."
- Perpetuating stereotypes that devalue certain ethnic groups—for example, the stereotype of the child from African-Caribbean descent as presumably "less good" in math than the Asian child; or the stereotyped image of African counting systems, prior to the coming of the Europeans, as "primitive systems" fit for the needs of a "simple society." This ignores the fact that the Ishango Bone from Zaire is the earliest recorded attempt to construct a lunar calendar; it also ignores the ingenious arithmetic of the Yoruba with its "subtraction principle" (see Joseph, 1991: 23–27, 44–46; Nelson, Joseph, and Williams, 1993: 97–100).
- Being ignorant or insensitive to the social position of minority groups in society, as if the existence of racial discrimination and the nature of power relations within the wider society were of no concern in a math class.

A multicultural/antiracist approach to teaching mathematics involves answering the following questions:

- What are the mathematical objectives for introducing a certain topic?
- What is the best approach for achieving these objectives from the point of view of teaching and learning?
- Is there any MC/AR lesson to be drawn from the topic? If so, what resources are required?

Most important, an MC/AR involves a sustained effort to empower students to believe that mathematics is within their reach and is an activity to which their ancestors, communities, and cultures have been active contributors. The consequences of the sense of confusion and intimidation which students from all backgrounds experience when confronted with a discipline whose cultural matrix seems irreducibly "other" have yet to be fully realized. They are already dramatically evident in the high rates of dropout from math classes at all levels. By contrast, there are reports of keen participation when the class takes place in a "context of inclusion."

REFERENCES

Ascher, M. (1991). *Ethnomathematics: A Multicultural View of Mathematical Ideas.* Pacific Grove, Calif.: Brooke/Cole Publishing Co.

Ascher, M., and R. Ascher. (1981). *Code of the Quipu.* Ann Arbor: Michigan University Press.

Avari, B., and G. G. Joseph. (1990). "Race Relations Training: The State of the Art." In P. D. Pumphrey and G. K. Verma, eds., *Race Relations and Urban Education*. London: Falmer Press, 121–39.

Bernal, M. (1987). *Black Athena: The Afroasiatic Roots of Classical Civilization*, Vol. 1. London: Free Association Books.

Bishop, A. (1990). "Western Mathematics: The Secret Weapon of Cultural Imperialism." *Race and Class* 32(2): 51–65.

Colenso, J. W. (1874). *Arithmetic—Designed for the Use of Schools* (2nd ed., 1892). London: Longman, Green and Co.

Department of Education and Science. (1988). *Mathematics for Ages 5 to 16*. London: H.M.S.O.

Dharampal. (1971). *Indian Science and Technology in the Eighteenth Century*. New Delhi: Biblia Impex.

Gerdes, P. (1985). "Conditions and Strategies for Emancipatory Mathematics Education in Underdeveloped Countries." *For the Learning of Mathematics* 5(1): 15–20.

———. (1986). "How to Recognize Hidden Geometrical Thinking: A Contribution to the Development of Anthropological Mathematics." *For the Learning of Mathematics* 6(2): 10–17.

———. (1988a). "On Possible Uses of Traditional Angolan Sand Drawings in the Mathematics Classroom." *Educational Studies in Mathematics* 19(1): 3–22.

———. (1988b). "On Culture, Geometrical Thinking, and Mathematics Education." *Educational Studies in Mathematics* 19(3): 137–62.

Gillings, R. J. (1972). *Mathematics in the Time of the Pharaohs*. Cambridge, Mass.: MIT Press.

Herbertson, A. J. (1902). *Man and His Work: Introduction to Human Geography*. London: Blacks School Geography.

In London Education Authority. (1985a). *Everyone Counts*. London: ILEA.

———. (1985b). *Count Me In*. London: I.L.E.A.

Joseph, G. G. (1987). "Foundations of Eurocentrism in Mathematics." *Race and Class* 28 (3): 13–28.

———. (1990). "The Politics of Anti-Racist Mathematics." *Multicultural Teaching* 9(1): 31–33.

———. (1991). *The Crest of the Peacock: Non-European Roots of Mathematics*. London: I. B. Tauris. (Reprints: Penguin Books, London and New York, 1992 and 1993.)

———. (1994). "Different Ways of Knowing: Contrasting Styles of Argument in Indian and Greek Mathematical Traditions." In P. Ernest, ed., *Mathematics, Education and Philosophy: An International Perspective*, Studies in Mathematics Education, Vol. 3. London: Falmer Press, pp. 192–204.

———. (1995, January/March). "Cognitive Encounters in India During the Age of Imperialism." *Race and Class* 36(3): 39–56.

Joseph, G. G., V. Reddy, and M. Searle-Chatterjee. (1990). "Eurocentrism in the Social Sciences." *Race and Class* 31(4): 1–26.

Layton, D. (1973). *Science for the People*. London: George Allen and Unwin.

MacKenzie, John M. (1984). *Propaganda and Empire: The Manipulation of British Public Opinion, 1880–1960*. Manchester: Manchester University Press.

The Mathematical Association. (1988). *Mathematics in a Multicultural Society*.

Leicester: Mathematical Association.

Nelson, R. D., G. G. Joseph, and J. Williams. (1993). *Multicultural Mathematics*. Oxford: Oxford University Press.

Neugebauer, O. (1962). *The Exact Sciences in the Antiquity*. New York: Harper and Row. (New edition [1969]. New York: Dover.)

Playfair, J. J. (1789). "Remarks on the Astronomy of the Brahmins." *Transactions of the Royal Society of Edinburgh* 2(1): 135–92.

Stembridge, J. (1939). *The World—A General Regional Geography*, 1956 ed. London: Oxford University Press.

Swann Report. (1985). *Education for All. A Report on the Education of Ethnic Minority Children*. London: H.M.S.O.

Swetz, F. J., and T. I. Kao. (1977). *Was Pythagoras Chinese? An Examination of Right Triangle Theory in Ancient China*. Harrisburg: Pennsylvania State University Press.

Zaslavsky, C. (1973). *Africa Counts—Number and Pattern in African Culture*. Boston: Prindle, Weber, and Schmidt. (Paperback [1979]. New York: Lawrence Hill Books.)

6

Orientalism, Political Economy, and the Canonization of Indian Civilization

John Roosa

In the current debate over multiculturalism, India appears as one of the great "others" to Western Civilization, and "Indian civilization" is one of the outstanding candidates, within the spectrum of world cultures, for integration into a reformed college curriculum. Thus, the main question for the advocates of multiculturalism seems to be a quantitative one: How much should we teach Indian civilization?

What is lacking in this debate is a critical understanding of what we define as Indian civilization. It is necessary, however, to ask how India's canon was formed, so that we do not reinstate in our study of Indian history the same ahistorical and reductionist approach that we reject in the customary accounts of Western Civilization. For there is no more unity and coherence in the history and culture of the Indian subcontinent than there is in the purported Western. Any critical pedagogy, moreover, should question the very concept of civilization and not simply the variety of geographical adjectives prefixed to it.

The subject of this essay, then, is the history of the canonization of "Indian civilization," the history of how the societies of the subcontinent came to be subsumed under one, internally coherent cultural reality. As a brief essay on a broad topic, it pretends to be neither historically nor theoretically comprehensive. For instance, no attempt is made here to demonstrate the heterogeneity of Indian history and culture. Instead, this principle is taken as a given, although the reader should consult the work of the historian of ancient India, Romila Thapar, who has devoted much of her writing over the past decade to combating the assumption of a monolithic Indian tradition and a single "Indian mind" (1983, 1987, 1989a, 1989b).

This essay begins with the East India Company's takeover of India in the late eighteenth century and early nineteenth century for the reason that this London-based multinational corporation attempted the first codification of a uniquely Indian civilization. The company was committed to making Indian society conform to the imperatives of commercial growth, and it was therefore vitally interested in acquiring practical knowledge of the social "raw material" it was committed to change. Thus Indian tradition became fixed in British studies at the very moment when it was being radically altered in practice.

This combination, paradoxical at first, indicates that we need to see the development of Indology in relation to the company's economic project in India. Although Indology defined what Indian civilization had been, the emerging discipline of political economy defined what it should be, setting the goals to which it should progress. Today Indology, and its more general discipline, "Orientalism," seem at odds with political economy. Indology is concerned with defining Indians as a particular genus of humanity, "homo hierarchicus," according to the French Indologist Dumont (1970), who nearly inscribed caste into the Indian genes. Instead, political economy proclaims that its theories are founded on universal attitudes and inclinations constitutive of the essence of human nature. Yet both disciplines owe much of their development to the East India Company and in earlier periods were considered to be complementary.

The first section of this essay charts the early development of Indology, and the second traces that of political economy in its relationship to the East India Company. The third section examines the changing relationship of Indian nationalism to these disciplines. Finally, the fourth examines how the post–World War II U.S. academy borrowed from the protocols of the East India Company civilization project while adapting them to the new postcolonial context.

The essay moves between India, Britain, and the United States in an attempt to transcend the customary comparisons between neatly defined civilizations and to demonstrate that the idea of Indian civilization has been an integral part of the simultaneous construction of Western Civilization.

This point bears some emphasis given the wide circulation of Edward Said's critiques of colonial discourses. Said criticizes the excesses of Orientalism for denying a common, universal "human experience" to Western and non-Western peoples (Said, 1978: 328). Thus, Said contrasts the particularism of the Orientalist project with an ideal of universalism strangely reminiscent of the tenets of the "Western tradition" (Young, 1990). It must be stressed, however, that if colonialism produced specious particulars (the Indians as a unique species of humans), it also produced specious universals in the form of political economy. Moreover, today more than ever, we must question not only which particulars we affirm, given the great variety of possible social identities, but also which universals. Can we embrace, for example, the universals of the International Monetary Fund (IMF) which presumes its principles of political economy to be founded on natural and universal truths? Or can we develop alternatives to the austerity programs that the IMF now applies in India as in virtually every other country of the "Third World"? Few could fail to subscribe to Said's hope for "a collective as well as a plural destiny for mankind" (Said, 1989: 224), but the difficulty is precisely to define both the commonality and the difference. It is in view of this difficulty that a reconstruction of the history of "Indian civilization" and its relation to the development of political economy becomes necessary.

INDIAN CIVILIZATION: LOST AND FOUND

One of the first consequences of the East India Company's rule in eastern India was famine. In some districts of present-day Bihar, Orissa, and Bengal, as much as half the population died in the famine of 1770. A land that had been known for its fertility and wealth, that had rarely experienced a famine before, was quickly reduced to misery under the company's administration. Despite a public disavowal of responsibility for the "natural" catastrophe, the company privately recognized that its own hiking up of the land revenue demand, not a failure of the rains, had caused the famine. This recognition threw it into a scramble for reform, for as Sir James Steuart, Europe's leading political economist at the time, advised in 1772, the goal was not to kill the goose that lays the golden eggs but to nurture her. All the company's reforms over the next decades were haunted by the experience of 1770. The famine "stands out in the contemporary records in appalling proportions," wrote Sir William Hunter. "It forms the key to the history of Bengal during the succeeding forty years" (Hunter, 1897: 19).

In planning for the long-term security of a vast rent-collecting machine, the company officials concurred that it was necessary to govern India on the basis of its own traditions. The Governor General, Warren Hastings, announced a wide-ranging reform scheme in 1772 with the assurance that "we have endeavored to adapt our Regulations to the manners and understandings of the People, and exigencies of the country, adhering as closely as we were able, to their ancient usages and institutions" (Archbold, 1926: 53). The 1770 famine, however, had wreaked havoc with whatever may have been considered the tradition in eastern India. A third to a half of its living bearers were dead (in Hastings' estimate), and many peasants and artisans had fled their villages. It was under these conditions that the company began its search for the traditional laws of the Bengal area.

The company's early strategy for traditionalizing the legal system was inspired by its officers' own beliefs derived from their British experience. William Jones, a founder of the scholarly Asiatic Society of Bengal and the chief judge of Bengal, had been a high-ranking barrister in London before coming to Calcutta. He had been an ardent believer in "Common Law" as the expression of the ancient will of the English people, a supporter of constitutional reform, and an opponent of monarchical despotism. Like other members of London's upper class, however, he conceived of the "people" only insofar as they were property holders; and during the London riots of 1780, when the whole legal apparatus was under siege (the prison was burned down, the chief judge's house and the courts were attacked), Jones did not hesitate to advocate military terror against the "licentious rabble" against whom "no remedies can be too severe" (Jones, 1780: 2–3, 31).

Officials like Jones brought to India a tested experience concerning the use of "nature" and "tradition" to buttress commercial expansion. But in order to apply the lesson in India they first had to establish what constituted India's tradition. The sources to which they turned were the preexisting legal texts; the assumption being that a country's laws were the supreme expression of its civilization. Thus, in the wake of the 1772 reforms, British scholars set about studying and translating these texts. However, they soon discovered that there were two distinct sets of legal codes, one Hindu and one Islamic, and within these two sets there were rival schools of interpretations and various methods of implementation. Thus, the inevitable complaint, after each new code of traditional law was compiled, was that it failed to give precise instructions for giving judgments and administering punishments (Rocher, 1983: 63).

Jones labored for most of his tenure as a chief judge (1783–94) in order to "give our country a complete digest of Hindu and Mussalman law" (Jones, 1970: 699). Yet, even his code, *A Digest of Hindu Law*, was considered by his successor (as Britain's leading Sanskritist) H. T. Colebrooke to be deficient since it, again, did not provide definite judgments for specific cases. Under the precolonial regimes, the lack of a standard legal code and the leeway given to the judge met the need of a society made up of diverse communities. The British, however, demanded a complete code, one that would enable them to follow the text and presumably avoid imposing their own practices on India, even though customs were to be respected only as long as they were not "hurtful to the authority of government." When it came to law that directly affected the company's profits—for example, criminal and revenue laws—tradition was superseded. Thus, only in two areas was "the intention to leave the natives of these Indian provinces in possession of their own laws" observed: contracts and inheritances (Warren Hastings, quoted in Rocher, 1983: 53). The society's whole system of property was changing in the late eighteenth century as a result of the company's economic policies, but the transfer of property between individuals or family members was to be left under traditional laws.

Throughout their search for the true Indian legal tradition, the officials harbored no doubts that the ancient texts were impartial and had priority over the practices of the living bearers of that tradition. The past was pure, for it was beyond the reach of the self-serving and duplicitous Indians. "I can no longer bear to be at the mercy of our pundits who deal out Hindu law as they please," Jones complained after two years on the bench (Jones, 1970: 686).

The belief that the Indians' present state was depraved pervades nearly all the British writings about Indian society at the time. Yet the belief that India had once possessed a great civilization was equally pervasive. As Jones wrote, "How degenerate and abased so ever the Hindus may now appear," they were in the ancient past "splendid in arts and arms, happy in government, wise in legislation, and eminent in various knowledge" (Marshall, 1970: 251). Jones believed it was the duty of the British to return them to that golden age. In this context, the search for the authentic legal code became part of an endeavor to resuscitate the ancient Indian tradition.

It was in part to carry out this task that a group of company officials founded a research organization, the Asiatic Society of Bengal, in 1784. Jones served as its president and was later appointed editor of its journal, *Asiatik Researches*. In the course of its publishing career, from 1788–1839, this journal carried nearly the same number of articles on the natural sciences as on the social sciences. The 174 articles on plants, animals, geological formations, and manufacturing technologies catalogued the existent natural wealth in India, while the 172 articles on Indian history, language, literature, customs, and revenue systems catalogued its social wealth. The same perspective the British applied to nature, they applied to society. The study of the flora and fauna of India was part of an effort to reveal how they could be used in the making of various products: dyes, ropes, chemicals, food. In the same way, the study of Indian culture was supposed to uncover the keys by which human resources could be exploited. The link between the study of culture and economic strategies was made explicit by Jones's opinion that, if the company followed traditional laws that "are actually revered . . . by many millions of Hindu subjects," the Hindus' "well directed industry would add largely to the wealth of Britain" (Jones, 1825: xxi).

The Orientalists' method of studying Indian tradition was to prioritize the ancient over the living culture. Thus, they did not simply "discover" India's past, but wrote into it an anachronistic dualism of indigenous/foreign and a false dualism of authentic/inauthentic. For their efforts to locate an "original" culture led them to see Hindu civilization as the authentic, indigenous one and Islamic civilization as a foreign intrusion. A new history was in fact written in which a golden age of Hindu power had given way to an age of tyranny following the Muslim invasions. Jones virtually identified India with the Hindus; and at the College of Fort William (in Calcutta), founded in 1800 for British civil servants, H. T. Colebrooke and William Carey promoted the idea of a Hindu renaissance under British rule (Kopf, 1969: 102–3).

The Orientalists' inscription in Indian history of a Hindu-Muslim divide was to have disastrous consequences. We should therefore reconsider the praise many scholars have given to their work, which the American scholar David Kopf (1980) described as a heroic feat and a generous "gift" to the Indians.

Certainly, "the work of integrating a vast collection of myths, beliefs, rituals, and laws into a coherent religion, and of shaping an amorphous heritage into a rational faith known now as 'Hinduism' were endeavors initiated by the Orientalists" (Kopf, 1980: 502). But these endeavors hardly merit the uncritical praise that Kopf accords them. By erasing (through their selective translations) the diversity of history and reinscribing it within a singular tradition, the Orientalists encouraged a divide between the purportedly indigenous Hindus and the invading Muslims.

By the end of the eighteenth century, the company had translated two texts that were fundamental to its view of the true Hindu India. One was Jones's translation of the *Manu Dharmashastras*, or the law books of Manu, their legendary composer. The second was the *Bhagavad Gita*, which was translated from Sanskrit in 1785 by one of the founding members of the Asiatic Society, Charles Wilkins. Both of these texts had an enormous impact on the European intelligentsia at the time, and they remain basic texts in Indian civilization courses today.

Both texts focus on *dharma*. This term is often translated as "law," but it means much more. In Manu, *dharma* is a combination of religious precepts, social order, and personal duties. Manu presents a utopian vision for a world subject to a universal order. Because it is an all-encompassing term, *dharma*'s meaning is problematic. But it is clear in Manu, and in the rest of the ancient *dharmashastra* texts of which Manu is just one, that the basis of any social order was the preservation of the caste (*varna*) hierarchy. Under this framework, whole classes of people are either limited in their rights or deprived of their rights, while the brahman caste is given virtual immunity from wrong. Manu presents the brahmans as "lords of all the castes." Obviously, not everyone in ancient India abided by the *dharma* Manu decreed. But the British reading of this text helped to reinforce their idea that whatever Hindu civilization was, the brahman was at the center of it. The brahmanical world view, for many British officials, became the standard by which to define Hindu and thus Indian civilization (Kosambi, 1962).

Jones's friend and colleague, Charles Wilkins, translated another text famous for its treatment of *dharma*: the *Bhagavad Gita*, a small portion of the massive epic, the *Mahabharata*. Wilkins had been informed by his brahman informants in Bengal that this text was among their most sacred. The *Gita* dramatizes an episode before a great battle between two groups of the same lineage. Arjuna, a young warrior, hesitates to fight his own kin, but Lord Krishna urges him on, arguing that he has to follow his caste role as a warrior, for disobeying the duties imposed by caste is controverting nature itself and jeopardizing the existence of the universe (Miller, 1986: 41). But paradoxes abound. If caste is a matter of nature, how can Arjuna will its violation? And if nature is so defective that its creatures fail to recognize its imperatives, why must it be defended? As if to suppress such queries, Krishna supplements his arguments with the injunction that we must follow our nature without thinking. We must act without any concern for the reasons for the act or for its consequences. The only focus for the mind must be Krishna, the infinite being, the absolute, the only reality, pure and unchanging. Hence, the famed lesson of the *Gita* is: act but think not of the fruits of the act. As Krishna discloses that "all nature's qualities come from me," we realize that the nature that is threatened with apocalypse by Arjuna's refusal is Krishna himself, who for inexplicable reasons manifests his nature through the caste system, thus giving a cosmic blessing to human inequality.

The *Gita*, as both a text and an oral tradition 2,000 years old, has been read and recited in a variety of ways over the centuries. In fact, it appears that the verses were substantially rewritten about 1,000 years ago, and the older version may not have contained this strident insistence on caste duty. Even after its revision, the ambiguities in the text allow one to read it in a variety of ways. The British, however, concluded from the *Gita* that all Hindus were committed to following the duties of their respective castes and had little concern for the material world. They found in the *Gita*'s philosophy, especially in its prescription "Think not of the reward for your work, but content your mind with the inscrutable Krishna," a natively sanctioned apologia for their colonial strategies. The *Gita* became the manifesto for a philosophy of life demanding both indifference to human suffering and joy and appreciation of this indifference as a sign of intellectual profundity. Nevertheless, British officials never applied the *Gita*'s precepts to their lives. Even when many were becoming inured to the suffering of the presumably fatalistic Indians, they treasured the rewards of monetary accumulation. In fact, they developed a science for their own joyous pursuit of worldly wealth: political economy.

ACCUMULATE GLOBALLY, EXPLOIT LOCALLY

At the time the East India Company was patronizing the translations of *Manu* and the *Gita*, it was also presiding over the rise of political economy. This science emerged during a period of widespread revolt and repression in Britain. From 1790 to 1820, from the London Corresponding Society to the Cato Street Conspiracy, there was a popular alternative analysis of wealth which the political economists were attacking, even while they allowed little of this battle to appear amid their abstract formulations. It was also a science that emerged at the time of a rapid expansion of the British Empire throughout the world, especially in India. Between 1790 and 1820, the East India Company claimed through conquest the bulk of the Indian subcontinent. Thus, it is not a coincidence that two of the most oustanding promoters of political economy in its earliest phase (Malthus and James Mill) were employees of the East India Company.

In the postfamine rush for reform, the East India Company turned to three political economists to write studies of Bengal's economy. Political economy owed its earliest formulations to Scottish Enlightenment thinkers and the

French Physiocrats, and, not unexpectedly, the men hired by the company were all Scotsmen. Alexander Dow, a Scotsman in Bengal who corresponded with David Hume and Lord Mansfield, wrote *An Enquiry into the State of Bengal, with a Plan for Restoring that Kingdom to its Former Prosperity and Splendour* (1772). Henry Patullo, a Scotsman settled in France and affiliated with the Physiocrats, wrote *An Essay upon the Cultivation of the Lands, and Improvement of the Revenues of Bengal* (1772). Europe's most prominent political economist at the time, Sir James Steuart, was commissioned to write a study titled *The Principles of Money Applied to the Present State of the Coin in Bengal* (1772).

The assumption behind these books (and the Scottish Enlightenment's political economy) was that civilization depended on the commodification of natural wealth. Steuart explained how the company could create a "civilized" coinage in Bengal and put an end to the traditional monetary "barbarism." Money, he argued, was the basis of civilization and had to be managed by "statesmen" according to "the invariable principles which regulate all money and coin" (1772: 7). In sum, civilizing India meant increasing the power of money over the society, as well as privatizing land tenure.

The work of Dow and Patullo on the land revenue system contributed to the framing of the Permanent Settlement of 1793, which aimed to promote an Indian class of agrarian-based profit maximizers by fixing the amount of the land tax in perpetuity. (The landlords—it was argued—would then have the incentive to invest in agriculture since the profit would accrue to them and not to government [R. Guha, 1981].)

One of the better enunciations of the strategy behind the Permanent Settlement came from Henry Thomas Colebrooke, who, while pursuing Sanskrit studies, wrote *Remarks on the Husbandry and Internal Commerce of Bengal* (published in 1804), in which he analyzed the eighteenth-century Bengali agrarian world that so enriched the East India Company. Placed beside Colebrooke's other works on the Hindu laws of inheritance, this work shows how Indology and political economy were products of the same mind.

The book is a model work of political economy. Colebrooke's careful attention to empirical detail is unsurpassed in any eighteenth-century English text on Bengal. He studied the social division of labor and concluded that it was insufficiently specialized: "No apology can be offered for the peasants indifferently quitting the plough to use the loom and the loom to resume the plough" (11). He calculated the productivity of the land for various crops, the wage rates for agricultural laborers, and the rental income of the landowners. He also measured the daily diet of an average family of five: 2.5 ounces of salt, 2 pounds of split pulse, and 8 pounds of rice. He believed the prospects for marketing Bengal's agricultural produce in the world market were excellent since Bengali labor appeared to be even cheaper than slave labor in the West Indies: the Bengalis lived on "the simplest diet and most scanty clothing" and resided in "straw huts" (128). He noted that the Bengalis could be rendered even more productive if scarcity was created, so that a work ethic could be instilled in the people. At present, he complained, "a subsistence may be earned without the uninterrupted application of industry" (26).

Finally, following the lesson of the Physiocrats and the Scottish Enlightenment thinkers (McNally, 1988) and their prescriptions for the development of agrarian capitalism, he recommended expropriating the agricultural population ("the assemblage of peasants in villages, their small farms, and the want of enclosures, bar all great improvements in husbandry" (1804: 11) and promoting the creation of a class of profit-maximizers, in conformity with what became the company's solution for the civilization of Bengal (1804: 49).

The East India Company's contribution to the development of political economy can also be seen in its decision, in 1805, to entrust the instruction of its future civil servants to T. R. Malthus, whose appointment represented the first ever professorship in political economy. (Adam Smith was a professor of moral philosophy, and Steuart was a landowner.)

At Haileybury, the East India Company's college, Malthus played Krishna to his teenage students. We can imagine him pointing a stern hand at the poor of Europe and India and instructing future civil servants as to their duties toward accumulation. The starvation of the poor was nature's retribution for their overbreeding, their *karma*, as it were, and the company's officials were not to question or interfere with the operations of such a divinely sanctioned free market. "Look to your own duty, do not tremble before it," Malthus could have said, had he read the *Gita* (*The Bhagavad Gita*, Miller, 1986: 34).

Malthus frequently consulted with two other famous political economists: James Mill and David Ricardo. The three of them, despite some intellectual disagreements, were the best of friends, and maintained a regular and large correspondence in between their frequent meetings. Malthus, Mill, and Ricardo were (after the dual enlightenments in Scotland and France) the primary creators of political economy as the main science of capitalist power.

James Mill applied the lesson of the Scottish Enlightenment to the study of India. The result was the publication of six volumes of *The History of British India* on which he labored for twelve years (1806–1817). His decision to write on India was determined by his expectation that of all possible literary projects, one on India would reap the greatest profit. Ultimately, most of the profit from the book went to the publisher, but the company made it a standard textbook in Haileybury and its colleges in India. In addition, it appointed Mill to the well-paying post of "assistant to the examiner of India correspondence" in 1819. He worked his way up to the post of the head examiner in 1830 where he remained until his death in 1836.

To compose *The History of British India*, Mill fused the information from Orientalists such as Jones and Colebrooke with the tenets of political economy. He considered the book a study of human nature; his task was to understand "the whole field of human nature" and then analyze how the general principles are modified by India's particular circumstances (1966: 384). This was the approach taken by the Scottish theorists with whom he studied in Edinburgh. He wrote to Ricardo that his history of India "would make no bad introduction to the study of civil society" (Ricardo, 1952, vol. viii: 195). What defined civil society and human nature was the propensity to exchange commodities. Here Mill found the Indians lacking: "that ever the people of Hindustan were profusely supplied with commodities, every thing in their manners, habits, government, and history concur to disprove" (1975: 244).

The centuries of "priestcraft and despotism" which Jones had decried as the product of the "manners and morals" of Indians conspired, in Mill's view, to restrict the civilizing influence of commodity exchange and private property. For Mill, there was no greater proof of a "barbarous" civilization than the "violent desire of exhibiting precious metals," rather than using them as monetary mediums (1975: 244). Armed with Indology's version of Indian tradition and the tenets of political economy, Mill ranked "Hindus" very low on the evolutionary "scale of civilization" (1975: 244, 225).

The position in the company with which Mill was rewarded for the book was quite powerful. He wrote to a friend that his work involved him in "the very essence of the internal government of 60 millions of people" (quoted in Stokes, 1959: 48). Among his more important tasks was land revenue policy. Defining rent as the cultivator's surplus or "net produce" (that which was left over after the cultivator covered the costs of production and earned an average rate of profit), he argued that, whatever the productivity of the land, the state took only the superfluous product, that which remained after the cultivators had recouped their costs and pocketed a reasonable profit. This was "the most fortunate of circumstances that can occur in any country [Mill argued] because in consequence of this the wants of the state are supplied really and truly without taxation" (quoted in Stokes, 1959: 91).

However inaccurate Mills's theory of the company's revenue as "net produce," it did serve, like Indology's theories of tradition, as a guiding ideal. Many officials endeavored to gather the necessary data for determining the net produce: that is, the productivity of the land, the market value of the produce, the costs of production, and the average rate of profit.

The tradition of the triumvirate's theories of rent and political economy was continued by James Mill's son, John Stuart Mill, who was also a company employee. J. S. Mill, who worked in the company's examiner's office for thirty-five years (1823–58), is known for his philosophical and economic treatises, but most of his writing was devoted to memorandums on Indian affairs. In the course of his career, he wrote 1,713 dispatches to India which annually filled two bound volumes (J. S. Mill, 1990: Appendix A). His dispatches concerned the company's relations with the "native princely states" and other Asian governments. He recommended, as a policy guideline, that the company officials work through precedent and tradition in order to ensure political stability; nevertheless, he also viewed Indian civilization as an example of barbarism since for centuries it had restricted the sway of capital. Mill, however, blamed the poverty of India not only on its indifference to commodity trading (as his father had) but also on its lack of a will to save. He compared the disparity between India and Britain to that between the grasshopper and the ant in Aesop's fable (which at the time was very popular among British colonialists). The grasshopper squandered while the ant wisely planned for the future. Saving was for Mill the dividing element between a civilized society and a barbaric one. Liberty, he claimed in his famous text, is possible only for members of a "civilized community" while despotism, such as the company's government in India, was "a legitimate mode of government in dealing with barbarians, provided the end be their improvement and the means justified by actually effecting that end" (J. S. Mill, 1988: 10). Thus, a society could be entitled to freedom only upon the condition of possessing capital, and that capital conferred upon the society the right to rule over barbarians.

Mill's lesson on India's barbarism served to form popular perceptions of India at a time when the "laboring classes" were becoming literate and demanded entry into parliamentary politics (J. S. Mill, 1965: 756). Mill wished to teach the British people the necessity of capitalist production, and the necessity therefore of bringing backward areas of the world under capital's civilizing influence. His efforts, however, were frustrated by an unexpected turn of events. A mass rebellion in north India in 1857 nearly overthrew the company's rule. Soldiers, landowners, tenants, religious divines—a wide variety of people—organized armed assaults on everything and everyone British. For Mill, the uprising was a bid to restore India's barbarous conditions. He wrote the company's petition and memorandum to the British Parliament in 1858 that pleaded for the continuance of the company's rule (East India Company, 1858). "I was the chief manager of the resistance which the Company made to their own political extinction," he wrote in his autobiography (1960: 169). He tried to prove that the company had improved India and bore no blame for the revolt. He invoked the notion of "net produce" to present the company's revenue as having been of no burden for Indians (East India Company, 1858: 20). But the Parliament was intent on abolishing the company now perceived as an unreliable manager, and in 1858, India was placed directly under the control of the British government. Mill, after losing his job, turned to writing *On Liberty*.

NATIONALIST APPROPRIATIONS AND REVERSALS

The beneficiaries of the Permanent Settlement in eastern India, the landed gentry, had not supported the 1857 revolt. Over the preceding half century, they had become avid students and able practitioners of both political economy and

Orientalism. They were committed to learning from the British and were hardly prepared for revolting against them. The Bengali elite had not fulfilled the "improving landlord" role that the company had assigned them. They were unable to establish their absolute private rights over the land, expropriate the peasantry, and introduce technological improvements on a mass scale. However, even when many landlords remained rentiers, they were highly interested in political economy and such issues as agrarian productivity, technology, and the profits of enterprises (see Mukherjee, 1975). What became known as the "Bengal Renaissance" centered on a group of families who owned Bengal's major land holdings and business houses. Members of these families were behind nearly all of Calcutta's civic institutions in the first half of the nineteenth century: the Hindu School (1816), the Landholders Society (1838), and the British India Association (1851). Some were officials of the Asiatic Society of Bengal which began to accept Indian members, after forty-five years as an exclusively British organization, in 1829. The milieu of these elite Bengali Hindu families was one of close collaboration, and even friendship, with company officials, for both groups engaged in commercial enterprise and debates over Indian civilization, which both identified with the Hindu tradition. The Bengal Renaissance was in fact largely a Hindu Renaissance. By the mid- to late nineteenth century, "hardly any Bengali Hindu leader, writer or publicist" remained "untouched by this preoccupation with Hindu glory" (Raychaudhuri, 1988: xii). For the Bengali *bhadralok* (civilized people), a "burgeoning pride in the inherited culture co-existed easily with a total acceptance of colonial rule" (Raychaudhuri: 2). One of the leading Bengali writers of the latter half of the nineteenth century, Bankim Chandra Chatterjee, wrote of a "natural law": "When a relatively uncivilized nation comes into contact with a more civilized one, through this 'second channel' civilization comes forward very rapidly. There the social dynamics are such that the relatively less civilized race sets out to imitate the more civilized one in all its aspects" (Bagchi, 1991: 157).

In the post–1857 revolt period of increasing taxation, expatriation of wealth, famine, and racial discrimination, a sense of disillusionment gradually began to dampen this enthusiasm for imitating the "higher civilization." In the aftermath of the revolt, many more British officials, soldiers, and businessmen were also introduced into India to replace and supervise the Indians who were increasingly seen as unreliable and dangerous, and colonial racism became more open and institutionalized. Also, the economic exploitation of the country was intensified (Sarkar, 1983: ch. 2).

Despite these developments, many English-educated Indians still maintained a basic faith in the civility of the British, but desired to see their power tempered by greater Indian involvement in the government. Western Civilization began to be seen as schizophrenic, representing beauty, freedom, and truth, while at the same time promoting greed, murder, and racial chauvinism.

The early Indian nationalists argued against colonial power while relying on the same principles of political economy and Orientalism which they had learned from the British. Political economy was used to denounce the drain of wealth from India, and Orientalism was used to prove the greatness of the indigenous civilization and demonstrate their preparedness to assume greater powers within the government.

The first writer to document the drain of wealth from India was Dada Bhai Naoroji who wrote a detailed statistical account of India's economy in 1876. He calculated the amount of Britain's profit from India to be 500 million pounds and, reversing the colonial perspective, he asked: What if England were drained in the manner India was?

R. C. Dutt, one of the handful of Indian members of the Indian Civil Service, continued Naoroji's arguments during the famine of 1896–1900, insisting that the British be consistent and apply to India their own political and economic precepts (Dutt, 1900).

Naoroji and Dutt's use of the colonizers' teachings for a critique of colonial rule was also applied to Indology. While the British of the late eighteenth to early nineteenth centuries prided themselves on restoring India to its glorious ancient past, the British of the late nineteenth century were invoking that same past as proof of the country's barbarism and the need for continued colonial rule. The early nationalists set out to disprove India's alleged barbaric nature and to demonstrate that they were civilized enough to merit greater responsibility. To adduce such proof, the "educated Indians" usually resorted to the idea of Hindu civilization. Dutt is best known for his economic studies, but he also devoted much time to writing volumes on ancient Indian history and translating the Sanskrit epics into English. Like many other Bengali intellectuals of the latter half of the nineteenth century, he was as a scholar of Indian history nearly indistinguishable from the earlier generation of British Indologists. In several of his writings, he extolled the work of Jones and Colebrooke, and, in 1900, in the midst of writing about the famine, he delivered a eulogy on the death of the German Indologist Max Müller. He exhorted fellow Indians to build up a national pride in their past and to "demand under the British rule a larger share in the administration of our own concerns." This was the "political creed of educated Indians" (Dutt, 1986, part II: 154).

Around the same time, M. K. Gandhi and a group of militant Bengali anticolonialists endorsed the *Gita* as a central text of Indian civilization. Gandhi first read the *Gita* in London, in English translation, at the prompting of British friends, although he had previously learned some verses from his father (Gandhi, 1957: 67). Gandhi valorized the *Gita* even further than the Indologists had; he made it the supreme text of his life: "[it] contains for me all knowledge," he declared (Gandhi, 1960: 73). However, he reversed the Indologists' interpretation of it as a fatalistic text, arguing that its injunctions on duty called for unremitting service to others and political activism against colonial rule.

A nationalist politics was necessary to counter Britain's arrogance, but the problem was defining the national culture in which to take pride. The elaboration of separate Hindu and Muslim civilizations over the first half of the nineteenth century inhibited the ability to define the newly conceived Indian nation as anything but a combination of two distinct elements. The long association of Hindus and Muslims, in villages and towns throughout the country, and the need for unity against a common imperial power hardly allowed anyone to think of Hindus and Muslims as two separate nations. Moreover, the class, caste, linguistic, and ethnic divisions within both groups made it difficult for them to be considered any more unified than an Indian nationality. Yet the elaboration of distinct Hindu and Muslim civilizations over the previous decades was a legacy difficult to renegotiate. R. C. Dutt's own trajectory is indicative in this respect. Dutt wrote four historical novels in Bengali over the 1870s which glorified an ancient Hindu past and mourned its passing (Chandra, 1993: 17). But by the turn of the century he had ceased to idealize a Hindu past. Bankim Chandra Chatterjee, one of the leading Bengali writers of the mid- to late nineteenth century, imagined the redemption of the Indian nation from the humiliation of colonialism as a matter of Hindu empowerment. Yet, despite the sometimes strident anti-Muslim tone of his revivalism, Bankim Chandra Chatterjee refrained from endorsing a Hindu resurgence. For all the early nationalists, there was a deep ambiguity as to how the Hindu-Muslim identities should be incorporated into an Indian national movement.

The Indian National Congress (INC), launched in 1885, vigorously campaigned for Hindu-Muslim unity but in its early years was constrained to functioning as a de facto Hindu body maintaining friendly relations with Muslim organizations. The principle that gained the greatest acceptance was that the Hindus and Muslims would work separately but in parallel; the paths were different, but the goals were the same.

This "composite patriotism" in which the Hindu and Muslim "shall best contribute to the common progress of the nation by developing his own special excellences," as Bipinchandra Pal said in 1903 (Sarkar, 1973: 423), appeared to be a workable solution to national unity. But the widespread Hindu-Muslim riots over the 1920s indicated to many nationalists that this organizing principle allowed chauvinist tendencies to grow on both sides. Instead of a welded national culture, they found themselves with a nation even further sundered. In response, some nationalists called for a pure nationalism, redefining India as a nation indifferent to any religious content, and motivated instead by the desire for economic betterment. Such was the view of Jawaharlal Nehru who, over the 1930s, tried to reconstitute the Congress party as a mass party based in the working class and peasantry. The advent of the Russian Revolution and the rise of European left movements also had a powerful impact on Indian nationalists, as many Indian students returned from their education in Europe with a first-hand familiarity with the European situation. Europe appeared as a living contradiction in the wake of the slaughter of World War I and the bitter civil violence that erupted in many countries between the capitalists and workers in its aftermath. It was obvious that there was no single Western Civilization from which to learn. In this context, the commitment of the earlier nationalists to political economy and Indology was abandoned. Marx and Lenin replaced John Stuart Mill as a source of inspiration for a critique of colonialism. Instead of Jones and Colebrooke being adduced to demonstrate India's great civilization, the past was both denounced as feudalistic and rewritten to reveal the antinomian forces at work.

The leftist tendency inside and outside of the INC was largely responsible for transforming the national movement into an organized mass movement, which brought in workers and peasants, both Muslim and Hindu, and presented Britain with its most potent challenge. But Hindu and Muslim chauvinist organizations retained enough strength to foil any unity. Thus, when independence was gained, it came at the cost of a partition of the country. In the ruthless "transfer of populations" between the newly created "homeland for India's Muslims," Pakistan, and the secularly defined India, millions of people were uprooted and many killed. It was an independence that appeared to confirm Indology's old shibboleths on the incompatibility between the authentic, indigenous Hindu civilization and the foreign Muslim civilization. The many people who had worked to disprove such shibboleths were overwhelmed in a carnage instigated by an elite that wished to achieve decolonization without radical social change, an elite that more easily contemplated an internal slaughter as the cost for a quick negotiated settlement with the colonial power than a unified mass movement capable of seizing independence. The British left safely while the Indians were engulfed in terror.

MANU IN CHICAGO

Decolonization in India coincided with the rise of the United States as the world's leading power. The goal of U.S. planners with regard to the newly independent nations of the Third World was the expansion of capitalist relations under the aegis of indigenous bourgeoisies who would cooperate with U.S.-controlled multinational banks and corporations. The key question for the planners, then, was whether these indigenous elites could be simultaneously traditional and modern—that is, whether they could maintain ideological and political legitimacy in the eyes of their people while collaborating with Western capitalists. It was in this context that the universities' area studies departments and government offices of post–World War II United States continued many of the intellectual traditions of colonialism but adapted their meaning to a new era of Third World nationalism.

The University of Chicago was the first center for the elaboration of tradition versus modernity analyses, and it quickly became the leading U.S. center for Indian studies. Its scholars were uniquely equipped for the work since they had experimented with the tradition versus modernity logic in the home laboratory offered by the Native American reservations, like that of the Hopi in America's Southwest. In the 1950s, the University of Chicago became the center of "civilization studies," and nearly all its scholars were preoccupied with one question: How could a society be further opened to capitalist development without experiencing widespread resistance? Their answer was that its cultural values had to be redefined in such a way as to make change appear in conformity with tradition. This meant that the material losses due to capitalist development would have to be compensated by support for traditional rituals and spiritual beliefs. Thus, Robert Redfield, the University of Chicago's leading guru for the social sciences, wrote in 1954 that "the progressive spirit of Asia and Africa is not simply a decision to walk the road of progressive convictions that we have traversed, but rather . . . an effort of the so-called backward peoples to recover from their disruptive encounters with the West by returning to the 'sacred centers' of the ancient indigenous civilization" (Redfield, 1962: 350).

Redfield initiated and designed a mini-industry for the production of civilization analyses: the Comparative Civilizations Project which lasted from 1951 to 1961 (Davis, 1985: 29–40). Chicago professors from different departments and regional specializations were drawn together and asked to define and compare the world's "Great Civilizations": the West, Islam, and India. William McNeill presented the new summa on Western Civilization, *The Rise of the West: A History of the Human Community* (1963), while Marshall Hodgson authored its equivalent for Islam, the massive three-volume set, *The Venture of Islam: Conscience and History in a World Civilization* (1974). Still on Islam, Chicago sponsored Gustav von Grunebaum's edited volume *Unity and Variety in Muslim Civilization* (1955). Robert Redfield and Milton Singer (co-director of the Project) wrote a number of articles on Indian civilization in the 1950s. Singer compiled a collection of his writings in *When a Great Tradition Modernizes: An Anthropological Approach to Indian Civilization* (1972). In all four books, the central questions were those of "modernization," a term which in the 1950s began to be used as synonymous with "civilization." How did the West modernize while other great civilizations remained traditional? What is the internal capacity of traditional civilizations to modernize?

Complementary to Redfield's project, the Committee for the Comparative Study of New Nations was begun at Chicago in 1959. The committee, in the words of its chairman Edward Shils, was designed to define "the tasks of the elites of the new states [i.e., decolonized Third World states]." U.S. capitalists were counting on them to develop "new economic institutions and techniques, and persuading or coercing the ordinary members of the society into their acceptance" (Shils, 1963: 2). The work of Hodgson and Singer helped define the cultural traditions of the new nations, traditions that would either have to be obliterated or manipulated in order for modernization to prevail. As another member of the committee, Clifford Geertz, wrote, "the new states are abnormally susceptible to serious disaffection based on primordial attachments [i.e., kinship, language, religion, ethnicity]" (Geertz, 1963b: 109). The masses, he assumed, were prone to backslide toward tradition; thus, it was the task of the elite to forge the nation and "restrain primordial enthusiasm." The best way for the Third World elite to fulfill its task was in conformity to Warren Hastings's old method—to rework traditional symbols, customs, "ways of thinking," so that they could serve to reinforce new property relations and entrepreneurial behavior.

Redfield turned his attention to India in the early 1950s after having worked throughout the 1930s and 1940s on Mexican villages. The problem in the Yucatan, in Redfield's view, was the existence of the communal landholding villages that were the legacy of Zapata and the Mexican Revolution. How could the communal land-holding villages be broken up so that profit-oriented farmers could control rural relations (Redfield, 1950)? Redfield discerned a similar problem with India's rural resistance to "progress" and found its solution in the nationalist-minded urban elite. They could lead the primitive rural world, clinging to age-old village communities, into the modern age of capitalism while retaining a cultural legitimacy with the people.

To succeed, the elite had first to ensure the vitality of the "sacred centers" to which the Indians, "disrupted" by economic change, would resort for solace and affirmation of their identity. Redfield's close collaborator, Milton Singer, went to India in 1954 in order to discover those centers. Singer was searching for anything sacred: sacred buildings, sacred rites, sacred dates, sacred specialists. For him, sacredness was ubiquitous and proof of the health of a 5,000-year-old "Sanskritic tradition" (Singer, 1972: ch. 4). Singer even thought that Indians' "worldly ambitions" were guided by an ancient Sanskrit text (the *Arthasastra*) (1972: xiii). But if Indian civilization was to be defined as an integrated whole, then Chicago's program could not rest content with studying only the literati. The task was to harmonize the "folk tradition" with that of the intellectual elite so that all castes and classes could be made to share the same civilization. The model that the Chicago anthropologists chose was that of "Sanskritization." The Indian anthropologist, M. N. Srinivas, had proposed this as a model of social mobility in a 1952 ethnography. The premise was that when the lower castes attempted to move up the social ladder by emulating the higher castes, they "Sanskritized" themselves. Conflict could arise over whether claims to a higher status were legitimate, but everyone was presumably fighting over a shared conception of social order and status identified with the brahmanical tradition. Srinivas's argument that social mobility through Sanskritization was the unifying connection between the lowest and the highest castes shaped Chicago's search for a fundamentally harmonious Indian civilization (Srinivas, 1952).

After his first trip to India, Singer began to argue that this "Great Tradition," despite its apparent superstition and irrationality, posed no obstacle to modernization. Singer had been enchanted by the fact that businessmen in Madras managed to turn a well-calculated profit while still singing love songs to Krishna in their spare time. Apparently, the ancient "Sanskritic tradition" was not incompatible with the Protestant ethic of work, private property, and entrepreneurialism. He found "modern industrialists and engineers and lawyers" who were able "to combine their Hinduism, or their traditional religious commitments and loyalties, with modernization" (1976: 263). In Redfield and Singer's model, these urbanites seemed well suited to engage with the rural world that purportedly followed a similar, though simpler, form of the same religious tradition.

By encouraging the continuation of the Hindu tradition, Chicago anthropologists seemed to accord a great deal of cultural respect to it. Redfield advised his students "to stimulate investigations which would not impose upon primitive societies our analytical categories" but would instead produce "the most other-centered ethnology of which we can conceive" (quoted in Stocking, 1979: 35). This was the same approach taken by Edward Sapir (also at Chicago) and Benjamin Whorf in their studies of American Indians. The idea was to submerge one's self in the mental sea of the exotic other and then return to the shores of Western Civilization to convey the foreignness of the experience. But in attempting a nonethnocentric methodology, the Chicago anthropologists reinstated the Orientalist definition of Indian civilization as Hindu civilization, and produced a view of the Indian "other" that was so monological that it excluded all inconsistencies, counter tendencies, and historical changes. The "Indian," conceived of as a singular timeless essence, was accorded great respect, while the vast reality incompatible with their model of the "Hindu mind" was dismissed from consideration.

Chicago's search for the uniqueness and integrity of "Indian civilization" was pursued furthest by McKim Marriott. Like many other scholars engaged in postwar area studies, he was the product of the disgorging by the Office of Strategic Services of its intellectual cadre into the universities. During the war, Marriott had worked in India on Japanese codes. After the war, as an anthropology student at Chicago, he tried to decipher a "code" to Indian society, reminiscent of Jones's work on a "Code of Gentoo Laws." By now, Marriott has spent forty years inventing the authentic Indian consciousness and stressing its radical otherness to the West. His recent essay, "Constructing an Indian Ethnosociology" (1989), is a grand manifesto of this ultra-indigenous approach. If we are to write about Indian society, Marriott argues, we cannot use Western categories; rather, we have to comprehend Indian "perceptions and meanings" (1989: 4). Should we ask whether these "perceptions and meanings" encompass the material and objective aspects of Indian society, we would be informed that Indians themselves do not distinguish between the material and ideological realms, for they have no "non-material ideas" (1989: 2). They believe in *karma* where thoughts have material consequences. In Marriott's account, Indians are also unable to distinguish between the religious and the secular (because of the concept of *dharma*). Nor can they distinguish between the natural and the social; for them, what is social is natural, as Krishna says in the *Gita*. Nor do they ever think of equality between people, a thoroughly Western concept, since they maintain a caste (or *jati*) hierarchy.

One may ask how Marriott became an expert on the "semantic property-space in which Hindus conceptually and perceptually dwell" (whatever semantic property space hopes to mean) (1989: 22). It should not come as a surprise, after our excursion through late-eighteenth-century Bengal, to find that many of his citations are to the *Manu Dharmashastras* and the *Bhagavad Gita*. The texts authorized by the East India Company's officials as the keys for entry into "the Hindu mind," and thus into the "mind of India," are still considered canonic by some twentieth-century anthropologists. Nor are there any signs that this methodological approach to "Indian civilization" may soon lose its prestige. Given the present Indian government's economic austerity program as directed by the International Monetary Fund (widespread privatization of public resources, removal of subsidies on basic commodities, and slashing of social welfare spending) and the increasing power of a right-wing Hindu chauvinist movement claiming that India is a Hindu nation, it would appear that Malthus and Manu may still have a bright future.

REFERENCES

Ahmad, Aijaz. (1991). "Between Orientalism and Historicism: Anthropological Knowledge of India." *Studies in History* 7(1).
———. (1992). *In Theory: Classes, Nations, Literatures*. London: Verso.
Ambirajan, S. (1978). *Classical Political Economy and British Policy in India*. Cambridge: Cambridge University Press.
Archbold, W.A.J. (1926). *Outlines of Indian Constitutional History*. London: Curzon Press.
Bagchi, Jasodhara. (1991). "Shakespeare in Loin Clothes: English Literature and the Early Nationalist Consciousness in Bengal." In Svati Joshi, ed., *Rethinking English: Essays in Literature, Language, and History*. New Delhi: Trianka.
Banerjee, Sumanta. (1989). *The Parlour and the Street: Elite and Popular Culture in Nineteenth Century Bengal*. Calcutta: Seagull.
Cawnpore Riots Enquiry Report. (1931; 1976). Published as *The Roots of Communal Politics*, N. G. Barrier, ed. New Delhi: Arnold Heinemann.

Chandra, Sudhir. (1993). "Towards an Integrated Understanding of Early Indian Nationalism." In Alok Bhalla and Sudhir Chandra, *Indian Responses to Colonialism in the Nineteenth Century*. New Delhi: Sterling, p. 17.
Chaudhuri, K. N. (1981). "The English East India Company in the Seventeenth and Eighteenth Centuries: A Pre-Modern Multinational Organization." In L. Bluss and F. Gaastra, eds, *Companies and Trade*. Leiden: Leiden University Press.
Colebrooke, Henry Thomas. (1804; reprinted edition 1806). *Remarks on the Husbandry and Internal Commerce of Bengal*. London: Blacks and Parry.
———. (1844; reprint 1984). *Dayabhaga and Mitaksara: Two Treatises on the Hindu Law of Inheritance*. Delhi: Parimal Publishers.
Davis, Richard. (1985). *South Asia at Chicago: A History*. Chicago: Committee on South Asian Studies.
Doniger, Wendy, trans. (1991). *The Laws of Manu*. London: Penguin Books.
Dumont, Louis. (1970; 1966). *Homo Hierarchicus: The Caste System and Its Implications*. George Weidenfeld, trans. London: G. Weidenfeld and Nicolson, Ltd. Chicago: Chicago University Press.
Dutt, R. C. (1986). *Letters to Curzon*. Delhi, reprint.
———. (1900). *Famines and Land Assessments in India*. London: Kegan Paul, Trench, and Trubner.
East India Company (written by John Stuart Mill). (1858). *Memorandum of the Improvements in the Administration of India During the Last Thirty Years and the Petition of the East India Company to Parliament*. London: Box and Wyman.
Gandhi, M. K. (1957). *An Autobiography: The Story of My Experiments with Truth*. Boston: Beacon Press.
———. (1960). *Discourses on the Gita*. Ahmedabad: Navajivan Publishing House.
Geertz, Clifford. (1963a). *Agricultural Involution: The Processes of Ecological Change in Indonesia*. Berkeley: University of California Press.
———. (1963b). *Old Societies and New States: The Quest for Modernity in Asia and Africa*. New York: Free Press.
———. (1973). *The Interpretation of Cultures*. New York: Basic Books.
Gohain, Hiren. (1991). *The Idea of Popular Culture in the Early Nineteenth Century Bengal*. Calcutta: K. P. Bagchi.
Grunebaum, Gustav Edmund von, ed. (1955). *Unity and Variety in Muslim Civilization*. Chicago: University of Chicago Press.
Guha, Ranajit. (1981; first published 1963). *A Rule of Property for Bengal: An Essay on the Idea of Permanent Settlement*. Delhi: Orient Longmans.
Henderson, James P. (1983). "The Oral Tradition in British Economics: Influential Economists in the Political Economy Club of London." *History of Political Economy* 15: 2.
Hodgson, Marshall G. S. (1974). *The Venture of Islam: Conscience and History in a World Civilization*. Chicago: Chicago University Press.
Hunter, W. W. (1897). *Annals of Rural Bengal*. London: Smith, Elder and Co.
Inden, Ronald. (1986). "Orientalist Constructions of India." *Modern Asian Studies* 20: 3.
———. (1990). *Imagining India*. Oxford: Basil Blackwell.
Jones, Sir William. (1780). *An Inquiry into the Legal Mode of Suppressing Riots, with a Constitutional Plan of Future Defense*. London.
———. (1825). *Institutes of Hindu Law, or the Ordinances of Manu*. London.

———. (1970). *The Letters of Sir William Jones*, two volumes, Garland Cannon, ed. Oxford: Clarendon Press.
Kejariwal, O. P. (1988). *The Asiatic Society of Bengal and the Discovery of India's Past 1784–1838*. Delhi: Oxford University Press.
Kopf, David. (1969). *British Orientalism and the Bengal Renaissance: The Dynamics of Indian Modernization 1773–1830*. Berkeley: University of California Press.
———. (1980). "Hermeneutics versus History." *Journal of Asian Studies* 34: 3.
Kosambi, D. D. (1962). "Combined Methods in Indology." *Indo-Iranian Journal* 6: 177–202.
McNally, David. (1988). *Political Economy and the Rise of Capitalism: A Reinterpretation*. Berkeley: University of California Press.
McNeill, William Hardy. (1963). *The Rise of the West: A History of the Human Community*. Chicago: Chicago University Press.
Majeed, J. (1990). "James Mill's 'The History of British India' and Utilitarianism as a Rhetoric of Reform." *Modern Asian Studies* 24: 2.
Malthus, Robert Thomas. (1970). *The Pamphlets of Thomas Robert Malthus*. New York: A. M. Kelley.
———. (1982; first published 1798). *An Essay on the Principle of Population*. London: J. M. Dent.
Marriott, McKim. (1989). "Constructing an Indian Ethnosociology." *Contributions to Indian Sociology* 23: 1.
Marshall, Alfred. (1926). *Official Papers by Alfred Marshall*. London: Macmillan.
Marshall, P. J., ed. (1970). *The British Discovery of Hinduism in the Eighteenth Century*. Cambridge: Cambridge University Press.
Marx, Karl. (1959). *Capital*, Vol. 3. Moscow: Progress Publishers.
———. (1968). *Theories of Surplus Value*, Vol. 2. Moscow: Progress Publishers.
———. (1970). *A Contribution to a Critique of Political Economy*. Moscow: Progress Publishers.
———. (1975). *Selected Correspondence*. Moscow: Progress Publishers.
Mill, James. (1844). *Elements of Political Economy*. London: Henry G. Bohn.
———. (1966). *Selected Economic Writings*, Donald Winch, ed. Chicago: University of Chicago Press.
———. (1975; first published 1818). *The History of British India*, abridged by William Thomas. Chicago: University of Chicago Press.
Mill, John Stuart. (1960). *Autobiography*. New York: Columbia University Press.
———. (1965; first published 1848). *Principles of Political Economy with Some of Their Applications to Social Philosophy*. New York: A. M. Kelley.
———. (1988). *On Liberty*, Elizabeth Rapaport, ed. Indianapolis, Ind.: Hacket Publishing.
———. (1990). *Collected Works*, Vol. XXX: *Writings on India*, John Robson, Martin Moir, and Zawahir Moir, eds. Toronto: University of Toronto Press.
Miller, Barbara, trans. (1986). *The Bhagavad-Gita*. New York: Bantam.
Mukherjee, Nilmani. (1975). *A Bengal Zamindar, Jayakrishna Mukherjee, of Uttarpara and His Times, 1808–1888*. Calcutta: Firma K. L. Mukhopadhyay.
Mukherjee, S. N. (1987). *Sir William Jones: A Study in Eighteenth Century Attitudes to India*. Bombay: Orient Longman.

Naoroji, Dada Bhai. (1901). *Poverty and Un-British Rule in India*. Delhi: Low Price Publications.

Pandey, Gyanendra. (1990). *The Construction of Communalism in Colonial North India*. Oxford: Oxford University Press.

Raychaudhuri, Tapan. (1988). *Europe Reconsidered: Perceptions of the West in Nineteenth Century Bengal*. Delhi: Oxford University Press.

Redfield, Robert. (1950). *A Village That Chose Progress: Chan Kom Revisited*. Chicago: University of Chicago Press.

———. (1962). *Human Nature and the Study of Society: The Papers of Robert Redfield*, Margaret Redfield, ed. Chicago: University of Chicago Press.

Ricardo, David. (1951). *The Principles of Political Economy and Taxation*, Vol. 1.

———. (1952). *Letters, 1816–1818*, Vol. 8.

———. (1951–55). *The Works and Correspondence of David Ricardo*, 10 volumes, Piero Sraffa, ed. Cambridge: Cambridge University Press.

Rocher, Rosane. (1983). *Orientalism, Poetry, and the Milennium: The Checkered Life of Nathaniel Brassey Halhead, 1751–1830*. Delhi: Motilal Banarsidass.

Said, Edward. (1978). *Orientalism*. New York: Vintage.

———. (1985). "Orientalism Reconsidered." *Race and Class* 27: 2.

———. (1989). "Representing the Colonized: Anthropology's Interlocuters." *Critical Inquiry* 15: 205–25.

———. (1993). *Culture and Imperialism*. New York: Alfred A. Knopf.

Sarkar, Sumit. (1973). *The Swadeshi Movement in Bengal, 1903–1908*. New Delhi.

———. (1983). *Modern India, 1885–1947*. New Delhi: Macmillan.

Sen, Asok. (1977). *Iswar Chandra Vidyasagar and His Elusive Milestones*. Calcutta: Riddhi-India.

Shils, Edward. (1961). *The Intellectual Between Tradition and Modernity: The Indian Situation*. The Hague: Mouton.

———. (1963). "On the Comparative Study of the New States." In Clifford Geertz, ed., *Old Societies and New States: The Quest for Modernity in Asia and Africa*. New York: Free Press.

Singer, Milton. (1972). *When a Great Tradition Modernizes: An Anthropological Approach to Indian Civilization*. Chicago: University of Chicago Press.

———. (1976). "Religion and Traditional Values in Relation to Modernization." *Asian Thought and Society* 1: 3.

Srinivas, M. N. (1952). *Religion and Society among the Coorgs of South India*. Bombay: Asia Publishing House.

Steuart, Sir James. (1772; 1805). *The Works, Political, Metaphysical and Chronological, of the Late Sir James Steuart*, Vol. V: *The Principles of Money Applied to the Present State of the Coin in Bengal*. London: T. Cadell and W. Davies.

Stocking, George. (1979). *Anthropology at Chicago: Tradition, Discipline, Department*. Chicago: University of Chicago.

Stokes, Eric. (1959). *The English Utilitarians and India*. Oxford: Clarendon Press.

Tagore, Rabindranath. (1992; first published 1917). *Nationalism*. Calcutta: Rupa.

Thapar, Romila. (1983). "Syndicated Moksha." *Seminar* (September).

———. (1987). "Cultural Transaction and Early India: Tradition and Patronage." *Social Scientist* 165: 3–31.

———. (1989a). "Imagined Religious Communities? Ancient History and the Modern Search for a Hindu Identity." *Modern Asian Studies* 23: 2.

———. (1989b). "Epic and History: Tradition, Dissent, and Politics in India." *Past and Present*, No. 125: 3–26.

Young, Robert. (1990). *White Mythologies: Writing History and the West*. London: Routledge.

7

African Languages and European Linguistic Imperialism

Alamin Mazrui

> The domination of a people's language by languages of the colonizing nations was crucial to the domination of the mental universe of the colonized.
>
> Ngugi wa Thiong'o 1986: 16

The ongoing debate on the implications of language for the decolonization process has its roots in the African colonial experience, whose formal beginning was the so-called Berlin conference of 1885. The conference was attended by the leading politicians of the major European nations for the purpose of negotiating the criteria for "carving up Africa" without provoking inter-European wars. At the end of the conference, the same nations descended on Africa and divided it up into previously nonexistent entities called "nation-states." The French and British took the lion's share of these territories, but other European governments—Germany, Italy, and Belgium—also benefited from the partition.

The introduction of a formal colonial presence in Africa did not simply mean the imposition of alien economic structures and political systems; colonialism had a cultural aspect as well. Probably the most significant cultural institution to be imposed on the African continent was the use of European languages, which moved to the center stage of African civil life, while African languages were relegated to the periphery. Although some African languages gained from colonialism (some African languages were written down, others were standardized, and still others were used in the print and, later, the electronic media), of the nearly 2,000 languages that existed on the continent, the large majority were completely marginalized.

Christian missionaries were at the forefront of devising colonial language policies, yet it was not foreign religions but foreign languages that came to have an enduring effect on African life. Today we do not refer to regions of Africa on the basis of the religions to be found there. Rarely is reference made to, for example, "Protestant Africa." By contrast, it has become normal to refer to Africa in terms of Western languages, for example, "anglophone," "francophone," "lusophone." This, if anything, demonstrates the extent of the influence of European languages on Africa.

But colonialism did not have an easy time in Africa. It was resisted from the very beginning, and in the late 1950s and early 1960s one African country after another attained its independence from colonial rule. The era of decolonization was a period of great hope for a progressive Africa. No sooner had the dust of anticolonialism settled, however, that Africans began to feel that something had gone wrong. Many claimed that the independence achieved was nominal at best and that colonialism, expelled from the front door by the African people, was being brought back through the back door by the embryonic African bourgeoisie. Thus, political activists and intellectuals began to call this period not "postcolonial Africa," but "neo-colonial Africa," in order to emphasize that colonialism was still there but in a new guise. Indeed, some European institutions spread faster in the neo-colonial period than in the colonial period. In some countries, for example, European languages began to be taught as early as kindergarden or nursery school.

The presence of neo-colonialism led many Africans to rededicate themselves to the cause of liberating Africa from Europe. It is in this context that within the last couple of decades, a neo-nationalist school of thought has emerged in Africa, which argues that the struggle against imperialism calls for cultural and mental decolonization. Specifically, advocates of this school argue that resistance against imperialism and social progress in the continent must be rooted in the decolonization of the African mind—that is, in the destruction of the seeds planted by colonialism in the African's cognitive apparatus. Emphasis has been placed on the need to revive African traditions, perhaps with a modern mold, in an attempt to dislodge prevailing cultural institutions that have a colonial foundation.

In this process of mental decolonization, language is seen as playing a crucial role. The replacement of European languages inherited from the colonial era with African languages that have an indigenous base is considered a necessary, if not sufficient, condition in the mental liberation of the African people. The linguistic philosophy of the neo-nationalist school is the focus of this essay. The central arguments of this school are reviewed critically in order to demonstrate that the promotion of African languages per se is neither a sufficient nor even a necessary condition in the decolonization process, and that African languages can be as instrumental in furthering the interests of colonialism as European languages are deemed to have been. The first step in support of this claim is to look at the theoretical foundation of the neo-nationalist claim and then to examine the historical relationship between language and the colonial experience in Africa.

THE SAPIR-WHORF HYPOTHESIS IN AFRICA

Although the cultural nationalists are not a homogeneous group, the largest and most influential cultural-nationalist tendency argues that the imposition of European languages was indispensable in the colonization of the African mind and that mental decolonization must involve the retrieval of indigenous African languages and their use in the most important aspects of African civil life. This conception has two sources, one theoretical and the other historical. The first source is what can be called the "relativist conception of language," which was associated with both Edward Sapir, a pioneer American linguist, and his student, Benjamin Lee Whorf, a fire insurance agent who in the 1930s became a major theorist of the relation between language and culture (cf. Sapir, 1949; Whorf, 1987).

Linguistic relativity is the view that language is a reservoir of culture, which means that the form and structure of one's language affects our perception and action in a culturally specific manner. Most disturbingly, it implies that there is a culturally bound "tyranny of language," for the grammatical and semantic structure of one's language—which most speakers acquire and use unconsciously—determines and limits one's ability to think or act. Edward Sapir argued that human beings are very much at the mercy of their society's linguistic medium of communication and that the social world is built on the language habits of the group. In his view, no two languages are sufficiently similar to be able to represent the same social reality.

Although Edward Sapir was quite interested in the relation between language, culture, and cognition, it was his student, Benjamin Lee Whorf, who was the strongest proponent of linguistic relativity. Whorf based his view on his perception of fundamental semantic and grammatical differences between European languages and Native American languages. He observed that European languages tend to objectify and reify emotions, abstractions, and psychological states. But in Hopi, the indigenous American language he studied most intensively, Whorf claimed, one cannot objectify abstract spiritual processes (Whorf, 1987: 134–59).

Whorf also claimed that European languages are based on a linear conception of time which dissects temporality into separate segments—"the Past," "the Present," and "the Future." He noted that time itself is objectified or "spatialized" in European languages. An English speaker says that people "lose time" as they lose money, "gain time" as they gain strength, and "waste time" as they waste a bar of soap in washing. But in the Hopi language, Whorf claimed, time had a circular character: one does not "lose" a Friday, if nothing was done on Friday, because Friday will return. These contrasting views of time, Whorf argued, had a major impact on the behavior of European language speakers and Native Americans which is clearly seen in their contrasting attitudes to work and planning (Whorf, 1987: 134–59). Whorf's followers extended his efforts by investigating these linguistic differences in other languages and cultures besides those of the Native Americans.

The Sapir-Whorf hypothesis had an influence on African cultural nationalists, who sought a cause-and-effect relationship between European languages and mental colonization and, conversely, between African languages and decolonization. One of the most prominent advocates of linguistic relativity is Ngugi wa Thiong'o, a distinguisted creative writer and a political activist. In *Decolonizing the Mind* (1986), Ngugi wa Thiong'o argues that the domination of a people's language by the language of the colonizing nation is central to the domination of the mental universe of the colonized. His claim can be seen as an application of the Sapir-Whorf hypothesis, although Sapir and Whorf and other linguistic relativists were interested in how different languages condition the worldviews of their respective native speakers. African cultural nationalists such as Ngugi wa Thiong'o made a cross-cultural leap by suggesting that the worldview inherent in any particular language can be transposed to speakers of other unrelated languages. It is supposedly in this way that the European worldview came to exercise its domination over the collective mind of the African people.

This cultural nationalist current might be the strongest in terms of adherents, but it is the weakest in terms of its theoretical argument. The Sapir-Whorf hypothesis or, equivalently, the theory of linguisitic relativity, which is presupposed by these cultural nationalists, has been invalidated by linguistic research. In modern American linguistics, there has been a search for language universals (i.e., common traits of all languages), spurred by the work of Noam Chomsky (cf. Chomsky, 1972). This quest has led to research of numerous languages throughout the world. As a result, a large amount of data has been accumulated that questions the notion of a one-to-one correlation between language and cultural perception. For example, some of the features that Whorf thought were peculiar to Native American languages and explained both their perception of the world and their behavior, have been found to exist in European languages.

In general, the overwhelming evidence presented so far in support of linguistic-cultural relativity has been at the lexical level. The general thrust of evidence has been of a contrastive nature between languages, and it has taken the following form. Language X has three terms, while language Y has only one or no equivalent term for phenomenon Z. But in virtually all such cases, it is not difficult to relate the linguistic contrasts to environmental differences. There are good reasons why, in terms of semantic nuances, Somalis should be more interested in camels and Maasai in cows than English speakers would be. Certainly, for those Somalis and Maasai who continue to live as pastoralists, such semantic nuances are of significant cultural value. But the effect that such lexical structures would have on a cosmopolitan Somali or Maasai is not easy to determine. It is reasonable to assume, however, that it would not be the same as the effect it would have on their more traditional compatriots despite the linguistic commonality.

Proponents of the Whorfian hypothesis, however, associate linguistic relativity not only with lexical differences between languages, but also with structural or grammatical aspects. In its crudest form, the argument at this level proposes a relationship between the structure of language and the structure of cultural behavior. Linguists sympathetic to the Whorfian hypothesis have so far found it an uphill task, however, to isolate the grammatical features that might be said to have specific cultural and, therefore, behavioral correlates. It is the empirical vacuousness of the Whorfian hypothesis that led Wallace Lambert to conclude, after some thirty years of research on the social importance of language, "I have come to question the very commonly held notion that culture and/or language really affects personality. I am inclined rather to the position that culture and language may affect styles of expression, but likely not basic personality dynamics. Similarly, I am not persuaded by the evidence available that language or culture have any real impact on thought" (Lambert, 1979: 186–87).

Thus, it is still not clear in what sense our indigenous languages, even if they are idealistically static enough to maintain the purity of "traditional" cultures in their expression, are supposed to spare us the onslaught of imperialist culture in psychosocial and material terms. The bulk of existing evidence would seem to demonstrate that, in its expression, language is largely influenced by material conditions, which forge specific perceptions of the world around us. Language might have some influence on perception, but language-engineering efforts in several parts of the world have shown that language's influence on perception can be counteracted. As material conditions change, and with them our perception of the world, so does language at its symbolic level. Thus, to expect that any African language, merely by virtue of its Africanness, can control social change and perception in a liberative sense, in the wake of rapid economic transformations, is to expect of it a role that is well beyond its potential.

LANGUAGE AND COLONIALISM

In what sense can language and language policy be said to have aided the colonization process in Africa, and where were the African languages situated in this colonial linguistic equation? The neo-nationalist school has argued that the marginalization of African languages and the promotion of European languages among the "natives" were necessary steps in the mental colonization of the African. Is this proposition historically tenable?

No doubt, a rather uniform feature of colonialism in Africa was its treatment of European languages as ideological institutions whose particular relationship with the African colonial subject could either consolidate or undermine the colonial status quo. But the colonial language policies themselves were not uniform. They often varied on the basis of two major considerations: first, that language was a reservoir of culture and a vehicle of cultural transmission; second, that language was a reservoir of knowledge and a transmitter of ideas including ideas that could serve subversive ends and instigate resistance against colonial rule.

Colonial language policies, then, had to confront a seemingly paradoxical situation. If the colonial language in its role as a cultural transmission belt could numb the consciousness of the colonized to a point of acquiescence to the colonial status quo, would not language as a bearer of knowledge imbue the African with a counter-consciousness dangerous to the very survival of colonialism? These two considerations were in the foreground of colonial language policies in Africa.

The French had great confidence in their language as a transmitter of French cultural values and were convinced that any subversive knowledge that the Africans might acquire in the process of being educated in the French language would be neutralized by the "potency" of French culture. French colonialism, therefore, sought its security in linguistic and cultural assimilationist policies. Thus, it is in French (and to some extent Portuguese) colonies that we find the clearest evidence supporting the neo-nationalist thesis that the imposition of European languages was an important cultural aid to colonialism.

While the French looked confidently at language as a transmitter of culture, the Germans' approach to their language stressed its potential to impart German knowledge. Assuming an increasingly aggressive role in European geopolitics which had world ramifications, and racing to outstrip other European nations in technological advancement, the Germans regarded their language, complemented by its leading philosophical tradition, as a custodian of the "German knowledge" which they wanted to monopolize. An exclusivist language policy, which would deny colonial subjects access to the German language, was therefore believed to serve the greater interest of German colonialism. This policy contributed to the consolidation of the Swahili language in German East Africa, later known as Tanganyika, or Tanzania (after Tanganyika's union with Zanzibar).

The British, on the other hand, tried, though inconsistently, to strike a balance between the two considerations. In many instances, under British rule, the Africans were allowed regulated access to the English language. This meant regulated acculturation on the one hand and regulated induction into spheres of Western knowledge on the other. Both processes were carried out in such a way as to enable the Africans to function in the institutions the British had introduced, while limiting their exposure to any kind of knowledge that might have subversive potential.

For both the Germans and the British, language also served to maintain social distance between the colonial administrator, or settler, and the "native." Europeans would insist on speaking to a "native" in an African language, even though their command of that language was far inferior to the African's proficiency in the respective European language. In this way, Africans were linguistically placed where they belonged, so to speak, in the mind of the colonizer.

Despite their variation, colonial language policies had common ideological foundations. Whether encouraging the acquisition of the European language by the colonized or promoting the use of African languages, all colonial language policies at this macro-level were intended to consolidate colonial rule.

European languages also promoted the political interest of colonialism at the micro-level—that is, at the level of the images their words were made to carry. For centuries, these languages have brutalized Africans with their racist supremacist images. Thus, these languages played a crucial role in the colonial attempt to force Africans to accept an inferior status and lose confidence in themselves as productive members of the human race. With words forged like truncheons, the Africans have been battered into submission, and there is no doubt that Europe's imperial classes have molded language into a weapon in their domination of peoples of other cultures. However, we should not overlook the fact that the language policies of the colonial era sometimes cut across both European and African languages in the service of colonialism.

None of the colonizers was monolithic with regard to the question of language and power. In many cases, internal differences arose among their own ranks. One example of divergent colonial interests, with respect to linguistic politics, is that of Belgian colonialism in the Congo. Here the conflict was between the francophone Belgians, who controlled the Congo and the metropole politically, and the Flemish Belgians, who served as missionaries and educators in the Congo. French Belgian authorities imposed French as the official language of the Congo, ensuring the exclusion of Flemish. On the other hand, Flemish Belgians, through their local control of the schools and the church, subverted French assimilationism in the colony—thus minimizing the French impact—and promoted indigenous African languages.

A second example of intracolonial language disputes is that of Anglo-Afrikaner colonialism in South Africa. If the Congo served as an example of Romanic-Germanic differences, South Africa is more a case of inter-Germanic rivalry. Using a language policy supposedly designed to keep Africans "African" and European power unchallenged, Afrikaner officialdom introduced the so-called Bantu education. Under this educational system, Afrikaners attempted to preclude the cultural "Westernization" of Africans by restricting them to an "African tongue." Thus the African was allowed access to Afrikaans only at a later stage in education; except at the university level, the English language was given a subsidiary role in education by the Afrikaner political authorities. Partly in response to the coercive administration of Bantu education, Africans rose in the Soweto protest of 1976 against Afrikaans, favoring English, the language of much wider communication in Africa.

A final example of linguistic intracolonial rivalry is that of British colonialism in Kenya. Here the British colonial language policy had to mediate between three colonial forces. A substantial section of Christian missionaries (the so-called Livingstonians), guided by the principle that spiritual communication with the Africans was best achieved within the context of their tribal milieu and medium, insisted on using indigenous languages in their proselytization and evangelical activities. Ironically, then, the maintenance and use of the languages of the African peoples was regarded as an essential ingredient of the Christianizing mission—the attempted capture of the African soul.

The second important colonial force in Kenya was the community of colonial administrators. Colonial administration saw its interests in African education as one of creating a substantial pool of local native officers capable of serving at low administrative levels. In this context, teaching to the Africans the English language, the Christian religion, and some other English norms was deemed necessary for efficient management of the administrative machinery. At the same time, the administrators felt that it was necessary to provide an education "suited" to the African condition and minimally disruptive of African cultures. This policy was regarded not only as an example of philanthropic colonialism, but also as a matter of colonial interest. Although colonial administrators raised some opposition to this view, it continued to influence British colonial policy in education, even if rather inconsistently.

British colonialism in Kenya also had to respond to the more aggressive interests of the British settlers, who saw the Africans as their only source of cheap plantation labor and therefore discouraged their Europeanization, lest they become too civilized to accept the roles of wage laborers. They also discouraged the maintenance of African cultures in their "localized" forms, lest they impede the cultural proletarianization of the peasants.

The colonial settler generally preferred the promotion of Swahili (a transethnic African *lingua franca*) to that of "tribal" languages, since a certain degree of cultural fusion by partial "detribalization" was regarded as an important step in creating a wage labor force.

What emerges from our discussion, then, is that while, throughout the colonial era, the European languages served the ends of colonialism, they did not necessarily do so through their imposition on the African peoples. In some cases, European languages were deemed to serve the colonial interests best by being made inaccessible to the Africans. In other instances, it was the use of African languages that furthered the ends of colonialism. The thesis of the neo-nationalist school, therefore, requires some major qualification. What about the situation in the postcolonial era, or what is sometimes referred to as the neo-colonial era?

LANGUAGE AND NEO-COLONIALISM

The decolonization school has again argued that in the neocolonial era

1. African governments have continued to pursue colonial policies that subordinate African languages to European languages;
2. while local African languages are the medium of the African masses, the African ruling class has become the beneficiary of European languages, seeing itself as an Afro-Saxon class of rulers;
3. through these European languages, the African ruling class and its "imperialist masters" abroad continue to impose a Western imperialist culture on the African people;
4. the African ruling class tries to keep people ignorant, thereby mystifying its power through the continued use of European languages which are inaccessible to the majority.

Let us take a critical look at these propositions.

The marginalization of African languages characteristic of the colonial era has continued to some degree throughout most of Africa. Few serious attempts have been made to accord African languages a more central social role. The African situation is characterized by an expanding use of English and French. Many African governments are introducing English at an earlier phase in the educational process than the British themselves favor.

Some African governments have attempted to formulate policies and programs that could reform this linguistic imbalance. Most impressive has been the case of Tanzania, which has adopted Swahili as its national and official language. In the educational sphere, Swahili has gradually replaced English as a medium of instruction. More modest efforts are also visible in a few other countries. Nonetheless, it is still true that the policies pursued in most parts of Africa have continued to relegate African languages and, therefore, large sectors of the population, to the periphery. Thus, there is much to support the neo-nationalist proposition that, by and large, the African language is the language of the formally uneducated African masses. For this reason, radical neo-nationalists in Africa have often insisted that the democratization of both knowledge and the political process will ultimately depend on the degree to which African governments adopt African languages in every sphere of national activity and development.

What about the equally popular neo-nationalist suggestion that European languages have become the languages of the African minority ruling classes in their respective nation-states? As in the colonial era, when European languages were associated with the European ruling classes, the African ruling classes are now considered the beneficiaries of this colonial linguistic heritage. Not surprisingly, the neo-nationalist call for a return to the linguistically indigenous is often coated in anticapitalist phraseology. There is a tendency to look at the indigenous languages of Africa as the media of the masses which, within the African neo-colonial capitalist framework, are pitted against the European languages, supposedly the trappings of the African bourgeoisie.

H.B.C. Capo offers a good example of this neo-nationalist stand. After emphasizing the necessity for an interdisciplinary approach to language planning in Africa, Capo goes on to argue that the process involves primarily political determination:

The main political determination is a commitment to the promotion of African languages to the status of official languages through an explicit language policy. The derived political determination is to devote the necessary amount of money to the project. The present Afro-Saxon and Afro-Romanic rulers will often refer to the huge amount of money involved to mask their true position. Their ruling power is built upon the knowledge of the so-called international languages and the success of their mystification is due to the exclusion of African languages. . . . It is, therefore, transparent that the Afro-Saxon and Afro-Romanic ruling minorities will not supply the means to implement such projects even though they may pay lip service to the adoption and promotion of national languages. (Capo, 1985: 17–18)

Capo's suggestion is clear. Not only has the ruling minority in Africa capitulated to the Anglo-Saxons and the Gauls in its linguistic and cultural expressions, but also it has done so in order to promote its class interests and the status quo. Following in the tradition of the Germans, the ruling minorities in Africa have been accused of making European languages, which are least accessible to the common person, the primary vehicles for transmitting knowledge. In this way, they can presumably thrive on the ignorance of the exploited classes concerning the source of their rulers' power. In other words, the linguistic policies favored by the African ruling minorities in pursuit of their interests have supposedly dispossessed the exploited classes of their fundamental right to know.

This proposition is true to some extent, but we must also appreciate its limitations. Undoubtedly, it is a class need of every ruling class, not just those of Africa, to mystify the source of its power by cultivating ignorance in the society it rules. It has become evident, however, that the bourgeoisie is in a predicament. Although it does need to maintain a certain level of ignorance in society, it also needs to "penetrate" and "capture" that same society, in its market form, in order to consolidate its power. And what better way is there of establishing a hold on the market than through its popular languages?

The result of this predicament has been an increasing shift from reliance on language per se as a means of social control to manipulation of information through language. Chris Searle gives a good picture of this development when he asks about Britain:

When our youth look at newspaper editorials, for example, do they see the brain killers who fit, as William Blake put it nearly two hundred years ago, "mind forg'd manacles" on to our people, the multi-national buyers and sellers of misinformation, lies, and trivia, those who distort language in ways previously unparalleled so that they can redefine the word "peace" by making it mean that our country is occupied by 111 U.S. military bases and installations so we are the first servile line of defense of imperialism. (Searle, 1983: 65)

In addition to manipulating information, a large section of the African ruling class often resorts to extralinguistic means (oppression and censorship) to control information. In many African nations, the mass media are constantly muffled, and school books are censored and screened. Freedom of speech has come to signify solitary confinement under dreaded prison conditions.

If the African bourgeoisie has a specific class interest in promoting popular languages to consolidate its hold on the local market, why has it continued to favor foreign languages that only a smaller fraction of the national population use and understand? This state of affairs is partly due to the peripheral status within the world capitalist order of the African bourgeoisie, who sometimes grudgingly but acquiescently finds its survival in an unequal symbiotic relationship with the imperial bourgeoisie.

As expected, then, in many African nations, it is the transnational corporations, transnational publishing houses, and other imperialist organizations that increasingly flirt with the possibility of promoting popular African cultures. For this same reason, perhaps, the study of foreign languages has received fresh impetus in a country like the United States. Penetration of foreign markets is seen as something that can be achieved most effectively, not by promoting English, but by equipping the new missionaries, the functionaries of transnational corporations, with foreign language skills. In the words of the chairman of the National Governors' Association, Gerald L. Baliles, Governor of Virginia, "How are we to sell our products in the global economy when we neglect to learn the languages of the customer? How are we to open overseas markets when other cultures are only dimly understood?" (*Chronicle of Higher Eduction*, March 1, 1989: A19).

The above considerations suggest that there is no a-priori reason to believe that the promotion of African languages is in any way opposed to the interests of the ruling classes or of imperialism.

Does this mean that the European languages in Africa cannot be identified with any particular class? The acquisition of European languages in much of Africa is by and large associated with the modern educational system that itself tends to separate the educated from the uneducated. Against this background, one could suggest that it is to the educated section of the middle class that European languages in much of Africa can be most consistently correlated.

But there is also strong evidence that European languages are quickly spreading beyond this class. Virtually every African country is experiencing the pangs of rising unemployment. Even university graduates are finding it increasingly difficult to get white-collar jobs for which they have supposedly been trained. Many students leave high school, joining the so-called informal economic sector and becoming hawkers of all types. In this way, the educated youth is slowly becoming the pioneer of English and other European languages within the ranks of the proletarian.

European languages are also stretching their branches upward as members of the middle class are gradually percolating upward—a much more traditional phenomenon—to become state technocrats. As this class or subclass grows numerically, it is bound to affect the linguistic equation, with European languages becoming more established at the ruling-class level. Thus, at the macro-level, European languages are gradually ceasing to have class undertones. They are gradually cutting across class lines to establish themselves as a kind of national linguistic norm.

This developing national norm need not be a European language. Pidgin in parts of West Africa, Swahili in East Africa, and Lingala in Zaire have established themselves as languages of wider communication. Nonetheless, in some cases, there seems to be little resistance from local-language users to the aggressive expansion of European languages. Would not a return to Africa's more indigenous languages spare the local population the pervasive entrapment of Western culture?

Culturally, the Africans have continued to be dislocated and imbued with an ethos that only serves the interests of imperialism. As a result, the emergent nationality of Afro-Saxons—those who are more articulate in, and feel more at home with European languages and mannerisms—seems to be steadily growing with new converts from other nationalities. But there is little evidence that neo-colonial language policies can be held responsible for the neo-colonial cultural characteristics in Africa. Certainly, the more glaring neo-colonial cultural attributes, which are so well depicted by many African novelists, defy such a reductionist linguistic explanation.

CONCLUSION

This essay has attempted, first, to demonstrate that, in championing the cause of African languages as a decolonizing strategy, the neo-nationalist school, in addition to being oblivious to the full range of the socioeconomic equation in Africa, has tended to simplify the relationship between language and culture and between language and knowledge. The situation presented in this discussion leads us to conclude that African languages per se are neither a sufficient nor a necessary tool in the decolonization of the African mind.

Second, this essay shows that African languages themselves are not completely innocent of the charge that they serve as linguistic instruments of colonial rule. The language policies of most religious missionaries in the colonial era, the practices of some colonial administrations, the linguistic thrust of economic missionaries of the neo-colonial era, the politics of language in the so-called Bantu education in apartheid South Africa—all contradict the view that African languages have some intrinsic decolonizing potential.

Third, while European languages in Africa served, and probably continue to serve, the interests of imperialism, in some cases they are known to have aided the anti-imperialist struggle. These are cases in which the colonized managed to transmute the language of the colonizers and use it to their advantage. A good example is French in colonial Algeria. Before the Algerian Revolution gained momentum, the African experience with the French language was both oppressive and humiliating. The majority of Algerians "identified everything written in the French language as the expression of colonial domination" (Fanon, 1967: 82). But with the creation by the *Moudjaidines* of the "Voice of Fighting Algeria," a radio broadcast in French which propagated the news of the struggle, the French language, the enemy's language, was liberated from its oppressive meanings. "The French language lost its accursed character, revealing itself to be capable also of transmitting, for the benefit of the nation, the message of truth that the latter awaited" (Fanon, 1967: 89). Thus, it was the Algerian Revolution, Fanon argues, that gave fresh impetus to the spread of French among Algerians (1967). While this liberation of the colonizers' languages was perhaps not a widespread phenomenon, the few known cases do suggest that there is nothing intrinsically colonial or imperialist in European languages.

In asserting the colonizing role of European languages in his *Devil on the Cross,* Ngugi wa Thiong'o describes one of his characters in the following terms: "Gatuiria spoke Kikuyu like many educated people in Kenya, people who stutter like babies when speaking their national languages, but conduct fluent conversations in foreign languages. The only difference was that Gatuiria was at least aware that the slavery of language is the slavery of the mind and nothing to be proud of" (Ngugi wa Thiong'o, 1988: 56). In spite of himself, Ngugi ends up depicting the university-educated Gatuiria as one of the most liberated of his characters, showing no mental slavery by virtue of his command of the English language.

The conclusion we can draw is that, as is true of any natural resource, language is open to control and exploitation in favor of the oppressor or the oppressed, depending on the political context. This applies as much to European languages as it does to African languages. Thus, for the purpose of cultural hegemony or liberation, control of the means of communication is far more important than control of the medium of communication. And within the existing political and economic framework, where the means of communication —mass media, publishing houses, international news agencies—are in the hands of neo-colonial interest groups, we cannot prevent African languages, just as we cannot prevent the rest of our natural resources from serving neo-colonial ends.

REFERENCES

Achebe, Chinua. (1966). *A Man of the People*. London: Heinemann.
Capo, H.B.C. (1985). "Comparative Linguistics and Language Engineering in Africa." Paper delivered at the Linguistic Association of Nigeria Conference, Zaria, August 16.
Chomsky, Noam. (1972). *Language and Mind*. New York: Harcourt Brace Jovanovich.
Chronicle of Higher Education. (1989). March 1, p. A19.
Fanon, Frantz. (1967). *A Dying Colonialism*. New York: Grove.
Lambert, Walter E. (1979). "Language As a Factor in Intergroup Relations." In Howard Giles and Robert N. Clair, eds., *Language and Social Psychology*. Oxford: Basil Blackwell.
Ngugi wa Thiong'o. (1986). *Decolonizing the Mind: The Politics of Language in African Literature*. London: Heinemann.
———. (1988). *Devil on the Cross*. London: Heinemann.
Sapir, Edward. (1949). *Selected Writings of Edward Sapir*. Berkeley and Los Angeles: University of California Press.
Searle, Chris. (1983). "A Common Language." *Race and Class* 25(2): 65–74.
Whorf, B. L. (1987). *Language, Thought, and Reality*. John B. Carrol, ed. Cambridge, Mass.: MIT Press.

8

They Came Before the Egyptians: Linguistic Evidence for the African Roots of Semitic Languages

Nicholas Faraclas

Mounting evidence from linguistics and other disciplines indicates that an understanding of African history and culture is both central and essential to an adequate understanding of what has come to be called "Western" history and culture. Martin Bernal has convincingly demonstrated that the origins of Greek culture (as well as the lexifier language of a hypothetical proto-Greek pidgin) are far more plausibly traced southward to Egypt than northward to Europe (Bernal, 1987, and in this volume). In a similar vein, this essay traces the origins of the Ancient Egyptian, Hebrew, Babylonian, Assyrian, and Arabic languages back to a Central African homeland. It suggests that many of the speakers of the languages from which all these languages developed may have participated in a black civilization that was driven out of Central Africa by the expanding Sahara Desert some 7,000 years ago. Given the scanty quantity of available evidence, the conclusions reached in this work can only be tentative. They allow us, however, to formulate new hypotheses and a new research agenda that may lead us to revise our view of the origin of the classical languages of the "West" and gain new insights into the links between African and European prehistory.

AFROASIATIC AND THE ORIGIN OF THE "MOTHER TONGUES" OF WESTERN CIVILIZATION—THE LINGUISTIC EVIDENCE

When we study African history, we are first told that our species originated in Sub-Saharan East Africa hundreds of thousands or even millions of years ago. Then, before we know it, it is 3000 B.C. and the pyramids are going up. But what did occur in Africa between 100,000 B.C. and 3000 B.C.? Where was the cultural fabric woven that allowed the Egyptians to organize their society in such a way that it could take on gigantic public works projects? Where was the science developed that gave the Egyptians the ability to build the pyramids? Admittedly, our knowledge of African prehistory is limited. Part of the problem is that, while much Greek soil has been sifted through by diligent archaeologists, large areas of sub-Saharan Africa still remain untouched, although when an adventuresome archaeologist has dared to leave the "safe zones" of the North he or she has often been rewarded with findings of great significance to human history (see Salibi, 1985; Shaw, 1984; Sutton, 1974). We do, however, possess crucial linguistic evidence, sufficient to challenge some of the traditional hypotheses regarding the migrations of peoples in Africa and the Middle East.

One of the main breakthroughs in this context came from the landmark work of J. H. Greenberg (1963), who established that most of the languages that can be shown to be related to the Semitic "mother languages" of "Western Civilization" are spoken in Africa. Greenberg rejected the traditional classifications of African languages, and posited four linguistic families, to which all of the thousands of languages spoken on the African continent belong. Before Greenberg, African languages were "classified" (one might say segregated) according to the "color" of their speakers. Linguists and historians, for the most part, had no theoretical or practical objections to equating language, race, and culture. The traditional classifications are summed up in Map 1 and Table 1.

Table 1
The Traditional Classification of African Languages

Language "Family"	Skin "Color"	Level of "Civilization"
Indo-European	White	High
Semitic	Off-white	Medium
Hamitic	Brown	Low
Nigritic or Sudanic	Black	Lowest

As objectionable as this classification might seem to a contemporary audience, it should be borne in mind that for nearly a century, indeed up until the 1950s, most academicians in Europe and the United States accepted it as the highest summation of linguistic, historical, and anthropological work in Africa. Many authors still use the terms "Hamitic" or "Nigritic" in their references to groups of African languages (see the present author's reviews of Muhlhausler, 1987 and Holm, 1988). A schematic view of Greenberg's classification is shown in Map 2 and Table 2.

Map 1
The Traditional Classification of African Languages and Cultures

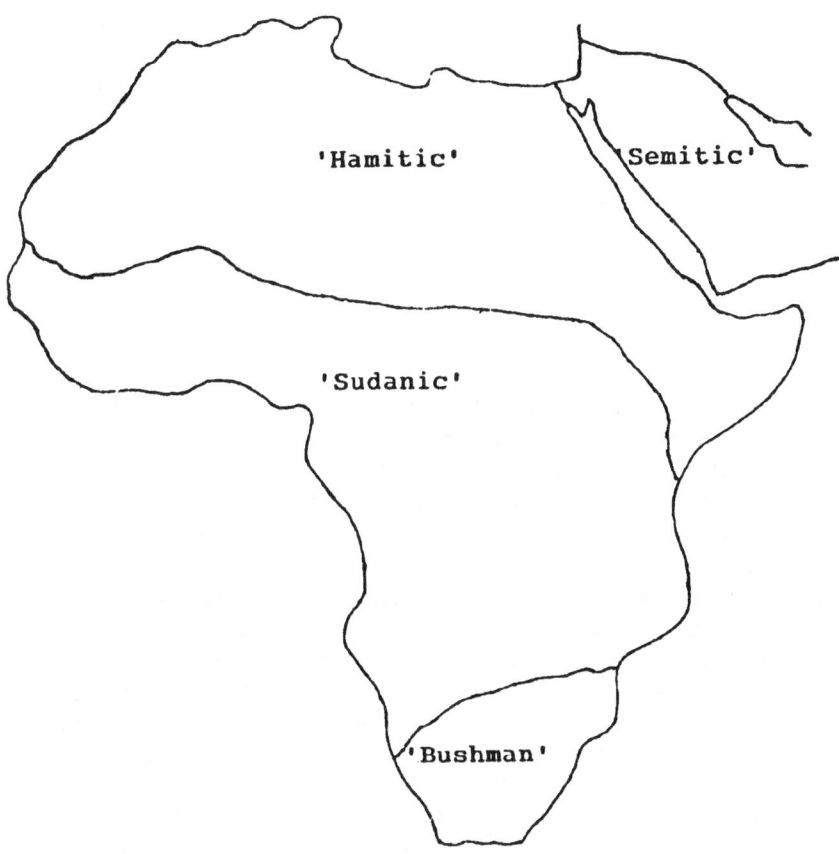

Table 2
Greenberg's (1963) Classification of African Languages[a]

Language Family	Approximate Number of Languages	Approximate Number of Languages in Africa	Approximate Number of Subgroups	Approximate Number of Sub-groups in Africa
Afroasiatic	200	195	5	4.5
Nilo-Saharan	200	200	6	6
Niger-Congo	1,000	1,000	7	7
Khoisan	100	100	3	3

[a] Figures for Africa do not include Arabia.

In addition to the families of languages listed in Table 2, one more family must be mentioned: the Austronesian family, whose hundreds of languages are spoken from Easter Island, off the coast of South America, to Madagascar. The case of Austronesian exemplifies the biases that have governed scholarly work and research. The discovery in the nineteenth century of the relationship of European languages to some of the languages spoken in Iran and on the Indian subcontinent was hailed as one of the key discoveries in the history of the social sciences and became the cornerstone of the entire discipline of philology (from which linguistics developed). The discovery in this century of the relationship between the languages of Madagascar and the languages of the Pacific has not generated a comparable research program. However, the history of the Austronesian-speaking peoples and their Indo-Pacific trading network has begun to be to documented (see Bellwood, 1978).

Greenberg's findings demonstrated that the Semitic languages (which include Babylonian, Assyrian, Hebrew, and Arabic) as well as Ancient Egyptian all belong within the Afroasiatic family. Greenberg also proved that almost all of the 200 or so languages in Afroasiatic (including the majority of the Semitic languages) are spoken in Africa. The Semitic languages (other than Arabic) that are spoken in Africa today include Amharic and Tigrinya, either one of whose speakers outnumber those of any Semitic language spoken outside of Africa, excluding Arabic. In fact, the majority of Afroasiatic languages today are spoken in Central and West Africa.

Greenberg's findings were controversial. It was difficult for biblical scholars, or specialists in Ancient Hebrew, Ancient Egyptian, or Ancient Mesopotamian language and culture, to accept the idea that the Chadic language group, most of whose languages are spoken in Nigeria and neighboring countries, belonged to the same language family as the "classical"

Map 2
Greenberg's Classification of African Languages (1950, 1955, 1963)

languages they had identified as the "mother tongues" of "Western Civilization." Paul Newman, a leading Afroasiatic and Chadic scholar, described their reluctance to come to terms with the evidence: "If Chadic languages had been spoken by Semitic-looking peoples in scattered oases in North Africa, their membership in Afroasiatic would have been settled long ago. But this is not the case. Chadic languages are spoken in sub-Saharan Africa by black people . . . and thus there has been not just a reluctance to accept Chadic, but rather a deep-seated resistance to the idea" (1980: 13).

Although modifications have been made regarding the groupings and subgroupings of the languages within each family, the contours of the four families that Greenberg established have withstood hundreds of challenges and tests, and remain as valid today as they were when they were first formulated. Harold Fleming (1983) has provided plausible evidence for the existence of two additional groups of Afroasiatic languages in Africa. Fleming's revisions of Greenberg's subgroupings have been gaining acceptance among Africanists and are summarized in Table 3. The rough geographic distribution of the groups within Afroasiatic, before the relatively recent Islamic Jihad (which spread Arabic across Northern Africa and displaced other groups of Afroasiatic speakers), is depicted on Map 3.

Table 3
Fleming's (1983) Revision of Greenberg's Language Groups Within Afroasiatic[a]

Greenberg's (1963) Language Groups in Afroasiatic: Name of Group	Fleming's (1983) Language Groups in Afroasiatic: Name of Group	Number of Subgroups/ Languages	Number of Subgroups/ Languages in Africa
Semitic	Semitic	9/15	6/10
Ancient Egyptian	Ancient Egyptian	(1/1)	(1/1)
Berber	Berber	4/24	4/24
Chadic	Chadic	25/125	14/108
Cushitic	Cushitic	8/29	8/29
	Omotic	3/23	3/23
	Beja	1/10	1/10

[a] Figures for Africa do not include Arabia.

Map 3
Approximate Location of Groups within Afroasiatic before the Expansion of Arabic during the Jihad

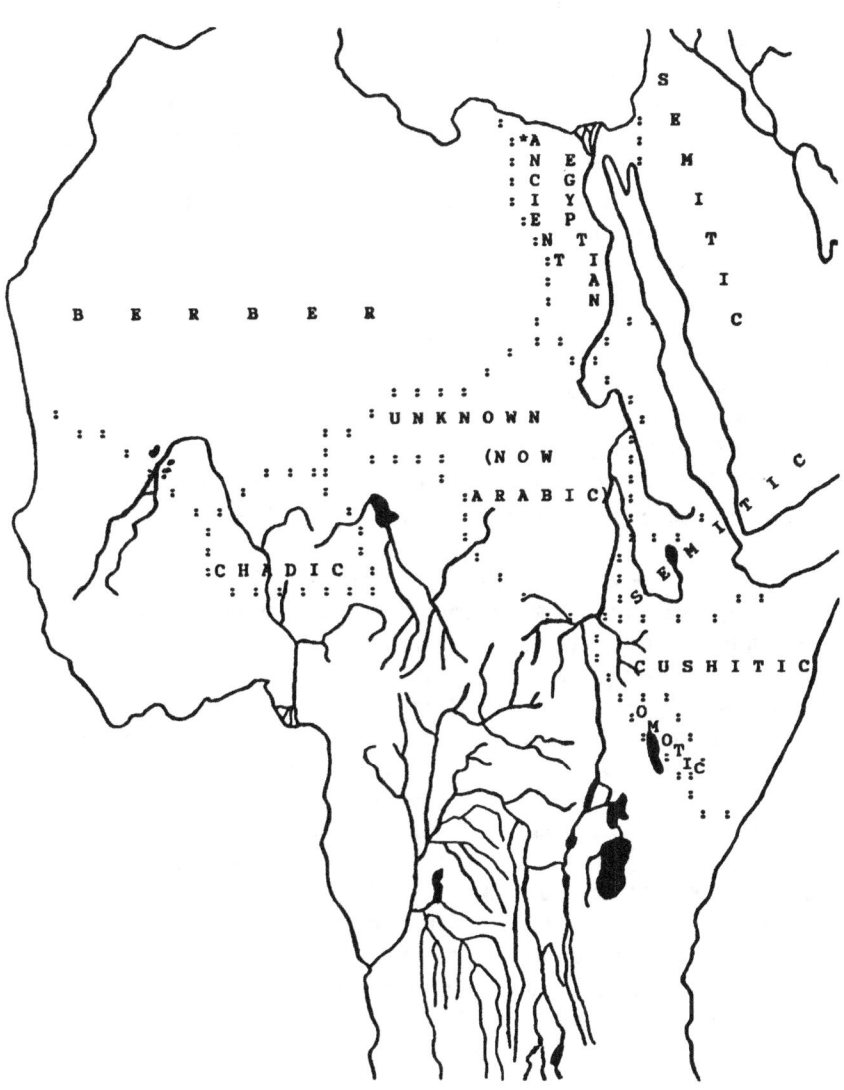

A CENTRAL AFRICAN HOMELAND FOR AFROASIATIC LANGUAGES

In light of this and other evidence, Sutton (1974), Williamson (1979), and Horton (1982) all follow Diakonoff (1965) in concluding that proto-Afroasiatic (the language from which all the Afroasiatic languages, including the Semitic languages and Ancient Egyptian developed) was originally spoken in Africa and not in the Middle East. Using generally accepted techniques, as originated by Edward Sapir (1921) and developed by Dyen (1965), Greenberg (1960), and Armstrong (1962), both Williamson and Horton located the Afroasiatic homeland (the place where proto-Afroasiatic was originally spoken) on the African continent.

When linguists attempt to locate the area where an original, or "protolanguage," was spoken before it gave rise over time to several "daughter" languages (as the protolanguage Latin gave rise to its daughter languages French, Spanish, Portuguese, Italian, and Romanian), they pay most attention to the area where the daughter languages are most divergent. The homeland (or area originally occupied by speakers of a given language grouping) can reasonably be assumed to have been in the area where the languages show greatest differentiation, resulting from a longer period in the area (Williamson, 1983: 1).

In determining the point from which speakers of related groups of languages dispersed from the same protolanguage community, linguists also pay attention to the boundary lines between the areas where the related languages are spoken. Where the various borderlines converge, there they locate the area from which the language originally diverged, all other factors being equal.

"Family tree" assumptions are supplemented by additional assumptions derived from the study of cases where there is independent evidence of the human movements that have given rise to particular patterns of language distribution. One such assumption, widely used in locating the original point of dispersal within a given territory old or new, is that the boundaries between daughter languages tend to converge on the area formerly occupied by the original protolanguage. A further assumption is that the present-day position of the point of convergence in relation to the total territory in question is a function of the particular pattern of dispersal from the original nucleus. Thus, where the dispersal has been in all directions from the periphery of the nucleus, the point of convergence will tend to be at the approximate center of the territory (Horton, 1982: 7).

Williamson and Horton each used this methodology to formulate a set of hypotheses concerning the movements of Niger-Congo speakers from a homeland in the area of the Inland Niger Delta. Sutton (1974) used similar methods to posit the dispersal of the Nilo-Saharan speakers from a homeland near Lake Chad. To my knowledge, however, no one has as yet proposed a specific area of the African continent as the homeland of the speakers of Afroasiatic languages.

If we use the criteria cited by Williamson and Horton above, we find that the epicenter of Afroasiatic expansion (the area where the boundaries of the Afroasiatic language groups in Table 3 converge) is the Darfur-Kordofan region along the present-day border between Chad and Sudan (see Map 3). I argue that this is the Afroasiatic homeland. Evidence for this claim is provided by climatological and ethnographical, as well as linguistic, evidence. The Sahara and the Sahel were not always desert. Lake-level measurements (Street and Grove, 1976; Van Zindern and Bakker, 1972), pollen counts (Suwonmi, 1981), and other climatological data (Burke, Durotoye, and Whiteman, 1971) indicate that the Sahara/Sahel region passed through several wet and dry phases over the past 30,000 years, as listed in Table 4.

Table 4
Wet and Dry Phases in the Sahara/Sahel During the Past 30,000 Years

28,000 B.C.–18,000 B.C.	Wet spell
18,000 B.C.–10,000 B.C.	Major dry spell
10,000 B.C. –5000 B.C.	Major wet spell
5000 B.C.–3000 B.C.	Drier
3000 B.C.–1000 B.C.	Wetter
1000 B.C.–Present	Drier

ARCHAEOLOGICAL EVIDENCE FOR AN AQUATIC CIVILIZATION OF MIDDLE AFRICA

During the wet phases, the Sahara/Sahel region was lush, green, covered by grass, swamps, lakes, and creeks; it could support a thriving population. Sutton (1974) first related the linguistic data to evidence from archaeology and climatography in order to show that the wet Sahara/Sahel region was originally the home to various hunting, herding, and fighting groups. Sutton, as summarized by Horton (1982), made two claims:

First, that the early stages of Niger-Congo, Nilo-Saharan, and Afro-Asiatic may have unfolded at a time when the Saharan and sub-Saharan areas were well supplied with rivers, lakes, and swamps: specifically, during the last major wet period. . . . Second, that all over the Saharan area as well as to the immediate south of it, archaeological sites that can be dated back to this period contain evidence, both of extensive consumption of shell-fish, fish, and other aquatic animals, and of implements for the catching and killing of such animals. The implication of these two main points, of course, is that in this area and during this period, we are dealing with peoples who may well have practiced hunting and gathering on dry land, but who were also, and perhaps even predominantly, fishermen and hunters of aquatic animals. The migratory movements of such peoples, it follows, may have been dictated by considerations relating to an aquatic rather than a terrestrial mode of life. (19–20)

On the basis of his extensive archaeological work in the Sahara and the Sahel, Sutton argued for the existence, during the last major wet spell, of a single cultural complex, stretching from the Atlantic Ocean to the Rift Valley, which included fishing, bone carving, and pottery making. Sutton called this cultural complex the "Aquatic Civilization of Middle Africa." According to Sutton, the Aquatic Civilization flourished during a time when Lake Chad was as big as the Caspian Sea, spilling into the Benue-Atlantic system, and the Rift Valley lakes were connected and flowed into the Nile.

Sutton contends that this Aquatic Civilization was likely one of the most "advanced" of its time and was a black civilization. The oldest recorded samples of pottery come from this culture and from another contemporary fishing culture in Japan. A wavy-line dotted motif typifies this pottery, suggesting that the pots were decorated to imitate fishing baskets. Wavy-line dotted pottery from this period has been found alongside skillfully carved bone harpoons all the way across the Sahara and the Sahel, from Mauritania to Kenya, as shown on Map 4.

In assuming that carved bones can constitute a yardstick for civilization as legitimate as carved stone, we follow B. W. Andah, who complains that scholars are too quick to link technological breakthroughs (metal working, bifacial tools) with socioeconomic breakthroughs. If culture first developed in Africa, we can expect to find here a much more varied and complex set of developmental models, combinations of technological, social, and economic patterns (Andah, 1979: 2). Sutton adds that an Aquatic Civilization defies the traditional European and Middle Eastern devices that anthropologists and historians use as measures of culture. For example, can an Aquatic Civilization be classified as paleolithic, mesolithic, or neolithic? And how do we classify a culture that had no use for stone, but whose techniques for carving bone harpoons was probably equal or superior to the stone-carving techniques of their contemporaries in Europe and the Middle East? How do we classify a culture that could support a greater population, and generate more leisure time, by fishing than could any agriculturists of the same era? Because of the narrowness of traditional academic definitions and measures of civilization, we are unable to gain a meaningful perspective on cultural configurations that predate written history, except for those of a few European and Middle Eastern stone-wielding farmers. Sutton suggests that the "slow spread of agriculture in Africa, sometimes considered an indication of 'backwardness,' may be partly explicable by the very success of the aquatic life and its distinct cultural tradition which was ascendant for a while across the widest part of the continent" (546).

THE LAST MAJOR DRY SPELL AND THE RETREAT TO THE WETLANDS

During the last Major Dry Spell (18,000–10,000 B.C.; see Table 4), Lake Chad probably disappeared and the Niger River stopped flowing out from the Inland Delta. This means that the populations living in the Sahara/Sahel would have had to leave the area by going north or south, or they would have had to retreat to the few well-watered places left in the region. These would have included the Inland Delta of the Niger River in the west, the basin of Lake Chad in the center, and the swampy lands of the Darfur-Kordofan region, on the Chad-Sudan border, to the east. Probably, in these three areas, the original languages were spoken that later gave rise to three of the four families of languages on the African mainland: (1) Niger-Congo, which radiates out from the Niger Delta; (2) Nilo-Saharan, whose nucleus is the Lake Chad area; and (3) Afroasiatic, which converges toward the Kordofan-Darfur region (see Maps 3 and 4).

The lexicostatistic counts of the level of similarity between the major groups within these three families (see, e.g., Armstrong, 1962; Greenberg, 1963; Gregersen, 1972; Williamson, 1979, 1983, ms.), while subject to further verification, support a scenario where each family started branching out around 10,000 B.C. This was a time when the last Major Dry Spell was coming to an end, and the new wetter conditions were allowing people to spread out once again across the Sahara/Sahel region. Referring to the speakers of proto-Niger Congo, who took refuge in the wetlands of the Inland Niger Delta during the dry spell, Horton (1982) notes:

In these conditions, the swamps and creeks would have been a refuge area for large numbers of people fleeing from drought. The result would have been a sizable, dense population exploiting with maximum intensity all available local resources. Prominent amongst such resources, of course, would have been aquatic ones. And we can assume that fishing loomed large as a mode of livelihood. At once congested and specialized in the intensive exploitation of aquatic resources, the population living at this time and in this place would be poised to take maximum advantage of any opportunity for riverine expansion offered by a return to wetter conditions and a new development of water courses. (29)

Sutton (1974) focuses on the expansion of groups of Nilo-Saharan speakers from the Lake Chad Basin (where they had taken refuge during the last Major Dry Spell, 18,000–10,000 B.C.; see Map 4 and Table 4) into other areas, as soon as the more favorable conditions offered by the following Major Wet Spell

Map 4
The Aquatic Civilization of Middle Africa, 15,000–5000 B.C.

x = Wavy-line/dotted pottery sites
* = Bone harpoon sites
(Map from Sutton, 1974; Watercourses from Horton, 1985; Mega-Chad from Grove and Warren, 1968)

(10,000–5000 B.C.) permitted such movements. Sutton proposes that the Nilo-Saharan speakers, already accustomed to an aquatic life, used river courses and other fishing grounds as their routes of expansion. It was during this period of expansion into unpopulated areas, rich in aquatic resources, that the Aquatic Civilization of Middle Africa was established across the Sahara and the Sahel. As shown on Map 5, Sutton's scenario is borne out by linguistic evidence, which puts the date of Nilo-Saharan dispersal at roughly 10,000 B.C. and divides the Nilo-Saharan family into three groups, each of which can be found along a separate watercourse radiating out from the Chad Basin.

Map 5 also shows that this same pattern of river-course migration can be applied to Niger-Congo and Afroasiatic with satisfactory results. In fact, Horton (1982) wonders why Sutton did not extend his finding to Niger-Congo and Afroasiatic: "A peculiar feature of Sutton's article is that, whilst it starts out by suggesting that the early stages of all three great diasporas (Nilo-Saharan, Niger-Congo, and Afro-Asiatic) may have involved primarily riverine migration, it ends up by suggesting that only the Nilo-Saharan diaspora actually was primarily riverine" (21).

By positing primarily riverine, rather than terrestrial, routes for the migrations of different groups of Niger-Congo speakers from the Inland Niger Delta, Horton (1982) argued at first that each of the major groups within Niger-Congo converged on the area of the Niger Bend, in a pattern that can be traced up and down the river courses of West Africa (see Map 5):

Linguistic and oral-traditional considerations suggest that the Niger-Congo dispersal started some 12,000 years ago in the general area of the Niger Bend. Paleogeographic considerations suggest that any sizable population living at this time and in this place would almost certainly have made an important contribution to the resettlement of Western Africa in the subsequent wet period. Being already equipped for aquatic life, it would have made this contribution through a primarily riverine expansion. (29)

Later, Horton (1984) amended this view, suggesting that the area from which the main boundaries of the Niger-Kordofonian languages (one of the subgroups of the Niger-Congo) radiate out was not the Inland Delta, but the Western Highlands, an area from which rivers (including the Niger) flow down in literally all directions into the lowlands of West Africa. Horton also postulated, in view of the geographical configuration of the Afroasiatic languages, their origin from a mid-Saharan homeland (Horton, 1984: 15).

Neither Horton nor Sutton, however, tried to identify the specific homeland of Afroasiatic or the possible riverine routes that each group of Afroasiatic speakers would have followed.

Map 5
Movements during the Last Major Wet Spell, 12,000–7000 B.C.

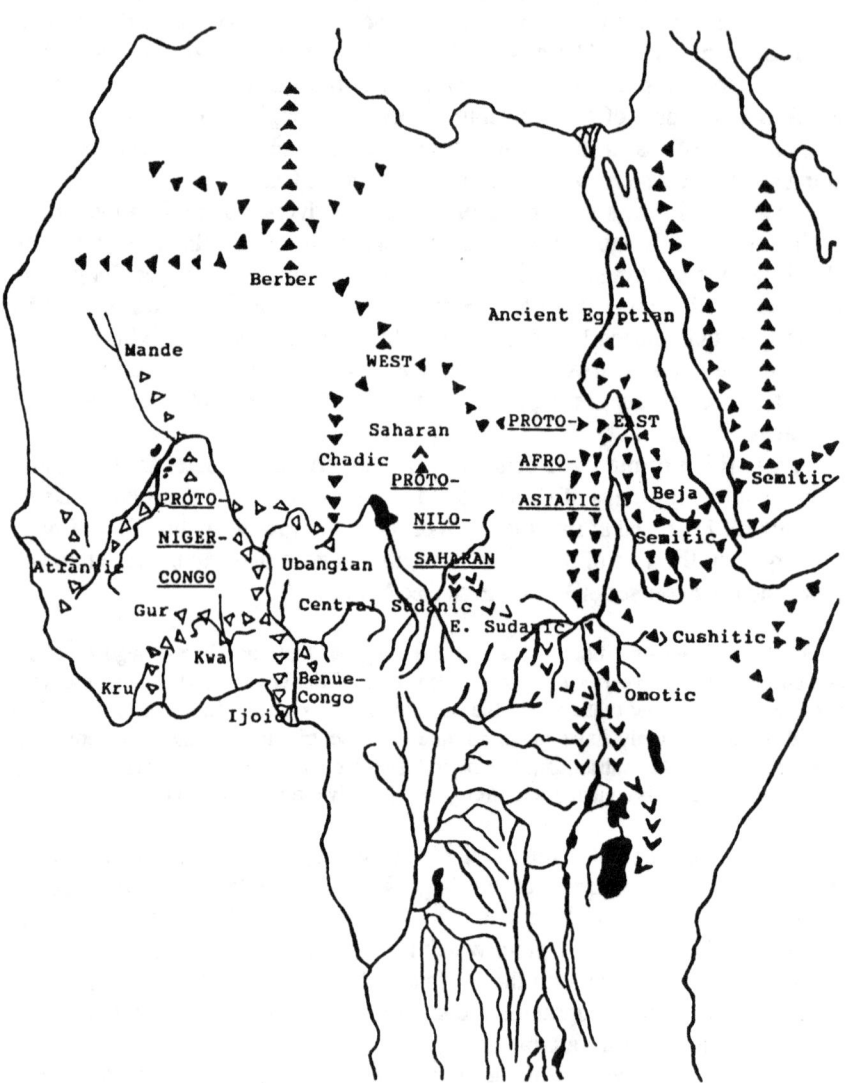

▶ = Afroasiatic speakers
▷ = Niger-Congo speakers
› = Nilo-Saharan speakers

THE RIVERINE EXPANSION OF AFROASIATIC DURING THE LAST MAJOR WET SPELL

Existing sources posit roughly the same date, 10,000 B.C., for the original splits within the Nilo-Saharan, Niger-Congo, and Afroasiatic families. This date corresponds to the beginning of the last Major Wet Spell and the onset of Sutton's Aquatic Civilization of Middle Africa. As mentioned above and illustrated on Maps 3, 4, and 5, the most probable area for the homeland of Afroasiatic during the last Major Dry Spell is the swampy Darfur-Kordofan region along the Chad-Sudan border. Map 5 shows how the same techniques that successfully explained the migrations of Nilo-Saharan and Niger-Congo speakers can be applied to the migrations of speakers of Afroasiatic languages. Once again, the archaeological, climatological, and linguistic facts suggest that the proto-Afroasiatic speakers may have inhabited a relatively compact wet zone during the last Major Dry Spell. Then, as conditions became wetter, the Afroasiatic-speaking community expanded and split, with each subgroup following a separate watercourse, just as did the Nilo-Saharan and Niger-Congo-speaking communities.

The archaeological evidence (see Map 4) suggests that speakers of languages of all the three families actively participated in the Aquatic Civilization of Middle Africa. Nilo-Saharan, Niger-Congo, and Afroasiatic speakers would have traveled down river courses in search of better fishing grounds provided by the onset of the last Major Wet Spell. In this process, members of all three groups would have had considerable contact with one another, and there would have been abundant opportunities for sharing technological and cultural innovations.

Skinner (1984) has traced the words for "reedbuck," "roan antelope," "waterbuck," and "hartbeeste" to proto-Afroasiatic. Assuming that these names referred then to the same species they refer to today, we have evidence that the original speakers of Afroasiatic knew about these animals, whose natural habitat stretches at present from the Darfur-Kordofan area, near the Chad-Sudan border, westward through the Lake Chad Basin, all the way to the Inland Niger Delta (see Map 6). If the present-day dry conditions in the Sahara/Sahel approximate those of the last Major Dry Spell, this evidence can provide critical support for a Darfur-Kordofan homeland for Afroasiatic.

Let us now consider the present distribution of the language groups within Afroasiatic, factoring out the recent spread of Arabic into North Africa during the Jihad (see Maps 3 and 5). To the east, all groups follow the river courses of the Nile Valley and converge, like spokes on a wheel, toward the area to the West of the great bend in the Nile before the Atbara confluence, that is, the Darfur-Kordofan region. To the west, the Chadic and Berber groups are presently cut off from the rest of Afroasiatic. However, the intervening groups of Arabic and Nilo-Saharan speakers can be shown to be relative newcomers to the region, which suggests that the Berber and Chadic speaking areas could have extended into the Darfur-Kordofan region.

When the evidence thus far considered is synthesized, the following scenario emerges. At the onset of the last Major Wet Spell, the Ancient Egyptian speakers would have made their way north down the Nile, while the Beja speakers would have gone eastward up the Atbara. The Omotic speakers would have headed south on the White Nile, followed and later almost completely displaced by the Cushitic speakers. The Chadic and Berber groups would have gone west into the marshes and swamps of the Chad Basin, where they finally divided and went their separate ways, the Berber speakers to the northwest and the Chadic speakers to the southwest. Fleming (1983) presents some evidence for a separate western grouping of Afroasiatic, which includes Chadic and Berber, indicating that these two groups may have remained together for some time in the area of Lake Chad. Finally, the Semitic group would have followed the Blue Nile to the Ethiopian highlands (where the majority of Semitic languages are found to this day) and would eventually have reached the narrow straits that separate the horn of Africa from the Arabian Peninsula. There is convincing toponymic evidence that the Semitic speakers first crossed over into the Middle East via this route (Salibi, 1985). Traces of different subgroups of Semitic are found all along the eastern and western shores of Arabia.

To my knowledge, the present work is the first to suggest the scenarios for Afroasiatic migration as a whole, and for Semitic migration in particular. As noted by Newman above, after twenty-five years scholars still resist the idea that Chadic and Semitic languages belong to the same family, despite the fact that available evidence points toward a Middle African origin not only for Afroasiatic as a whole, but also for the Semitic group. It is still currently assumed that (1) the Semitic group differentiated itself from the rest of Afroasiatic in Asia or on the Arabian Peninsula; (2) the Semitic speakers reached the Middle East via the Nile Delta during the time that the Ancient Egyptians occupied the same area; or (3) Afroasiatic influence "percolated" into the Middle East through a "filter" such as the Nile Delta or the Arabian Peninsula, or both.

These scenarios single out Semitic as a special case, as they assume that its origin and development are exempt from the climatic, geographic, social, economic, and linguistic processes that govern the origin and development of all the other groups within Afroasiatic and the other language families of Africa. Even so, the supporters of these hypotheses cannot account for the fact that the majority of the languages of the Semitic group are found in sub-Saharan Africa, along with all the other languages of the Afroasiatic family. Some further complicate these scenarios, in order to have some Semitic speakers in Ethiopia early enough, so that they could have the time to divide into more separate subgroupings and languages than can be found in Arabia

The African Roots of Semitic Languages 191

**Map 6
Area Inhabited by Animals Whose Names Can Be Traced Back to Proto-Afroasiatic (Enclosed by the Triangle)**

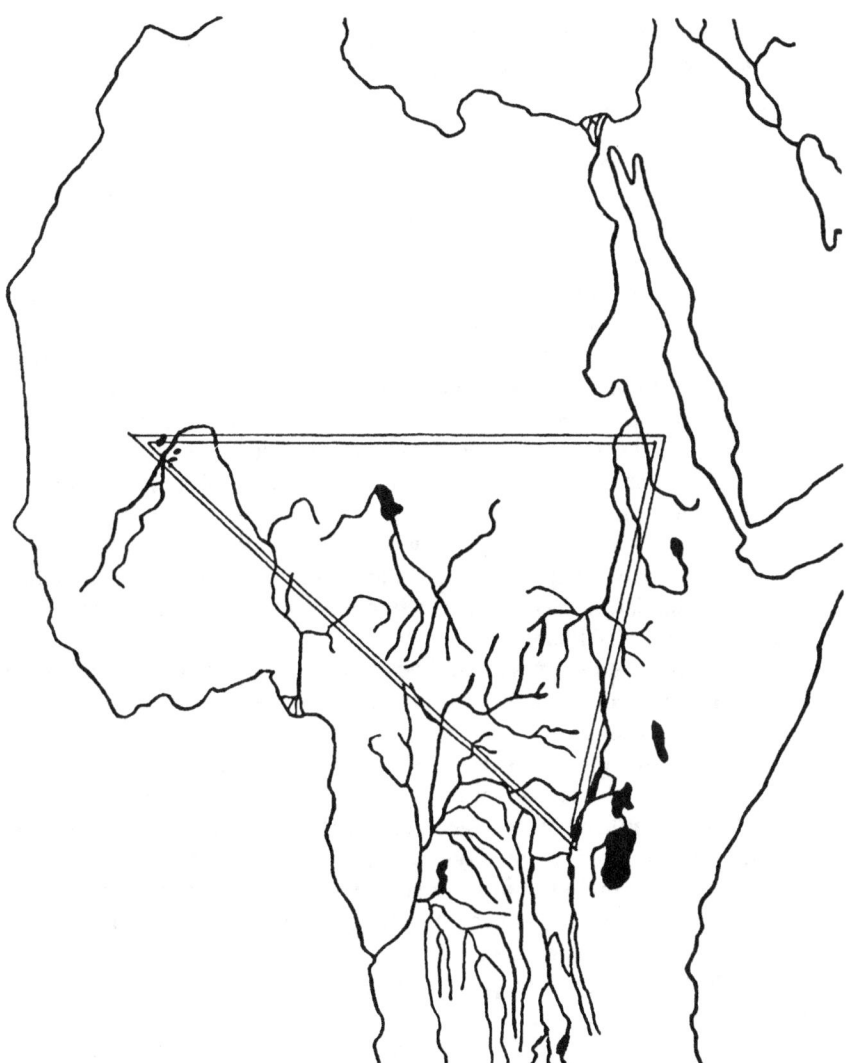

Source: Skinner, 1984.

and Asia put together. They, too, assume that the processes posited for the expansion of Niger-Congo and for Nilo-Saharan cease to be valid in the case of Afroasiatic.

THE SECOND RETREAT: DRIER CONDITIONS FROM 5000–3000 B.C. AND THE CHANGE FROM FISHING TO AGRICULTURE AND HERDING

If we replace these hypotheses with that of a Middle African homeland for both Afroasiatic and Semitic, subsequent developments during the drier phase in the Sahara/Sahel region between 5000 and 3000 B.C. may be accounted for more satisfactorily.

As conditions became drier, fish and other aquatic animals became less plentiful and many aquatic cultures turned from a water-based to a land-based agricultural or herding economy. When the wetlands dried up, the migratory pressure down the river courses, in both a southward and a northward direction out of the Sahara, increased dramatically. As shown on Map 7, the drier period of 5000-3000 B.C. led to another set of riverine migrations, away from the most arid areas of the Sahara/Sahel. In the west, the Mande speakers pushed up the Niger, displacing the Atlantic-speaking peoples (Horton, 1982). Toward the center, vast numbers of increasingly agriculturally oriented Niger-Congo, Afroasiatic, and Nilo-Saharan speakers moved toward the Niger-Benue confluence, forcing the Ubangian and Bantu speakers out of the Niger-Benue Basin and into the Zaire Basin (Williamson, 1979, 1983).

Increased population pressure and advances in agriculture thus led to the great Bantu expansion from the Eastern Nigeria-Western Cameroon region, across the wet rain-forest areas of Central, Eastern, and Southern Africa. The movements of different subgroups of Bantu speakers can be traced to major river courses, in much the same way as we can trace the movements of Afroasiatic, Nilo-Saharan, and other Niger-Congo speakers (Vansina, 1984). In this case, however, the river-course migration pattern may have been due to the impenetrability of the rain forests of Central Africa, rather than to depen-dence on fishing by the Bantu speakers, whose agricultural yields probably outstripped those of their contemporaries in Europe or the Middle East. As we know, one hectare of yams and palm oil trees feeds twice as many people as a hectare of wheat (Nzewunwa, 1980).

In the east, the drier climate drove the Ancient Egyptian speakers north, forcing them to depend less and less on fishing and more and more on the optimal conditions for agriculture provided by the Lower Nile Valley. Meanwhile, the Semitic speakers would have been driven northward along the Arabian coasts toward the Jordan Valley and Mesopotamia. There is no need to postulate a supernatural intervention to have speakers of Semitic languages

The African Roots of Semitic Languages

Map 7
Riverine Agriculture, 7000–3000 B.C.

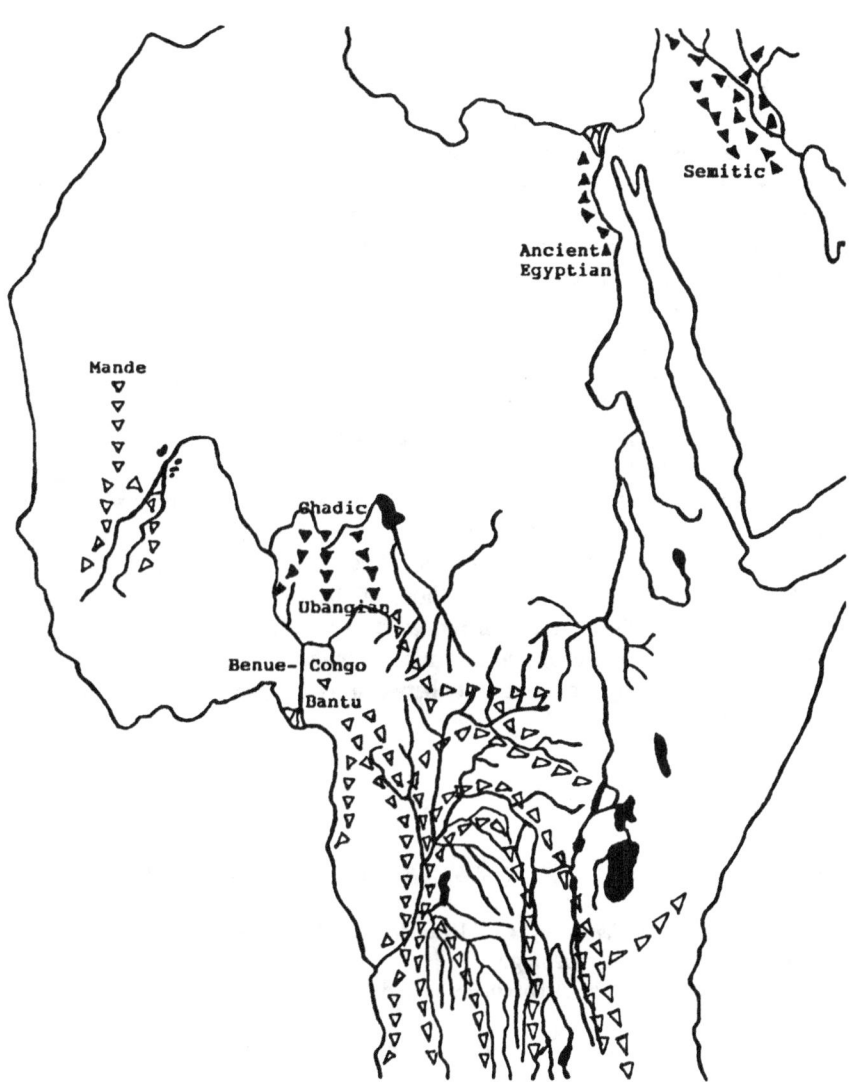

▶ = Afroasiatic speakers
▷ = Niger-Congo speakers

present at the foundation of the civilizations of the Nile, Jordan, and Tigris Valleys, if we assume that the homeland of their languages and cultures was in Central Africa.

CONCLUSION

To this day, only a few scholars and a few documents, many as yet unpublished, touch on the possibility of a Middle African origin for Semitic languages. For all that can be proven so far is that the overwhelming number and most diverse clusters of Afroasiatic and Semitic languages are today spoken in sub-Saharan Africa. Yet, as the essay has argued, this hypothesis deserves to be investigated, for the sake of historical coherence and understanding, as well as in view of the ideological benefits to be derived from recognizing the continuity between the cultures of Africa, Europe, and the Middle East. Here a note of caution must be introduced. Linguistic continuity is not yet evidence of the continuity and transmission of cultural and material achievements. It is, however, a crucial step toward it. Moreover, if proven, the hypothesis of a "migration" of Semitic languages from Africa may also throw light on the current debate concerning the actual "perimeters" of the African continent which, according to some, has been arbitrarily severed, owing to purely political considerations, from those of the Arabian landmass to which Africa was united before the rift. If indeed it can be proved that Central Africa was the homeland to Arabic and Semitic languages, then the hypothesis of a cultural, as well as physical continuity between Africa and the Middle East will be strengthened.

REFERENCES

Ajayi, J., and M. Crowder, eds. (1976). *History of West Africa*, Vol. 1. Rev. ed. London.
Andah, B. W. (1979). *Perspectives on West Africa's Past*. Special book issue of *West African Journal of Archaeology* 9.
Anozie, F. N. (1976). "The Archaeology of the Niger Delta." Seminar, University of Calabar.
Armstrong, R. (1962). "Glottochronology and African Linguistics." *Journal of African History* 3(2): 283–90.
Bellwood, Peter. (1978). *The Polynesians: Prehistory of an Island People*. London: Thames and Hudson Ltd.
Bernal, M. (1987). *Black Athena*, Vol. 1. London: Free Association Books.
Bright, William, ed. (1992). *International Encyclopedia of Linguistics*. New York: Oxford University Press.
Burke, K., A. B. Durotoye, and A. J. Whiteman. (1971). "A Dry Phase South of the

Sahara 20,000 Years Ago." *West African Journal of Archaeology* 1: 1–8.
Dalby, D. (1970). "Reflections on the Classification of African Languages with Special Reference to the Work of Sigismund Koelle and Malcolm Guthrie." *African Language Studies* 11: 147–71.
David, N. (1977). "Early Bantu Expansion in the Context of Central African Prehistory." Revised and expanded version of a paper delivered at the Colloque International du C.N.R.S., Viviers.
Dyen, I. (1965). "Language Distribution and Migration Theory." *Language* 32: 611–26.
Diakonoff, I. M. (1965). *Semito-Hamitic [sic] Languages*. Moscow: Nauka.
Faraclas, N. (1988). "Review-Article of P. Muhlhausler, 1987, *Pidgin and Creole Linguistics*" (Oxford: Basil Blackwell). *Journal of Pidgin and Creole Languages* 3(1): 119–36.
———. (1989). "Review of John A. Holm, 1988. *Pidgins and Creoles*, Vol. 1: *Theory and Structure*" (Cambridge: Cambridge University Press). *Journal of African Languages and Linguistics* 11(1): 103–10.
Fleming, Harold C. (1983). "Chadic External Relations." In *Studies in Chadic and Afroasiatic Linguistics*, Ekkehard Wolff and Hilke Meyer-Bahlburg, eds. Hamburg: Helmut Buske, pp. 17–31.
Greenberg, J. H. (1960). "Linguistic Evidence for the Influence of the Kanuri on the Hausa." *Journal of African History* 1(2): 205–12.
———. (1963). *The Languages of Africa*. The Hague: Mouton.
Gregersen, E. A. (1972). "Kongo-Saharan." *Journal of African Languages* 11(1): 68–89.
———. (1977). *Language in Africa: An Introductory Survey*. New York: Gordon and Breach.
Grove, A. T., and A. Warren. (1968). "Quaternary Landforms and Climate on the South-Site of the Sahara." *Geographical Journal* 134(2): 194–204.
Hetzron, Robert. (1980). "The Limits of Cushitic." *SUGIA* 2: 7–126.
Hoffmann, C. (1970). "Ancient Benue-Congo Loans in Chadic?" *Africana Marburgensia* 3(2): 3–24.
Holm, John A. (1988). *Pidgins and Creoles*, Vol. I: *Theory and Structure*. Cambridge: Cambridge University Press.
Horton, R. (1982). "The Niger-Kordofanian Diaspora: Another Aquatic Saga?" Port Harcourt (Unpublished).
———. (1984). "Environment and People: Some Formative Processes." Port Harcourt (Unpublished).
Ki-Zerbo, J., ed. (1981). *UNESCO General History of Africa*, Vol. 1. London: UNESCO.
Mokhtar, G., ed. (1981). *UNESCO General History of Africa*, Vol. 2. London: UNESCO.
Muhlhausler, Peter. (1987). *Pidgin and Creole Linguistics*. Oxford: Basil Blackwell.
Newman, P. (1980). *The Classification of Chadic within Afroasiatic*. Leiden: Universitaire Pers.
Nzewunwa, N. (1980). "The Niger Delta: Aspects of Its Prehistoric Economy and Culture." Cambridge Monographs in African Archaeology 1, Bar International Series 75.
Posnansky, M. (1981). "Introduction to the Later Prehistory of Sub-Saharan Africa." In G. Mokhtar, ed., *UNESCO General History of Africa*, Vol. 2. London: UNESCO.

Salibi, K. (1985). *The Bible Came from Arabia*. London: Jonathan Cape.
Sapir, Edward. (1921). *Language*. New York: Harcourt Brace and World.
Shaw, T. (1972). "Early Crops in Africa: A Review of the Evidence." Paper delivered to the Burgwartenstein Symposium 56 on the Origin of Africa Plant Domesticates.
———. (1981). "The Prehistory of West Africa." In J. Ki-Zerbo, ed., *UNESCO General History of Africa*, Vol. 1. London: UNESCO.
———. (1984). "Filling Gaps in Africa Maps: Fifty Years of Archaeology in Africa." Hans Wolff Memorial Lecture. African Studies Program, Indiana University.
Skinner, A. N. (1984). "Afro-Asiatic Vocabulary: Evidence for Some Culturally Important Items." *Africana Marburgensia*, Special Issue 7: 1–65.
Smith, H.F.C. (1976). "The Early States of the Central Sudan." In J. Ajayi and M. Crowder, eds., *History of West Africa*, Vol. 1. Rev. ed. London, pp. 152–58.
Street, F. A., and A. T. Grove. (1976). "Environmental and Climatic Implications of Late Quaternary Lake-Level Fluctuations in Africa." *Nature* 261(59): 385–90.
Sutton, J.E.G. (1974). "The Aquatic Civilization of Middle Africa." *Journal of African History* 15(4): 527–46.
Suwonmi, M. A. (1981). "Late Quaternary Environmental Changes in Nigeria." *Pollen and Spores* 23: 125–48.
Vansina, J. (1984). "Western Bantu Expansion." *Journal of African History* 25: 129–45.
Vansina, J., R. Mauny, and L. Thomas. (1964). *The Historian in Tropical Africa: Studies Presented and Discussed*. London: Oxford University Press.
Van Zindern, E. M., and S. R. Bakker. (1972). "Late Quaternary Lacustrine Phases in the Southern Sahara and East Africa." In E. M. Van Zindern and S. R. Bakker, eds., *Paleoecology of Africa and the Surrounding Islands and Antarctica*, Vol. 6. Cape Town: Balkema.
Vogelin, C. F., and F. M. Vogelin. (1973). *Index of the World's Languages*. U.S. Department of Health, Education, and Welfare.
Williamson, K. (1979). "Prehistory and the Spread of the Niger-Kordofanian Languages." Seminar, University of Calabar.
———. (1983). "The Application of Linguistics to the Study of Nigerian Prehistory." Paper delivered to the 4th Annual Conference of the Linguistic Association of Nigeria, University of Benin.
———. (1988). "Linguistic Evidence for the Prehistory of the Niger Delta." In E. J. Alagoa, F. N. Anozie, and N. Nzewunwa, eds., *The Early History of the Niger Delta*. Hamburg: Helmut Buske Verlag.
———. (n.d.). "Lexicostatistic Estimates for Some African Language Families" (manuscript).

Index

Act of Union (1707), 16–17, 33n
Adelard of Bath, 123
Aeschylus, 5
Africa, 7, 8, 67, 71, 161–74, 177–94; Algeria, 173; Cameroon, 192; Central Africa, 175, 178, 192, 194; Chad-Sudan border, 183, 185, 189; colonial language policies in, 161, 165–69, 172–73; colonialism in, 161–69; Congo, 167; cultural nationalists in, xv, 163, 164; Darfur-Kordofan region, 183, 185, 189–90; division into nation-states, 161; Ethiopia, 190; Eastern Africa, 166, 172, 177, 178, 192; England's relation to, 54; European languages in, xv, 161–74, 176; history of, xv, 175–76; Horn of, 190; Kenya, 168, 184; Mauritania, 184; Middle Africa, 192, 194; neo-colonialism in, 162, 169–74; neo-nationalism in, 165, 168–70, 172; Niger-Benue Basin, 192; Nigeria, 178, 192; North Africa, 180, 189; portrayal in British education, 121, 122; progressive spirit of, 152; Rift Valley, 184; ruling class in, 162, 169–72; Sahara, xv, 175, 183–89, 192; Sahel, 183–89, 192; South Africa, 167–68, 192; Sub-Saharan, 175–76, 180, 190, 194; Tanzania, 166, 169; West Africa, 172, 187; Zaire, 172; Zaire Basin, 192. *See also* Lake Chad, Niger River, Nile River
African languages, xv, 161–74, 177–94; Bantu, 192; Berber, 189–90; Chadic, 178–80, 189–90; classification of, 176–180; and decolonization, 161–62, 164, 173; Hamitic, 176t; Mande, 192, 199; Niger-Congo, 179t, 182, 183, 185–89, 190–93; Niger-Kordofonian, 187; Nigritic, 176t; Nilo-Saharan, 179t, 182, 183, 185–89, 190–92; Pidgin, 172; Sudanic, 176t; Swahili, 166, 168, 169, 172; Ubangian, 192. *See also* Afroasiatic languages, Semitic languages, *individual languages*
Afroasiatic languages, 124, 178t, 180, 180t, 181m, 182–83, 185–93; expansion of, 183, 192; homeland, 182–83, 187, 192; proto-Afroasiatic, 182, 189, 191m. *See also individual languages*
Afro-Saxons, 169, 170, 172
Aksakov, K. S., 45
Algeria, 173; Algerian Revolution, 173
Altertumswissenschaft, 4, 8. *See also* Classics
Amharic language, 178
Ancient Model, xiii, 4–8, 10–11
Andah, B. W., 184
Anderson, Benedict, 54–55
anti-colonialism, 67–68
anti-communism, 68, 79, 80, 82

anti-Semitism, 9, 10, 49
Aquatic Civilization of Middle Africa, 183–85, 186m, 187, 189
Arab: language, 175, 178, 180, 181m, 189–90, 194; mathematics, 123, 124, 125, 128, 132
Arabia, 190, 192; Arabian Peninsula, 190; Jordan Valley, 192; Mesopotamia, 124, 128, 178, 192. *See also* Middle East
Arendt, Hannah, 63, 77, 78, 79, 80, 85
Arithmetic. *See* Mathematics
Arjuna, in *Bhagavad Gita*, 142–43
Arthasastra, 153
Aryan: conquests of India, 4–5; invasions, 4, 9, 10; homeland for European languages, 67; Model, xiii, 4, 5, 9–10; tribes, 67; westward migration, 67
Aschheim, Steven, 49
Asia, 8, 71; Asiatism, 68; languages in, 192; nationalism in, 67–68; progressive spirit of, 152. *See also* Orient
Asiatic Society of Bengal, 139, 141, 142, 148
Asiatik Researches, 141
Assyrian language, 175, 178
Australia, 54, 122
Austro-Hungary, 49
Austronesian language, 178

Babylonian language, 175, 178
Bagehot, Walter, 29
Balfour, Arthur J., 53–55
Baliles, Gerald L., 171
Balkan States, 49–50
Bantu education, 167–68, 173
Barbarism: in India, 146–47, 149; as opposed to civilization, 15, 32; and Scottish Enlightenment, 29; of Scottish Highlanders, 27–29; and stages of civilization, 28–29
Barraclough, George, ix, x, 70–71
Barrett, William, 80, 82
Battle an as Inner Experience, The (Junger), 80
Baudrillard, Jean, 33n
Beccaria, Cesare, 23, 33n

Beckett, Samuel, 63
Beja language, 180t, 190
Belgium, 161; Belgian colonialism, 167
Bengal: and agrarian capitalism, 144, 145; anticolonialists in, 149–50; *bhadralok*, 148; brahmans in, 142; civilization of, 145; and East India Company, 139, 142, 143–45, 148; economy of, 143–45; elite of, 148; and Hindu revivalism, 148–59; famine, 139; history of, 139; political economy in, 144–45, 148; Renaissance, 148–49; traditional laws, 139; writers and intellectuals in, 58, 148–49. *See also* Hindu, India, Indian
Berber language, 180t, 189–90
Berlin Conference (1885), 161
Bernal, Martin, 124, 175
Bhagavad Gita, 142–43, 145, 149–50, 155; Gandhi on, 149–50; and Hinduism, 143; translation of, 143, 149
Black Athena (Bernal), xiii, 3–4, 10
Blackstone, William, 23
Boers, 79; Boer War, 53, 54
Bolshevism, 57, 68; Bolshevik Revolution, 44, 50, 57, 58, 68
Boswell, James, 15, 17, 32; and Samuel Johnson, 15, 32
Brahe, Tycho, 77
Britain: cultural diversity of, 119–20; cultural tradition of, 119–20; immigrants to, 120; role in world politics, 53; "splendid isolation" of, 53. *See also* British Empire, England, English
British Commonwealth, 53
British Empire, 24, 32; in Africa, 17, 54, 166–67, 168; "bio-political defense" of, 53; "citizenship" of, 54–55; decadence of, 54; destiny of, 40; dissolution of, 53; economy of, 14; East/West configuration of, 43; in India, xv, 17, 39, 139–51; and nationalism, 147–51; and "new imperialism," 37, 53; and race, 54–55; superiority of, 54; and "the West," 37, 40, 54, 55; westward movement of, 41,

43, 55; and Orientalism, 39, 141–42.
  See also colonialism, imperialism
British India Association, 148
British Isles, as "western isles," 42–43
Buddhism, 68
Burke, Edmund, 31
Burnett, James (Lord Monboddo), 17, 29
Bury, J. B., 5
Byzantium, 70. *See also* Constantinople

Caffentzis, George C., 83n
Cameroon, 192
Camus, Albert, 80
Canada, 54
Capitalism: in Britain, 19; expansion of, 68, 151, 153; and imperialism, 14, 79, 147, 170; and political economy, 145; in the United States, 68; and Western Civilization, 68, 84n
Capo, H.B.C., 170
Carey, William, 141
Cassirer, Ernst, 71, 72, 73–74, 81
Catholic Church, 18, 71, 73
Cato Street Conspiracy, 143
Central Africa, 175, 178, 192, 194
Cesaire, Aimé, 79
Chadic language, 178–180, 189–90
Chamberlain, Joseph, 53, 54
Chatterjee, Bankim Chandra, 148, 150
Chatterjee, Partha, 58
Chernyshevsky, N. G., 45, 46
China, 67; Chinese mathematics, 124, 127, 128, 132; colonial penetration of, 66
Chomsky, Noam, 164
Christendom, 40, 58, 65–66, 83n, 84n
Christianity, 6, 31, 65, 68, 70–71, 73, 75, 168; Christian art, 70; Christian missionaries, 161–62, 168
Christoff, Peter, 45
Civil Law: of Rome, 14–16, 26, 32, 32n; of Scotland, 14, 15–19, 21–23, 25, 27, 31–32, 32n, 33n
civilization: and culture, 70, 84–85n; development of concept, xiii, 13–14, 66, 137; of English legal system, 18–20, 22, 23–27, 31; in England, 13–32; European, 65–66; etymological development, 14–15, 32, 83n; French, 70; Greco-Roman, 84n; Greek, 3–11; Indian, 138–42, 152, 154; Islamic, 141, 152; as legal term, 14–15; and money, 144; origins of, 40; and Scottish Enlightenment, 19, 22; and Scottish Highlanders, 19, 27–31; stages of, 28–29. *See also* Western Civilization
Clair, Louis, 80
Classics, x, 3, 4, 8, 10, 42
Colebrooke, Henry Thomas, 140, 141, 144–45, 149, 151; and Hindu Law, 140; and Hindu Renaissance, 141; and political economy of Bengal, 144–45
colonialism: in Africa, xv, 161–69, 172–73; Anglo-Afrikaner, 167–68; Belgian, 161, 167; British, 47, 54–55, 57–58, 121–22, 138–51, 161, 166–67, 168; as "civilizing mission," 68; colonial administration in Africa, 167–68, 173; critique of, 149–50; decline of, 67; and education, 47, 119–20; European, 161–69; expansion of, xiii, 7, 67, 74; French, 161, 166, 173; German, 161, 166–67; in India, 138–55; and language, 161–62, 165–70, 172; and racism, 79, 81, 123, 148; resistance to, 37. *See also* British Empire, imperialism
Committee for the Comparative Study of New Nations, 152
Common Law, of England, 15–25, 32n, 33n, 140
communism, 9, 44, 57, 78–79, 84n; in Russia, 44, 57
Comparative Civilizations Project (University of Chicago), 152
Congo, 167
Congress for Cultural Freedom, 82
Constantinople, 70
Control of the Tropics, The (Kidd), 52
Copernicus, Nicolas, 76–77; Copernican Revolution, xiv
Courts of Chancery, 22
Cowper, William, 27
Creon, xiv, 91–115
Crystal Palace, 45, 46

Culloden, battle of, 29, 30, 31–32
cultural nationalists, in Africa, xv, 163, 164
cultural relativism, 58
culture: African, 125, 171; Ancient Greek, 4, 72, 124, 175; British, 119–20; European, ix, 37–38, 40–41, 46; German, 67, 70; relationship to language, 169–72; Western, 169. *See also* multiculturalism
curriculum: American undergraduate, ix, 63, 137; British school, 119–20, 128–29, 130–31; Eurocentric, x, 119–30; in France, 132; mathematics, 120–21, 123, 128–30, 131-33l; multicultural, xi, 131–33; reform, xi
Cushitic language, 180t, 190

Dadaism, 68
Darfur-Kordofan region, 183, 185, 189–90
Dawes, Richard, 129–30
Decline and Fall of the Roman Empire, The (Gibbon), 31
Decline of the West, The (Spengler), 43, 48, 50–52, 57, 71–72
decolonization, 53, 54, 58; in Africa, 161–66, 169, 172; in India, 151–55; of the mind, xv, 162–66, 172–73
Decolonizing the Mind (Thiong'o), 164
Defense de l'Occident (Massis), 67
Deism, 6
Delphi, 96–98
Derrida, Jacques, xiii, 72
Destiny of Western Man, The (Stace), 78
Devil on the Cross (Thiong'o), 173
dharma, 142, 155
Dharampal, 122
Diakonoff, I. M., 182
Digest of Hindu Law, A (Jones), 140
Dilthey, Wilhelm, 71
Diodorous Siculus, 5
Disraeli, Benjamin, 40–41
doctrine of "consideration," in Common Law, 21
Dostoyevsky, Fyodor, 45–47, 49, 80–82; and *Partisan Review*, 82; Pushkin speech, 46, 49; and Russian debates, 45
Dow, Alexander, 144
Dumont, Louis, 138
Duras, Marguerite, 63
Dutt, R. C., 149–150
Dyen, L., 182

East, the, 37–39, 40–41, 50, 67–68. *See also* Orient
East India Company, xv, 137–41, 143–47, 155; abolition of, 147; and conquest of India, 137, 143; economic policies, 140; and famine, 139; and Indian civilization, 146–47; and Indian tradition, 139–43; land revenue policy of, 146; and political economy, 143–47; rebellion against, 147
education, 129–30, 171–72; imperialism and, 120–23; multicultural, ix, xi, 63, 119–23, 130–33
Egypt, 5–7, 11, 66, 175–76
Egyptians, 5, 7, 8; Ancient Egyptian language, 175, 178, 180, 180t, 190, 192; civilizing influence on Greece, 8; colonization of Greece, 8–9; mathematics, 124, 128, 132
Elias, Norbert, xiii, 65
England, 14–32; "financial revolution" in, 20; and Western Civilization, 76
English: capitalism, 19–21; Common Law, 15–25, 32n, 33n, 140; contract law, 21–22; financial system, 14; language, 37, 40, 168, 169, 172; Romantic poetry, 41; Romanticism, 43, 44. *See also* Britain, British Empire, England
Enlightenment, 48, 124; philosophers, xiii, 6, 66, 67. *See also* Scottish Enlightenment
Enquiry into the State of Bengal, with a Plan for Restoring that Kingdom to its Former Prosperity, An (Dow), 144
"equity," and Common Law, 22
Essay upon the Cultivation of the Lands, and Improvement of the Revenues of Bengal, An (Patullo), 144
Ethiopia, 190
Ethnocentrism, 119–20

Euripides, 5
Eurocentrism, xiv, 63; in school curriculum, x, 119-30. *See also* Ethnocentrism
Europe, 11, 14, 64; concept of, 39-41, 50; Central, 49-50; Eastern, 44, 49-50, 57; hegemony of, 38; medieval, 70; Mitteleuropa, 50; superiority of, 8, 39-40; and the West, 37-59, 63-64, 66
European: culture, ix, xiv, 4, 37, 39, 40-41, 44, 46; history, 38, 41, 44, 46, 51, 64; identity, 39, 40-41, 46, 57; languages in Africa, 161-74, 176; literature, 66; nationalism, 57
Everyone Counts (ILEA), 133
evolution: Darwinian theory of, 67; theories of, 6
existentialism, 80

Fairfax, Edward, 65-66
Fascism, 68, 75. *See also* Nazism
Fathers and Sons (Turgenev), 45
Feaveryear, Sir Albert, 20
Feminism, x, 64, 72, 74
Ferguson, Adam, 29
Fielding, Sir John, 24
Fire and Blood (Junger), 80
Fleming, Harold, C., 180, 180t, 190
Foucault, Michel, 33n, 72
France, 53, 68, 75, 76
"Free World," 68
Freemasons, 6
French: in Africa, 161, 166, 172; colonialism, 161, 166, 173; Physiocrats, 83n, 144, 145; Revolution, 6, 7
Freud, Sigmund, 81

Gandhi, M. K., 149; and anti-colonialism, 149-50; and *Bhagavad Gita*, 149
Geertz, Clifford, 153
Genius of the West, The (Rougier), 73
Gerdes, P., 125, 127
German: in Africa, 161, 166-67; colonialism, 161, 166-67; as cultural norm, 69; culture, 67, 70; idealism, 71; language, 166; "Problem," 75; scholarship, 67, 71, 84-85n, 166, 170
Germanic invasions, 4-5
Germany, 53, 68, 70, 71, 75-76, 80-81, 161
Gherardo of Cremona, 123
Gibbon, Edward, 31
Gladstone, William, 9
Gordon Riots, 26-27, 31, 33n
Goudsblom, Johann, 48
Gramsci, Antonio, 37, 58
Grand Inquisitor, The (Dostoyevsky), 81
Greece, 64, 73, 75, 76, 124; Ancient, xiii, 3-11; as birthplace of Western Civilization, 4; Bronze Age, 5, 10; colonization of, 5, 8-9, 10; as ethnic melting pot, 7; Hegelian view of, 67; history of, xiii, 4, 8, 64
Greek: art, 7; civilization, xiii, 10-11; culture, 4-5, 43, 175; language, 4, 5, 9, 10; literature, 8; mathematics, 124, 127-28; mythology, 42-43; philosophy, 7, 64; Rationalism, 77; religion, 5
Greenberg, J. H., 176, 178-81, 182; classification of African languages, 176, 178-81
Grunebaum, Gustav von, 152
Guenon, Rene, 67

Haileybury, 145
Hamitic language, 176, 176t
Hastings, Warren, 139, 140, 153; and legal reform in India, 139, 140
Hay, Denys, 39
Hebrew, 175, 178; Ancient Hebrew, 178
Hegel, G.W.F., 38, 67, 71, 75; Hegelian philosophy, 51, 67, 71-72
Heidegger, Martin, 49, 51, 80
Hellenism, 6, 69; Hellenistic Age, 5
Herder, Johann Gottfried, 43-44, 67
Herodotus, 5; *The Histories*, 5
Hesse, Herman, 68, 83n
Heward, Edmund, 24
Hindu, 141, 143, 150, 155; chauvinist movement, 151, 155; civilization, 141, 142, 149, 150, 151; "glory," 148; India, 142, 155; law, 140, 144; "mind," 155;

as religion, 68, 141–43, 154; renaissance, 141, 148; School, 148; tradition, 148
Hindu-Muslim: divide, 141, 142, 150; riots, 150; unity, 150
historical linguistics, 10
historical relativism, 51, 58
Historical View of the English Government, An (Millar), 18
Histories, The (Herodotus), 5
History of British India, The (James Mill), 145–46
History of Greece, A (Bury), 5
Hitchcock, Alfred, movies of, 81
Hodgson, Marshall G. S., 152–53
Holdsworth, Sir William, 21
Holland. *See* Netherlands
Holt, Sir John, 20–21
Home, Henry (Lord Kames), 17, 22, 29, 30
Homer, 7, 42
Hopi Indians: and civilization studies, 152; language, 163–64
Horton, Robin, 182–84, 187
Humboldt, Wilhelm von, 7
Hume, David, 17, 18–19, 29–31, 144
Hunter, Sir William, 139
Huntington, Samuel, ix
Husserl, Edmund, 72, 77–78

Ibn Sina (Avicenna), 128
Ideas on the Philosophy of the History of Mankind (Herder), 43–44
Imperialism, 3–4, 10, 79, 173; in Africa, 161–74; British, xv, 40, 52, 53, 119–23; culture of, 165; and education, 120–23; expansion of, 43; ideology of, 54, 119–23; linguistic, 161–62; and mathematics education, 120–23; "new," 41, 52, 53; and Orientalism, 3; Roman, 54. *See also* British Empire, colonialism
India, 39, 54, 55, 66, 67, 137–55; Ancient, 47, 137; Aryan conquests of, 5; brahmans in, 142, 153–54; British in, 39, 138, 141, 145-46, 148; colonialism in, 137–55; and East India Company, 137, 139–47; economic exploitation of, 148–49; as Hindu nation, 141, 155; Hinduism in, 140–44; history of, 137, 141–42, 145–46, 149; Islam in, 141–42; Permanent Settlement in, 144, 147; political economy of, xv, 138–39, 143–48; poverty in, 147; rebellion in, 147. *See also* Bengal
Indian: astronomy, 122; barbarism, 146–47, 149; caste system, 138, 142–43, 150, 153, 155; civilization, xv, 137–55; history, 137, 141–42, 145–46, 149; legal tradition, 139–43; mathematics, 122, 124, 125, 127–28; "mind," 137, 155; nationalists, 138, 147–151; "sacred centers," 153; science and technology, 122; tradition, xv, 137–38, 139–43, 146, 154. *See also* Bengal, India, Indology
Indian National Congress, 150–51
Indo-European language, 9, 10, 176; and influence on Greek, 4
Indology, xv, 138, 146, 149; development of, 138; and East India Company, 146; and Indian nationalism, 149; and political economy, 138–39, 144–45, 149, 151; and tradition, 146. *See also* Orientalism
"intelligentsia," 56–57, 58
International Monetary Fund, 138–39, 155
Introduction to a Scientific System of Mythology (Müller), 8
Irrational Man (Barrett), 80
Islam, 40, 58, 152; in India, 140, 141–42; Islamic Jihad, 180, 181m, 189. *See also* Hindu-Muslim, Muslim
Isocrates, 5
Italy, 58, 75–76, 161

Jaspers, Carl, 80
Jerusalem Delivered (Tasso), 65–66
Jews, 9–10; as Europeans, 9–10; genocide of, 9
Jocasta, xiv, 91–115
Johnson, Samuel, 14–15, 27–28, 30, 32
Jones, Sir William, 139–41, 142, 145, 146, 149, 151, 154; and Indian

tradition, 140–41; and translation of *Manu Dharmashastras*, 142
Jordan River Valley, 192–93
Junger, Ernst, 80
Junius, 24–25

Kames, Lord. *See* Home, Henry
Keats, John, 42–43, 59
Kenya, 168, 184
Keynes, John Maynard, 83n
karma, 145, 155
Khoisan language, 179t
Kidd, Benjamin, 52–53, 54, 55
Kierkegaard, Soren, 80
Kingsley, Charles, 40–41
Kissinger, Henry, 82
Koestler, Arthur, 80
Kohn, Hans, 75–76
Kopf, David, 141–42
Krishna, 142–143, 145, 154–55; in *Bhagavad Gita*, 142–43, 155
Kuhn, Thomas, 72

LaCapra, Dominick, 46–47
Lake Chad, 182, 184–85, 190; Lake Chad Basin, 185, 187, 189–90
Lambert, Wallace, 165
Landholders Society, 148
Language: and colonialism, 162, 165–69; and cultural behavior, 163–165; and decolonization, 161; indigenous, 165, 168, 170; Native American, 163–64; and neo-colonialism, 169–74; and perception, 164–65; politics of, 173; relativist concept of, 163–65; and social control, 170–71. *See also* African languages, European languages, *individual languages*, Sapir-Whorf Hypothesis
Larner, Christina, 16
Law. *See* Civil Law, Common Law, Roman Civil Law
Lewis, Bernard, 3
Lexicostatistics, 185
Life of Johnson (Boswell), 15
Lingala language, 172
Linguistic-cultural relativity, 163, 164
Livingstonians, 168

Locke, John, 29
London Corresponding Society, 143
Lyotard, Jean-François, 33n

Macaulay, Thomas Babington, 39–40, 41, 47, 55
Maghreb region, 58
Mahabharata, 142
Malthus, Thomas R., 143, 145, 155
Mansfield, Lord. *See* Murray, William
Manu, 142, 155
Manu Dharmashastras, 142, 143, 155
Marriott, McKim, 154–55
Marshall Plan, 78
Marx, Karl, 38, 69, 75, 151; Marxism, 69, 84n
Massis, Henry, 67, 84n
mathematics, xiv-xv, 119–33; African, 125, 127, 133; Arab, 123, 124, 125, 132; Chinese, 124, 127, 132; curriculum, 120–21, 128–33; development of, 123–28; Eurocentric approach to, 120–28; Greek, 124; history of, 128–30; ideology of, 128–30; Indian, 124, 125; multicultural, 123, 130; multicultural/antiracist approach (MC/AR), 120, 131–33; plastic, 125, 127; practical, 128–30; of science, 129–30; and society, 128
Mauritania, 184
McCarthyism, 82, 84n
McNeill, William, 152
Melchior, Eugene (Count de Vogüé), 44, 47–48
Mexican Revolution, 153
Middle Africa, 192, 194; Aquatic Civilization of, 183–85, 186m, 187, 189
Middle East, 3, 7, 11, 40, 66, 176, 182, 184, 190–92, 194
Migration: from Africa, 190, 194; within Africa, 175, 176, 182, 185–87, 188m, 192–94; riverine, 187, 189–92
Mill, James, 143, 145–46; and East India Company, 143, 146
Mill, John Stuart, 146–47, 151; and East India Company, 146–47

Millar, John, 17, 18–19, 31
Milner, Alfred, 54–55
Milsom, Menachem, 3
"Minute on Indian Education" (Macauley), 39–40
Modernization: and civilization studies, xi, 152; of non-Western societies, 39, 68; and tradition, 152–54
Monboddo, Lord. *See* Burnett, James
Moore, William, 24
Moseley, Michael, 129–30
Moudjaidines, 173
Müller, Karl Ottfried, 8–9
Müller, Max, 47, 149
multiculturalism, xi, xiv, 83n; in Britain, 119–20; in education, ix, xi, 63, 119–23, 130–33; in mathematics, 123–28, 130–33
Murray, William (Lord Mansfield), 13, 22, 23–27, 144
Muslim, 150–51; civilization, 150–51; invasions, 141, 142. *See also* Hindu-Muslim, Islam
mysticism 45, 48; oriental, 68
Myth of the State, The (Cassirer), 73–74, 79, 81
"Mythical," the, 81

Naorji, Dada Bhai, 149
Napolean, 6, 7–8
nationalism: in Africa, 165, 169–70, 172; British, 54–55; cultural, 163; European, 57; Indian, 58, 147–51; rise of, 6, 67, 84–85n, 123–24; Third World, 69, 151–52, 153
Native Americans, 152, 154, 163–64. *See also* Hopi Indians
NATO, 68, 69
Nazism, 63, 64, 68, 77–82. *See also* Third Reich
Nehru, Jawaharlal, 150
neo-colonialism, 4, 53; in Africa, 162, 169–74. *See also* colonialism
neo-Hellenism: in Germany, 7; and social regeneration, 7
Neo-Kantians, 71–72
neo-nationalism, in Africa, 165, 168–170, 172. *See also* nationalism

Netherlands, 17–18, 19
New Europe: Some Essays in Reconstruction, The (Toynbee), 57
"new imperialism," 41, 52, 53
Newman, Paul, 180, 190
Nietzsche, Friedrich, 48–49, 75; and nihilism, 48
Niger River, 185, 187, 192; Niger Bend, 185, 187; Niger Delta, 182, 185, 187, 189–90
Nigeria, 180, 199
nihilism, 44–49, 51, 57; Russian, 44–49, 51
Nile River, 184, 189–90; Blue Nile, 190; Lower Nile Valley, 192; Nile Delta, 190; Nile Valley, 189, 194; White Nile, 190
Nirvana, 47
North Africa, 180, 189
Notes from Underground (Doystoyevsky), 46–47

Objectives of Education in a Free Society, The (Harvard University Committee), 84n
Occident, 65–66; Occidental, 44. *See also* the West
Oedipus, xiv, 91–115; Oedipus myth, xiv; *Oedipus the King*, xiv
Okey, Robin, 49–50
Omotic language, 180t, 190
"On First Looking into Chapman's Homer" (Keats), 42
On Crimes and Punishments (Beccaria), 33n
On Isis and Osiris (Plutarch), 5
On Liberty (J. S. Mill), 147
On the Malice of Herodotus (Plutarch), 5
Open Society and Its Enemies (Popper), 75
Orient, 3; mathematics of, 124; mysticism of, 68; philosophies of, 58–59, 68
Orient et Occident (Guenon), 67
Orientalism, xv, 3, 39, 40, 47–48, 83n, 138, 141–42, 149; and East India Company, 138; and Hindu-Muslim divide, 141–42; and India, 149, 154;

and Indian tradition, 141–42; and political economy, 138, 145, 149; and Russian nihilism, 47–48; Edward Said on, xv, 3, 38–39, 40, 47, 138
Orientalism (Said), xv, 3
Origins of Totalitarianism, The (Arendt), 79
Orwell, George, 80
Ottoman Empire, 57, 65

Pakistan, 151
Pal, Bipichandra, 150
Panslavism, 44, 46, 49
particularism, xiv
Partisan Review, 78–79, 80, 82
Pascal Triangle, 125, 127
Patullo, Henry, 144
Pausanias, 5
Pelasgians, 5
Permanent Settlement (1793), 144–45, 147–48; and Indian political economy, 144–45, 147–48
Philhellenism, 8
Philosophy of History, The (Hegel), 38, 67
Phoenicians, 5, 7, 8–9, 10
Physiocrats, 83n, 144, 145
Plague, The (Camus), 80
Plato, xiii, 6–7, 69, 75, 124; and Western Civilization, 75; *Timaeus*, 6–7
Plato of Tivoli, 123
Playfair, John, 122
Plutarch, 5
Political economy: of Bengal, 144; and East India Company, xv, 143–47; and Indology, 138–39, 144–45, 148, 149, 151
Pollock, Sir F., 21
Popper, Karl R., 75
Possessed, The (Dostoyevsky), 45
postmodernism, theories of, ix–x
poststructuralism, 72, 74
Pre-Hellenes, 4, 5
Principles of Equity (Home), 22
Principles of Freedom Committee, 73
Principles of Money Applied to the Present State of the Coin in Bengal, The (Steuart), 144

Progress Theory, 6
Protestant Reformation, 16, 18, 33n, 65; in England, 18, 33n
Protestant work ethic, 71, 154
Proto-Afroasiatic language, 182, 189, 191m
Proto-Indo-European language, 9
Ptolemy, 123; *Almagest*, 123; Ptolemaic theory, xiv, 76–77, 82
Pythagoras, 125; Pythagorean theorem, 124, 127

"quasi-contract," in Common Law, 21–22
Quine, W. O., 72

racism, 4, 6, 7, 10, 52, 54–55, 67–68, 79, 81–82, 148; in Africa, 167; in British education, xiv, 121; combating, 132–33
rationalism, xiv, 48, 68, 72
Redfield, Robert, 152–54; and University of Chicago civilization studies, 152–54
Reformation. *See* Protestant Reformation
Reflections on the Revolution in France (Burke), 31
Remarks on the Husbandry and Internal Commerce of Bengal (Colebrooke), 144–45
Renaissance, 7, 40, 41, 123, 124
Retamar, Roberto, 44
La Revue Universelle, 84n
Ricardo, David, 145–46
right of self-determination, 57–58, 76
Rise of the West: A History of the Human Community, The (McNeill), 152
Robert of Chester, 123
Roberts, J. T., 74
Rolland, Romain, 68
Roman Empire, 4, 54, 64, 70–71, 75, 77; Civil Law in, 18, 31, 32n
Romanticism, 6, 41; English, 43; and Progress Theory, 6
Rougier, Louis, 73–74
Russian debates, 37, 44, 48, 50, 57. *See also* Slavophile-Westerner debates
Russian: cultural identity, 45; empire, 49; ideas of the West, 44–51, 58; literature

and culture, 44–50; nihilism, 44–49, 51; novelists, 47; political thought, 49; "soul," 46, 49

Russian Revolution, 9, 37, 44, 57, 150; and Indian nationalism, 150–51

Sahara, xv, 175, 183–88, 192; climate changes in, 183–88, 192; Sahara/Sahel region, 183–88, 192

Sahel, 183–88, 192

Said, Edward, xv, 3, 38–39, 40, 47, 138; on Orientalism, xv, 3, 38–39, 40, 47, 138

Sanskritic tradition, 153–54; Sanskritization, 153–54

Sapir, Edward, 154, 163–65, 184; and study of Native Americans, 154, 163–65; Sapir-Whorf hypothesis, 163–65

Sapir-Whorf hypothesis, 163–65

Schlesinger, Arthur, 80, 81

Schliemann, Heinrich, 5

"science of common things," 129

scientific positivism, and nihilism, 45

Scotland, 14–32

Scottish: Civil Law, 14, 15, 17–19, 21–23, 25, 27, 31–32, 32n, 33n; Clearances, 31, 33n; Enlightenment, 15, 17, 18, 19, 22, 23, 27, 29, 32n, 143–144, 145; Highlanders, xiii, 14, 17, 19, 28–31, 33n; Lowlands, 16, 17, 19, 23, 28, 33n

Searle, Chris, 171

Semites, 7, 9; Semitic languages, xv, 176, 176t, 178–80, 180t, 182, 190, 192–94

Shils, Edward, 152–53

Singer, Milton, 152, 153–54

Skinner, A. N., 189

Slavery, 6, 9, 73, 78, 123, 173

Slavophiles, 44, 45, 46, 49, 50; Slavophile-Westerner debates, 44–45, 49, 50

Smith, Adam, 17, 28–30, 145

Smith, T. B., 31

Social Darwinism, 52

Social Evolution (Kidd), 52

Sophocles, xiv, 94–115

South Africa, 167–68, 192; Afrikaner language policies in, 167–68; Bantu education in, 167–68, 173; Boer War, 53, 54; Boers, 79; colonialism in, 167–68; Soweto protest in, 168

Spain, 74, 76, 123; Spanish Inquisition, 74

Spanish-American War (1898), 52

Spengler, Oswald, 43–44, 48, 50–52, 57, 71–72

Srinivas, M. N., 153–54; and Sanskritization, 153–54

Stace, W. T., 78

Stern, Fritz, 82

Steuart, Sir James, 139, 144, 145; on money, 144

Stocking, George, 67

Study of History, A (Toynbee), 38, 43, 52

Sub-Saharan Africa, 175–176, 180, 190, 194

Sutton, J.E.G., 182–87, 189

Swahili language, 166, 168, 169, 172

Swann Report (*Education for All*), 119, 132

Tancred, or The New Crusade (Disraeli), 40–41

Tanzania, 166, 169

Tasso, Torquato, 65–66

Thapar, Romila, 137; and ancient India, 137; and Indian tradition, 137

Thatcher, Margaret, 130

Thiong'o, Ngugi wa, 161, 164, 173

Third Reich, 69

Third World: xi, xii, 10, 68, 51–53, 138; nationalism, 68, 151–53

Thirlwall, Connop, 8

Thunder of Steel (Junger), 80

Tigrinya language, 178

Tigris River Valley, 194

Timaeus (Plato), 6–7

Tiresias, 94–115

Toynbee, Arnold, 38, 43–44, 51–52, 56–58

Turgenev, Ivan, 44, 45, 49

Turks, 66, 83n

Unionist party, 53, 54

United States, 64, 66, 68–69, 76, 82, 138, 151; and colonialism, 52, 78, 151; cultural diversity of, 63; and foreign language, 171; as "New World," 43, 66; and Western Civilization, 68–69, 76, 78, 80, 84n
Unity and Variety in Muslim Civilization (Grunebaum), 152
universalism, xiv, 138
University of Chicago, 152–54; and study of India, 153–55; and study of Native Americans, 152, 154

Venture of Islam: Conscience and History in a World Civilization, The (Hodgson), 152
Verstehen, 72

Wallerstein, Immanuel, ix
Walpole, Horace, 25
Weber, Max, 71–72
West, the, xii, 14, 37–59, 63–73, 154; American, 58; Americas as, 43, 66; Bolshevik Revolution and, 44–50, 58; "boundless," 41–42; as capitalist construct, 38; changing definition of, 50, 57, 70–71; as cultural construct, 42, 43, 48, 55, 58; "decline of," xi; and decolonization, 53, 54, 58; defense of, 82–83; development of concept of, 66–73; and the East, 37, 38–40, 43, 50–58, 67–68, 73–74; and education, 55; in English Romantic poetry, 41–43; and Europe, 39, 41, 49, 50, 65–66, 70; "genius of," 72–73; in geographical terms, 37, 43, 58–59, 65, 66; as historical construct, 38, 48, 51, 53, 55, 57, 58; in Hegel, 38, 67; in imperialist rhetoric, 37, 40–43, 53–55, 66; in Kidd, 52–53; in literary tradition, 40–42; in Marx, 38, 69; in Nietzsche, 48–49; and nihilism, 44–49; as political construct, 42, 43, 48, 53, 55, 65, 76, 78; as postcolonial construct, 58; as racially defined, 53–55, 74; rehabilitation of, 78; rise in usage of, 43; Russian idea of, 44–51, 58; as social construct, 43; Spengler on, 50–51; "temperament of," 54, 55; Toynbee on, 51–52, 56–58. *See also* Western Civilization
West Africa, 172, 187
Western: cultural identity, 37, 47, 83; culture, 37, 39, 48; education, 39; history, 37–39, 41, 51, 74; ideals, 76; "isles," 42–43; knowledge, 166; literature, 39–43; "Logocentrism," xiii; "Mind," 64, 69–72, 122; philosophy, 37, 48, 51; reason, 73, 79–81, 82; "soul," 72; "spirit," 76; tradition, 51, 64, 70, 78, 138; values, x, 68, 70–71, 81, 120; Westernized "other," 47. *See also* the West, Western Civilization
Western Civilization, ix–xv, 10, 13, 38, 41, 42, 43, 44, 47, 48, 51–53, 56–57, 58, 63–85, 148, 151, 152, 154; alternatives to, x; ascendancy of, 52; and capitalism, xii, xiv, 69, 78; and Cold War, 75, 78; concept of, xii, xiii, 64–67, 72; crisis of, ix, 77–81; as cultural construct, 64, 69, 71, 72, 75; debate, ix, x, 38; definition of, 50; development of, 52, 65–69; in education, xiv, 51–52, 55, 63–64, 68, 73, 74–77, 84n; and European culture, 63–64, 68; as exclusionary, 55–56, 67, 75–76; Greece as birthplace of, 4; historical function of, 64, 70–72, 73, 75, 77; as ideology, xii, 52, 65, 68, 70; and Indian civilization, 137–38; "legacy of," 76; and Nazism, 64, 77–80; as organic form, 72–73; as paradigm, 59, 64, 76, 77, 79, 82; as philosophy, 70; as political reality, 65, 68; racialism and, 67, 71; and rationalism, xiv, 68, 72; and Russia, 44–51; salvaging of, 77–78, 81–83; threat to, 48, 56–57; universal education and, 55; universalism, 71, 77. *See also* the West, Western
Westward Ho! (Kingsley), 40–41
What Is Existentialism? (Barrett), 80
What Is to Be Done? (Chernyshevsky), 45, 46
When a Great Tradition Modernizes: An Anthropological Approach to Indian

Civilization (Singer), 152
Whorf, Benjamin L., 154, 163–65
Wilkes, John, 24; Wilkites, 24, 31
Wilkins, Charles, 142
Willamovitz-Moellendorff, Ulrich, 3

Williamson, Kay, 182–83
Winkelmann, J. J., 7
witch-hunt, 13, 16, 82; in Scotland, 16; in England, 16
World War I, 44, 52, 53. 68, 76, 151

About the Contributors

MARTIN BERNAL is Professor of Governmental Studies at Cornell University. He is the author of *Chinese Socialism to 1907* (1976) and *Black Athena: The Afroasiatic Roots of Classical Civilization*, a projected four-volume work that has already been acclaimed as a milestone in its field. Two volumes of *Black Athena* have been published. They are Vol. I, *The Fabrication of Ancient Greece, 1785–1985* (1987), and Vol. II, *The Archaeological and Document Evidence* (1991).

GEORGE C. CAFFENTZIS is Associate Professor of Philosophy at the University of Southern Maine. His published work includes numerous essays on social and political philosophy and the first of a three-volume work on the philosophy of money of the British empiricists, *Clipped Coins, Abused Words, and Civil Government: John Locke's Philosophy of Money* (1989).

NICHOLAS FARACLAS is Senior Lecturer in Linguistics at the University of Papua, New Guinea. He has taught, done research, and facilitated community-based critical literacy in South America, Africa, and the South Pacific. He has published works in the areas of social-historical, descriptive, and theoretical linguistics, as well as in the areas of literacy and development from a critical perspective.

SILVIA FEDERICI is Associate Professor of Philosophy and International Studies at Hofstra University. She has written essays on feminist theory, international politics, and cultural studies. She is the co-author, with L. Fortunati, of *Il Grande Calibano: Storia del Corpo Sociale Ribelle Nella Prima Fase del Capitale* (*The Great Caliban: History of the Rebel Social Body in the First Phase of Capitalism*) (Milano, 1984).

CHRIS GoGWILT is Associate Professor of English at Fordham University. He has published articles on turn-of-the-century literature and culture in *Mosaic*,

New German Critique, and *Conradiana*. He is the author of the book *The Invention of the West: Joseph Conrad and the Double Mapping of Europe and Empire* (1995). Currently, he is working on a book entitled *Geopolitics: Afterimages of Culture*.

GEORGE GHEVERGHESE JOSEPH is Reader at the School of Economic Studies of the University of Manchester (England). His teaching and research have ranged over a broad spectrum of subjects in applied statistics. In recent years, he has been mainly concerned with the social and historical aspects of mathematics, with emphasis on the non-European contributions to the discipline. His publications include *Women at Work: The British Experience* (1983), *The Crest of the Peacock: Non-European Roots of Mathematics*, (1991), and *Multicultural Mathematics* (with B. Nelson and J. Williams) (1993).

ALAMIN MAZRUI is Associate Professor at the Department of African Studies and Coordinator of the African Languages Program at Ohio State University at Columbus. He has published widely on the politics of language and on African literature and politics. He is the co-author, with Ibrahim Shariff, of *The Swahili: Idiom and Identity* (1994). He has also published two plays: *Kilio Cha Haki* (1982) and *Shadows of the Moon* (1992).

JOHN ROOSA is a Ph.D. candidate at the University of Wisconsin at Madison in South Asian history. He has done most of his research work in India and Pakistan, and he is presently completing his dissertation on the former state of Hyderabad. His study concentrates on the agrarian ecology of the State, its social structure, and political movements. Roosa is an occasional translator of Urdu literature.

SOL YURICK is one of the most outstanding contemporary American fiction writers and essayists. He is the author of novels and short stories that have been widely reviewed, anthologized, used as classroom texts, and translated in several languages. They include *The Warriors* (1965); *Fertig* (1966); *The Bag* (1968); *Someone Just Like You* (1974); *An Island Death* (1974); and *Richard A* (1982). He has also published various essays, including "Behold Metatron, The Recording Angel" (1985). In 1974, he received a Guggenheim Fellowship.

www.ingramcontent.com/pod-product-compliance
Lightning Source LLC
Chambersburg PA
CBHW061444300426
44114CB00014B/1821